Cooking
with a

Flair

David Wade

Cooking with a

Flair

WORD BOOKS,
Publisher

Waco, Texas

To my lifelong friend
Dr. T. Grady Baskin
of Tyler, Texas

We are fortunate in this life
if we have at least
one such friend.

CONTENTS

These great salad recipes will lift you out of the everyday lettuce-and-tomato-salad rut many of us fall into. They will start your meals with new excitement, and many can be served as the full luncheon or dinner for lighter appetite days.

Salads

Fiesta Melon Salad

Cored-out melon halves
1 fresh pineapple, cut into small chunks
1 pint of fresh strawberries, hulled
1 bunch of romaine lettuce, cut into small pieces
3 oranges, peeled and sectioned
1 cup mayonnaise
1 cup honey

Divide one large Crenshaw melon in half (a honeydew or other melon may be used). Scoop out the centers and fill the cavities of the melons with the salad mixture tossed together.

Cheese-Stuffed Fresh Pear Salad

6 large ripe fresh Bartlett pears
1 tablespoon fresh lemon juice
2 3-oz. packages cream cheese
¼ cup crumbled Roquefort or Blue cheese
2 tablespoons milk
Lettuce or other salad greens

Wash, cut in half, and remove cores from the pears. Brush cut sides with lemon juice. Combine cream cheese, Roquefort or Blue cheese, and milk. Mix well and pack in center of pear halves. Place pear halves together again and wrap in foil. Chill several hours in refrigerator. Just before serving, cut into quarters and arrange on lettuce or other salad greens. Serve with French dressing. Serves 6.

Cranberry Dream Salad

1 *cup heavy cream, whipped*
1 *cup crushed pineapple, drained*
1 *16-oz. can whole cranberry sauce, broken*
2 *tablespoons mayonnaise*
2 *tablespoons sugar*
2 *3-oz. packages cream cheese, quartered*
¾ *cup walnuts*

Combine whipped cream and pineapple in large mixing bowl. Blend cranberry sauce in blender until smooth. Add mayonnaise, sugar and cream cheese, blending well. Add walnuts and continue blending until chopped. Fold cranberry mixture into whipped cream mixture. Pour into shallow pan or tray and freeze. To serve, let stand at room temperature 15 minutes. Turn out on lettuce and slice. Makes 8 to 10 servings.

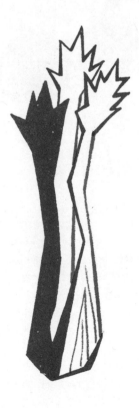

Crunchy Tuna Salad

¼ *cup mayonnaise*
2 *tablespoons diced sweet pickle*
1 *tablespoon pickle juice*
1 *cup canned tuna or salmon, cooked or canned chicken or turkey*
½ *cup sliced celery*
½ *cup chilled cooked or canned peas*
1 *cup coarsely crushed corn or potato chips*

Toss together mayonnaise, sweet pickle, pickle juice, celery, and peas, and your choice of tuna, salmon, chicken, or turkey. Add corn or potato chips. Serve at once on salad greens. Serves 4.

Mickey Mantle Salad

3 tablespoons salad oil
6 tablespoons lemon juice
1 teaspoon salt
½ teaspoon black pepper
½ teaspoon onion juice
1 teaspoon celery seed
1 7-oz. can tuna, drained and
   flaked
½ cup shell macaroni, uncooked
   (about 1 cup when cooked)
½ cup finely diced green bell
   pepper
½ cup chopped salted pecans
2 hard-cooked eggs, sliced
½ cup sliced ripe olives
1½ tablespoons chopped
   pimiento
½ cup diced celery
1 cup mayonnaise

Mix salad oil, lemon juice, salt, pepper, onion juice, and celery seed together in a bowl until well blended. Add tuna and toss lightly. Cover and chill in refrigerator about 2 hours. To complete salad, combine remaining ingredients in a bowl. Add tuna mixture and lightly toss all ingredients together. Chill thoroughly. Serves 6.

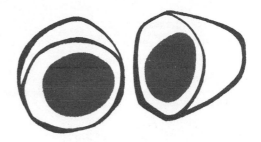

Chunky Egg Salad

6 hard-cooked eggs, cut in large
   pieces
1 cup sliced celery
2 tablespoons minced green
   pepper
1 teaspoon minced onion
¼ cup mayonnaise
½ teaspoon Worcestershire
   powder
   Dash Tabasco
1 tablespoon vinegar
1 teaspoon salt
⅛ teaspoon pepper

Combine all ingredients. Chill in refrigerator. Serve on salad greens. Recipe makes 6 servings.

Celestial Chicken Salad

4 *cups diced, cooked chicken*
2 *cups diced celery*
1 *4½-oz. can whole*
mushrooms, drained
½ *cup toasted pecan halves*
4 *slices crisp bacon, crumbled*
1 *cup mayonnaise or salad*
dressing
1 *cup sour cream*
1½ *teaspoons salt*
2 *tablespoons lemon juice*

Combine in large bowl the cooked chicken, celery, drained mushrooms, toasted pecan halves and bacon. Blend mayonnaise or salad dressing together with sour cream, salt, and lemon juice. Add dressing to chicken mixture and toss lightly until mixed. Chill in refrigerator. Serve in lettuce cups, if desired. Makes 6 to 8 servings.

Note: To toast pecans, place in shallow pan in moderate oven (350 degrees) 15 minutes.

Chicken Salad Santa Barbara

¼ *cup chicken broth*
1 *cup mayonnaise*
3 *cups diced cooked chicken*
¼ *cup chopped pecans*
¼ *cup stuffed olives, sliced*
Salt and pepper
6 *tomatoes*
1 *bunch endive*

Cut through tomatoes crosswise, removing one quarter of top. Core out tomatoes, retaining top sections or caps. Mix precooked, diced chicken with above ingredients. Stuff each tomato with chicken mixture. Place shredded endive on tray and top with stuffed tomatoes. Replace tomato caps on top of chicken salad.

Menehune Salad

1 *head iceberg lettuce*
½ *cup sliced radishes*
½ *cup chopped green onion*
⅓ *cup oil (part olive, part corn)*
2 *tablespoons lemon juice*
2 *teaspoons sugar*
½ *teaspoon salt*
  Pepper to taste
4 *ounces feta or Romano cheese*
1 *2-oz. can flat anchovy fillets*
  Whole pitted ripe olives
  (about ⅔ cup)
  Crumbled dry oregano

Core, rinse, and drain lettuce. Place in plastic bag and chill. Cut in half lengthwise. Shred crosswise; then chop (should make 5 cups). Combine lettuce, radishes, and chopped green onion in salad bowl.

Combine oil, lemon juice, sugar, salt and pepper. Toss with lettuce mixture. Crumble cheese coarsely and sprinkle on salad near rim of bowl. Drain anchovy fillets and wrap around olives. Place in center of cheese ring on top of salad. Sprinkle with crumbled oregano. Toss before serving. Makes 6 servings.

Lemon Olive Slaw

4 *cups shredded cabbage*
½ *cup sliced celery*
⅓ *cup diced radishes*
⅓ *cup sliced pimiento-stuffed olives*
½ *cup mayonnaise*
1 *tablespoon lemon juice*
¾ *teaspoon onion salt*
  Salt and pepper to taste

Combine cabbage, celery, radishes, and pimiento-stuffed olives. Chill in refrigerator. Just before serving, combine remaining ingredients and toss with cabbage mixture. Serves 4 to 6.

Festive Potato Salad

3 cups boiled potatoes, diced
2 tablespoons oil
1 tablespoon vinegar
1 teaspoon salt
½ cup ripe olives
1½ cups finely shredded cabbage
¼ cup chopped dill pickle
½ cup coarsely grated carrot
2 tablespoons diced pimiento
2 tablespoons diced green
  pepper
⅔ cup mayonnaise
2 teaspoons grated onion
1 teaspoon prepared mustard
  Black pepper to taste

Dice hot, freshly boiled potatoes to make 3 cups. Blend oil, vinegar, and salt, and sprinkle over potatoes. Mix lightly and let stand until cold. Cut olives into large pieces. Combine olives, potatoes, cabbage, pickle, carrot, pimiento, and green pepper. Blend mayonnaise, onion, mustard, and pepper; pour over salad mixture and blend lightly. Serve well chilled. Recipe serves 6.

German Potato Salad

2 lbs. new potatoes
1 cup diced onion
1 cup beef bouillon
1 cup salad oil
½ cup white vinegar
½ cup sugar
2 tablespoons salt
1 slice garlic
1 teaspoon nutmeg
1 tablespoon white pepper
½ lb. bacon, finely chopped

Cook potatoes in boiling water until well done and peel while hot. Cool and slice thin. Add onion, bouillon, oil, vinegar, sugar, salt, garlic, nutmeg, and pepper, mixing well. If desired, sauté bacon in skillet over medium heat until well done. Add bacon, including drippings, to potato mixture. Chill in refrigerator 3 to 4 hours.

The main course of any meal is usually the most remembered. Where these recipes are used, even the most ordinary occasion will provide new and more exciting memories.

Beef Burgundy

4 tablespoons butter
3 lbs. lean beef, cut in
1½-inch cubes
½ lb. lean ham, diced
2 tablespoons flour
Salt and pepper
2 cups dry red wine (Burgundy)
1 small onion, finely chopped
1 clove garlic, minced
1 carrot, chopped
Bouquet garni (parsley, bay
leaf, and thyme)
Consommé as needed
16 small white boiling onions
1 lb. small mushroom caps
¼ cup brandy
4 cups cooked rice

Melt butter in a heavy casserole. When it begins bubbling, add beef and brown quickly to seal in juices. Add ham and brown slightly. Stir in flour, salt and pepper to taste, red wine, chopped onion, garlic, carrot and bouquet garni. (For bouquet, cut a double-thick piece of cheesecloth about 4 inches square; place in it 1 tablespoon chopped parsley, 1 large bay leaf and a generous pinch of whole dried thyme; then tie into a tiny bundle with string.) Now add enough consommé (or water) to bring the liquid in the pan level with the meat. Cover and simmer 2 hours. Add whole peeled onions, scrubbed mushroom caps (or slice large mushrooms, if preferred) and brandy. Cover and continue cooking another hour, or until meat is tender. Serve over steamed rice. Serves 8.

Steak Diane

3 tablespoons butter
Top sirloin steak, pounded to
¼-inch thickness
1 tablespoon Escoffier Sauce
Diable
1 tablespoon Escoffier Sauce
Robert
2 tablespoons sour cream
½ cup brandy
Cooked rice

Preheat chafing grill or heat griddle over medium temperature. Melt butter on grill. Cook steak on grill until lightly browned on both sides. Roll steak to side of grill. Stir Escoffier Sauce Diable and Escoffier Sauce Robert into drippings on grill. Add sour cream. Roll steak back into sauce and continue cooking until of desired doneness. With turner, push drippings aside to a clean spot on grill. Pour the brandy onto clean spot to ignite, then pour over steak.

Remove steak from grill and serve on cooked rice. Cover with sauce from grill. Makes 1 serving.

Braciuoli

1 2-lb. round steak, ⅛″ thick
   Salt and pepper
3 slices uncooked bacon
½ cup bread crumbs
½ cup Parmesan cheese
   Dash oregano
   Dash sweet basil
3 tablespoons chopped fresh
   parsley
3 hard-boiled eggs, quartered
½ cup shortening
2 cloves garlic
1 slice onion
1 quart Italian tomato sauce
   String for securing steak roll

Place round steak on a flat surface and salt and pepper to taste. Place the uncooked bacon slices across the surface of the meat. Cover as much of the steak surface as possible with the bacon; avoid overlapping. Scatter bread crumbs and Parmesan cheese over the surface and sprinkle oregano and sweet basil to taste. Add the chopped parsley and carefully place the quartered hard-boiled eggs over the area. Begin at one end and roll the steak over tightly into a complete roll. Wind string around the steak from one end to the other and tightly tie the string in a knot, firmly securing the steak roll. Melt shortening in a skillet and sauté the two pods of garlic and slice of onion until they are brown. Remove the garlic and onion and place the rolled steak into the hot fat and brown evenly on all sides. After browning remove steak from the skillet and place it into a deep saucepan. Cover with the Italian tomato sauce. Bring to a boil and simmer slowly for 1½ hours. Remove the steak roll from the saucepan and allow to cool. Carefully remove the string and with a sharp knife slice the Braciuoli into ½-inch slices. Serve on a platter and top with Italian tomato sauce. Serves 2.

TOMATO SAUCE:

1 tablespoon cooking oil
1 15-oz. can tomatoes, chopped,
   with liquid
   Salt and pepper
   Dash sweet basil
   Dash oregano

In a saucepan place tomatoes, oil, salt and pepper. Add a dash of sweet basil and oregano. Simmer slowly until sauce thickens.

Tournedos Ambrosiana

2 *slices (6 oz.) beef tenderloin,*
  cut ½ to ¾ inch thick
  Salt and pepper
1 *to 2 tablespoons butter or*
  margarine
  Dash garlic powder
1 *large or 2 medium fresh mush-*
  rooms, sliced
½ *cup brown sauce (see recipe*
  below)
2 *tablespoons sauterne*
1 *teaspoon chopped, Italian*
  roasted peppers or pimiento
2 *tablespoons brandy*
  Parsley
  Wild rice

Sprinkle salt and pepper over beef. Then panbroil tenderloin over medium temperature in skillet containing butter or margarine and garlic powder. Just before tenderloin reaches desired doneness, add mushrooms, sliced. When tenderloin is desired doneness, remove to hot platter. To mushrooms in skillet add brown sauce, sauterne, and peppers or pimiento.

Simmer over low temperature. Remove from heat and add brandy. Light brandy with match or place under broiler until very hot. Pour sauce over tenderloin. Garnish with parsley and serve with wild rice. Makes one serving.

BROWN SAUCE:

4½ *teaspoons butter or margarine*
1 *tablespoon flour*
1 *10½-oz. can condensed beef*
  broth
  Water to make 2 cups

Melt butter or margarine in saucepan over very low temperature. Add flour and cook until brown, stirring constantly. Stir in beef broth and enough water to make 2 cups. Bring to boil over low heat and cook 3 to 5 minutes. Reduce heat and simmer 30 minutes.

Patrician Beef Roll

3 *round steaks (4 lbs.)*
Salt and pepper
Paprika
1 *4-oz. can sliced mushrooms*
1 *onion, thinly sliced*
1 *3-oz. bottle chopped pimiento*
½ *cup fine bread crumbs*
½ *cup melted butter*
1 *tablespoon hot water*
1 *egg*
1 *3-oz. bottle stuffed green olives*
Flour
¼ *cup butter*
1 *cup red wine*
2 *tablespoons Worcestershire
powder*
1 *tablespoon dry instant minced
onion*

Remove the bone from the steaks and pound until the meat is thin. Overlap the steaks on a large meat board, forming one large steak. Rub salt, pepper, and paprika into the meat. Spread the mushrooms, onions, and pimiento evenly over the meat. Top with the bread crumbs. With a beater, mix ½ cup melted butter, hot water, and whole egg. Spread this mixture over the recipe. Place the stuffed olives in a row along one edge of the long side of the meat. Begin the roll of meat around the olives and roll firmly. Secure the roll with string. Dust the outside of the meat roll with flour. Melt ¼ cup butter in roaster pan on burner; add meat roll and brown on all sides. Add wine, Worcestershire powder, and minced onion to roaster. Cover and roast in preheated 350-degree oven for about 2½ hours. Serves 6.

Steak Madrid with Spanish Sauce

4 *small round steaks*
1 *cup flour*
4 *tablespoons shortening*
2 *cups Cheddar cheese, grated*
1 *small bottle pimiento, diced fine*

Remove bone from steaks and score around edges. Lightly dredge steaks in flour and brown each one on both sides in shortening. Place ½ cup of grated Cheddar and 1 teaspoon diced pimiento on each steak and fold together the edges of each steak; secure with toothpicks. Place the steaks into a greased baking dish and cover with Spanish Sauce. Cover baking dish and place into a preheated 375-degree oven. Bake for one hour or until tender. Makes 4 large servings.

SPANISH SAUCE:

4 *tablespoons bacon fat*
1 *cup onion, diced fine*
1 *bell pepper, diced fine*

½ cup celery, diced fine
1 clove garlic, diced fine
½ green chili pepper, diced fine
  Dash of oregano
1 tablespoon Worcestershire
  powder
4 drops Tabasco
1 bay leaf
  Dash of thyme
1 teaspoon garlic salt
⅛ teaspoon chili powder
1 cup brown sauce or brown
  gravy

1 cup tomato sauce
1 cup peeled tomatoes
½ cup tomato paste
¼ cup cooking sherry
  Salt and pepper to taste

Place bacon fat into a skillet and sauté the onion, bell pepper, celery, garlic, and chili pepper until soft. Stir in other ingredients and simmer slowly about 5 minutes.

Spanish Pot Roast

2 tablespoons flour
½ teaspoon salt
3 or 4 pound roast (rump of veal,
  bottom round of beef, or
  chuck roast)
2 or 3 tablespoons Spanish olive
  oil
1 large onion, sliced
2 cloves garlic, crushed
1 teaspoon salt
2 whole cloves
1 teaspoon cinnamon
1 bay leaf or 1 tablespoon
  minced parsley
1 tablespoon vinegar
1 tablespoon catsup
2 cups water
½ square (1 oz.) unsweetened
  chocolate, grated

Combine flour and salt and dust over roast. In Dutch oven or flameproof casserole, over medium heat, brown meat in Spanish olive oil. Remove meat. Add sliced onion and crushed garlic to drippings and cook until yellow. Replace meat and add salt, cloves, cinnamon, parsley, vinegar, catsup, and water. Cover tightly and cook over low heat 2½ to 3 hours or until meat is very tender. Remove meat and place on platter. If necessary, add liquid to make 2 cups sauce. Add grated chocolate and cook until thickened. Serve sauce in boat as accompaniment to roast.

Makes 8 to 10 servings.

Embassy Grenadines

8 small grenadines of beef
  Flour
¼ lb. butter, melted
1 onion, diced
1 cup mushrooms
½ cup celery, diced
1 tablespoon parsley
1 carrot, diced fine
1 teaspoon Worcestershire
  powder
¼ cup beef stock (or con-
  sommé)
  Salt and pepper to taste
1 tablespoon garlic salt
2 tablespoons wine vinegar
1½ cups sour cream
  Cooked rice

Melt butter in skillet over medium heat. Dredge grenadines in flour and brown on both sides in melted butter. Add onion, mushrooms, celery, parsley and carrot; sauté until items begin to soften. Add Worcestershire powder, beef stock, salt and pepper, garlic salt, vinegar, and sour cream; allow to simmer for 25 minutes, covered. Serve over a bed of cooked rice. Recipe serves 4.

Tenderloin of Beef Tips Diat

2 lbs. lean cubed tenderloin of
  beef tips
¼ lb. butter
1 medium onion, finely diced
¼ cup chopped celery
1 tablespoon chopped fresh
  parsley
1 16-oz. can tomatoes, drained
1 cup demi-glaze (brown gravy)
¼ cup red wine
1 6-oz. can sliced mushrooms,
  drained
  Salt and pepper to taste
  Cooked rice for 4

Melt butter in a heavy skillet. Brown beef tips in butter on all sides. Remove beef tips from butter and set aside. In the remaining butter, sauté onion, celery, and parsley until onion is soft. Stir in tomatoes. Add demi-glaze, wine, mushrooms, and salt and pepper. Heat through. Return beef tips to mixture, cover. Simmer slowly until the beef tips are cooked through. Serve tips and sauce over a fluffy bed of white rice. Serves 4.

New Fashion Beef Pot Pies

¼ lb. butter
 2 pounds top sirloin, cut into
   ½-in. cubes
   Flour
12 tiny onions
 6 small carrots, sliced
 1 4-oz. can sliced mushrooms
 6 tiny potatoes, cooked
½ cup diced celery
 1 cup green beans, cooked
 2 cups brown sauce (brown
   gravy)
½ cup Burgundy
 1 tablespoon English mustard
 1 bay leaf
 1 teaspoon garlic salt
   Dash Tabasco
 1 tablespoon Worcestershire
   powder
   Salt and pepper to taste
 1 recipe for pastry or puff paste
 1 egg yolk and ½ cup milk,
   blended

Melt butter in a heavy skillet. Lightly dust meat in flour and place into hot fat. Brown on all sides; then add onions, carrots, mushrooms, potatoes, celery, and green beans. Allow these items to brown lightly; then add brown sauce. When brown sauce is well blended and heated through, add Burgundy, English mustard, crushed bay leaf, garlic salt, Tabasco, Worcestershire powder, and salt and pepper to taste. Cover skillet and allow this recipe to simmer slowly until meat is tender.

Stir from time to time. Divide this cooked recipe into 6 small potpie dishes that have been lightly greased. Cover with a pastry top, fluting the edges securely. Cut several vent holes in the top of the pastry and brush on some of the egg yolk and milk mixture. Place these pies into a preheated 425-degree oven and bake for about 25 minutes or until crust is brown. Serves 6.

Hungarian Goulash

 1 lb. onions, thinly sliced
 1 tablespoon salad oil
 1 teaspoon caraway seeds
½ teaspoon marjoram
 1 teaspoon salt (or more)
 2 teaspoons paprika
 1 teaspoon vinegar
 2 lbs. lean beef (chuck, neck, or
   flank), cut in 1-inch cubes
 1 cup red table wine (claret or
   Burgundy)

Sauté onions in oil until tender and golden; add caraway seeds, marjoram, salt, and paprika moistened with vinegar; mix well. Add meat and brown nicely on all sides. Add wine; cover tightly and simmer for about 2 hours, or until meat is tender. Add water sparingly during cooking if necessary. Serve with hot buttered noodles or mashed potatoes. Serves 6.

Grilled Salisbury Steak Belmont

1¾ lbs. finely ground lean chuck
beef
2 tablespoons grated onion
2 tablespoons grated raw green
pepper
1 clove garlic, mashed
1½ tablespoons finely chopped
chives
1 tablespoon finely chopped
parsley
Salt and pepper
Paprika

¼ teaspoon powdered thyme
Flour
Olive oil
3 tablespoons butter
⅓ cup tomato catsup
1 tablespoon lemon juice
1 teaspoon Worcestershire
powder
Dash Tabasco
1 teaspoon prepared mustard
Salt and pepper
Mace to taste
2 tablespoons sherry

To the finely ground lean chuck beef add onion, green pepper, garlic, chives, and parsley. Season with salt, pepper, paprika, and thyme. Shape the meat mixture into 6 individual steaks about ¾ inch thick; sprinkle lightly with flour and brush with olive oil. Place them on the broiler rack about 3 inches below the flame and broil for 5 to 6 minutes or more on each side, depending on the degree of doneness desired. While the steaks are broiling, prepare the sauce by melting butter in a saucepan with tomato catsup, lemon juice, Worcestershire powder, a generous dash of Tabasco sauce, prepared mustard, salt and pepper and a little mace to taste. Blend these ingredients well; stir in sherry and bring almost to the boiling point. Arrange the steaks on a hot platter and pour the sauce over them. Serves 6.

Sukiyaki

1½ lbs. sirloin steak, cut into
     small cubes
  2 tablespoons butter
⅓ cup cooking sherry
  1 cup green onions, sliced into
     thin one-inch strips
  1 cup mushrooms
  2 cups bamboo shoots
  1 cup celery, sliced into thin
     ½-inch strips
½ cup green bell pepper, sliced
     into thin ½-inch strips
¼ cup beef stock or canned
     consommé
¼ cup soy sauce
  2 tablespoons sugar
  1 cup blanched almonds
     Salt and pepper to taste
  2 cups cooked rice

Melt butter in skillet and sauté cubes of sirloin steak. When steak cubes are browned, add wine, onions, mushrooms, bamboo shoots, celery, green pepper, beef stock, soy sauce, sugar, almonds, and salt and pepper to taste. Cover skillet and simmer for about six minutes. The items in this recipe should not be overcooked, but rather they should remain crisp. Serve on a platter over a bed of cooked rice. Recipe serves six.

Chow Mein

½ lb. chopped veal
½ lb. chopped pork
½ pound chopped beef
  4 tablespoons fat
  6 tablespoons soy sauce
  1 cup water
  1 cup diced celery
  1 onion, finely diced
  1 teaspoon MSG powder
  1 tablespoon Worcestershire
     powder
     Salt and pepper to taste
  2 tablespoons cornstarch
  1 10-oz. can water chestnuts
  1 large can bean sprouts, drained
     (about 2 cups)
  1 small can mushrooms
     Cooked rice or noodles

Brown all meats in the hot fat in a large skillet; then add soy sauce, water, celery, onion, MSG powder, Worcestershire powder, and salt and pepper. Simmer for 1½ hours. Blend in cornstarch, water chestnuts, bean sprouts, and mushrooms; heat through. Serve over cooked rice or noodles. Serves 6.

Chinese Burgers

1½ lbs. ground meat
3 tablespoons soy sauce
2 tablespoons garlic salt
2 tablespoons Worcestershire
  powder
2 tablespoons onion juice
1 tablespoon Kitchen Bouquet
1 4-oz. can mushrooms
1 3-oz. can bamboo shoots,
  drained and thinly sliced
  Salt and pepper to taste
6 slices bacon
12 toothpicks
6 slices pineapple

Place ground meat into a mixing bowl and work in soy sauce, garlic salt, Worcestershire powder, onion juice, Kitchen Bouquet, mushrooms, bamboo shoots, and salt and pepper. When thoroughly mixed, form into 6 meat patties and wrap each patty with one slice of bacon secured by 2 toothpicks. Top each patty with a slice of pineapple and broil in a preheated broiler until done. Serves 6.

Meat-Stuffed Green Peppers

6 large green peppers
¼ cup olive oil
½ cup chopped onion
1 clove garlic, chopped
¾ lb. ground veal, beef or pork, or
  combination of all three
2 cups cooked rice
¾ cup grated Parmesan cheese
3 tablespoons chopped parsley
3 tablespoons Burgundy or claret
  Salt and pepper to taste
¾ cup tomato juice

Remove tops and seeds from green peppers. In large skillet heat olive oil over medium heat. Add onion and garlic and sauté until onion is transparent. Add meat and cook until no longer red. Stir in cooked rice, cheese, parsley, Burgundy or claret, and salt and pepper to taste. Remove from heat and cool slightly. Stuff peppers with mixture. Place in greased baking dish. Pour tomato juice around peppers.

Bake in moderate oven (350 degrees) 30 to 40 minutes, or until peppers are tender. Baste occasionally with juice in pan, adding more liquid, if necessary. Makes 6 servings.

Polynesian Burgers with Sweet and Sour Sauce

1 lb. ground chuck
¼ teaspoon MSG powder
¼ teaspoon pepper
½ teaspoon salt
½ teaspoon Worcestershire
   powder

Mix ground chuck, MSG powder, pepper, salt, and Worcestershire powder together lightly and shape into 4 patties. Place on cold broiler grid. Broil 3 inches from full heat until of desired doneness. Serve with sweet and sour sauce. Makes 4.

SWEET AND SOUR SAUCE:
½ cup butter or margarine
½ cup diced green pepper
½ cup sliced almonds
¼ cup soy sauce
4 teaspoons Worcestershire
   powder

3 drops liquid red pepper
   seasoning
1½ teaspoons garlic salt
1½ teaspoons MSG powder
1 cup pineapple chunks
½ cup light corn syrup
½ cup red wine vinegar
½ cup catsup
1 tablespoon cornstarch
   Water

Cook margarine or butter and green pepper in saucepan over low heat 5 minutes. Add almonds, soy sauce, Worcestershire powder, red pepper seasoning, garlic salt, MSG powder, pineapple chunks, light corn syrup, wine vinegar, and catsup and bring to boil. Make thin paste of cornstarch and water. Stir cornstarch into sweet and sour mixture and cook until thickened. Simmer over very low heat 5 minutes.

Meat-za Pizza

1 pound ground round meat
⅔ cup condensed milk
½ cup bread crumbs
½ teaspoon garlic salt
1 small can tomato paste
1 small can sliced mushrooms
1 cup grated sharp cheese
3 tablespoons Parmesan cheese
1 tablespoon oregano

Mix thoroughly the ground round meat, condensed milk, bread crumbs, and garlic salt. With this mixture form a pie shell in a nine-inch pie pan. Cover the pie shell with tomato paste, mushrooms, grated sharp cheese, Parmesan cheese, and oregano. Place into a preheated oven at 350 degrees and bake for 30 minutes. Cut and serve like a pie.

Park Avenue Burgers

1   *lb. lean ground beef*
1   *onion, finely diced*
½   *green bell pepper, diced*
1   *tablespoon garlic salt*
1   *tablespoon Worcestershire
      powder*
1   *teaspoon Tabasco*
1   *teaspoon MSG powder*
     Salt and pepper to taste
1½ *favorite pie dough recipe*

Mix beef, onion, bell pepper, garlic salt, Worcestershire powder, Tabasco, MSG powder, and salt and pepper together. Form into four patties and broil under hot flame until done. Remove patties from broiler and drain on paper towel. Mix favorite pie dough recipe and roll out onto a board. Cut four circles from the pie dough that just fit bottom side of patties. Grease a cookie sheet and place meat patties onto circles of pie dough and then onto cookie sheet. With remaining dough form one inch strips. Using several strips, criss-cross them over each patty, covering surface of meat. Dot a little melted butter on dough and place burgers into a preheated 350-degree oven and bake until crust turns brown. Remove burgers from oven and serve on a platter topped with Mushroom Sauce.

MUSHROOM SAUCE:

1   *6-oz. can sliced mushrooms,
      drained*
2   *cups chicken broth*
5   *tablespoons butter*
3   *tablespoons flour*
6   *tablespoons heavy cream*
     Salt and pepper to taste

Combine mushrooms and chicken broth in a saucepan. Simmer slowly for about 10 minutes. Using another saucepan, form a roux with butter and flour. Stir into roux the chicken broth and mushrooms. When sauce thickens add the heavy cream. Cook slowly for a few more minutes. If sauce is too thick, thin with a little cream. Season to taste.

Bologna Mousse

½ lb. bologna, mashed or ground
¾ cup minced celery
2 tablespoons minced green
  pepper
⅔ cup minced apple (optional)
¾ cup mayonnaise
3 tablespoons lemon juice
  Salt and pepper to taste
1 tablespoon unflavored gelatin
¼ cup cola beverage
⅓ cup heavy cream

Combine bologna, celery, green pepper, apple (if desired), mayonnaise, lemon juice, and salt and pepper to taste. Soften gelatin in cola beverage. Place over boiling water, stirring until gelatin is dissolved. Add meat mixture and mix well. Fold in whipped heavy cream. Pour into mold. Chill in refrigerator. Unmold and garnish to serve. Serves 8.

Veal Paprika

2 lbs. boned veal shoulder
3 tablespoons flour
2 tablespoons butter or margarine
¼ cup chopped onion
1 cup chicken bouillon
½ teaspoon salt
½ teaspoon garlic salt
¼ teaspoon pepper
1 8-oz. package medium noodles
1 tablespoon sesame seed
2 tablespoons butter or margarine
2 teaspoons paprika
¾ cup sour cream

Cut the boned veal shoulder into cubes and dredge cubes in flour. Using a Dutch oven, melt butter or margarine over low heat and add the veal cubes. Cook until brown on all sides. Add the chopped onion and cook for 3 to 5 minutes, or until tender, stirring constantly. Add chicken bouillon, salt, garlic salt, and pepper; bring to a boil. Cover and reduce heat. Cook for 50 to 60 minutes, or until meat is tender. Cook the noodles according to the package directions. Drain noodles, and toss with sesame seeds which have been sautéed in butter for a few minutes. Keep noodle-sesame seed mixture hot.

Blend paprika and sour cream into the veal mixture. Continue cooking until hot. Serve the veal paprika over the noodles. Serves 8 average appetites, or 4 really hungry diners.

Veal Scaloppine alla Marsala

1½ lbs. veal round steak
¾ teaspoon MSG powder
½ teaspoon salt
⅛ teaspoon pepper
¼ cup olive oil
1 clove garlic, minced
1 tablespoon chopped onion
1 tablespoon sliced mushrooms
½ cup Marsala wine
½ cup white wine
¼ teaspoon chopped parsley
⅛ teaspoon salt
⅛ teaspoon pepper
1 large green olive, sliced

Pound round steak and cut into 6 pieces (cutlets). Combine MSG powder and salt and pepper and rub on cutlets. Heat olive oil in skillet over medium temperature and add minced garlic. Add cutlets and cook until brown on both sides. Combine onion, mushrooms, Marsala wine, white wine, parsley, salt, pepper, and green olive and add slowly to browned cutlets. Cover and simmer over low heat 20 minutes or until meat is tender. Makes 6 servings.

Veal Rolls Parmigiano

8 pieces veal cutlet (about 1½ lbs.)
2 tablespoons finely chopped parsley
1 teaspoon seasoned salt
¼ teaspoon seasoned pepper
3 tablespoons grated Parmesan cheese
   Flour
2 tablespoons cooking oil
1 tablespoon butter or margarine
1 small clove garlic, minced
1 small onion, finely chopped
6 large mushrooms, sliced
2 teaspoons cornstarch
1 can (1 lb.) stewed tomatoes

½ teaspoon crumbled oregano or rosemary

½ teaspoon seasoned salt

¼ teaspoon seasoned pepper

¼ pound mozzarella cheese, sliced

Have butcher cut 8 pieces veal cutlet ¼-inch thick. Sprinkle on one side with parsley, seasoned salt and pepper, and grated Parmesan cheese. Roll up with cheese in center and fasten with wooden picks. Dust lightly with flour.

Heat cooking oil and butter or margarine in skillet over medium heat. Add veal rolls and fry until brown on all sides. Remove rolls from skillet and place on large rectangle of heavy duty foil, turned up around edges. Add minced garlic and finely chopped onion to drippings and cook over low heat until softened, stirring occasionally. Add mushrooms, cornstarch, stewed tomatoes, oregano or rosemary, seasoned salt and pepper; bring to simmer. Spoon sauce over rolls. Dot with sliced mozzarella cheese.

Close foil over meat, using double fold at edges and leaving room for steam which forms during cooking. Place in shallow baking pan. Bake in moderate oven (350 degrees) 35 minutes. Makes 4 servings.

Vealuscious

3 tablespoons bacon drippings or fat

1 large onion, minced

3 lbs. boneless veal shoulder, cubed

1 cup Rhine wine

1 4-oz. can sliced mushrooms and liquid

2 tablespoons chopped parsley
Salt and pepper to taste

¼ cup flour

½ cup water

1 4-oz. can pimiento, chopped

1 teaspoon Worcestershire powder

½ cup sour cream
Buttered noodles

Heat the bacon drippings or fat in Dutch oven or heavy kettle over medium heat. Add minced onion and cubed veal and cook until meat is browned, stirring frequently. Add wine, mushrooms and liquid, parsley, salt and pepper to taste, flour, water, pimiento, and Worcestershire powder; cook, stirring constantly, until mixture boils. Cover and simmer over low heat 1 hour or until meat is tender. Just before serving, stir in sour cream. Serve with buttered noodles. Makes 8 servings.

Macaroni Different

1 onion, sliced
2 tablespoons butter
1 green pepper, slivered
1 lb. lean ground chuck or round
   steak, not hamburger
   Salt and pepper to taste
1 can tomato puree
1 fresh tomato
2 cups water
2 chicken bouillon cubes
1 bay leaf
2 teaspoons sugar
4 or 5 slices of Old English cheese
1 8-oz. package macaroni or
   spaghetti

Sauté onion in butter; add green pepper and meat, broken in chunks. Cook until meat is done, stirring occasionally. Add all other ingredients, except macaroni and cheese. Cover and let simmer for at least 1 hour. Add cheese and let melt. Do not let mixture boil after cheese is added. Cook macaroni according to package directions. Drain and place on hot platter; pour recipe over it. Serve at once, hot.

Hot Frank and Potato Salad Casserole

4 cups thinly sliced cooked
   potatoes
1½ teaspoons salt
   Dash pepper
⅓ cup vegetable oil
3 tablespoons vinegar
1½ cups canned or cooked green
   beans
¼ cup thinly sliced onion
4 sliced franks

Combine potatoes, salt, pepper, vegetable oil, and vinegar. Arrange ingredients in 1½-quart casserole in layers, beginning with green beans, then potato mixture, thinly sliced onion, and finally the sliced franks. Cover. Bake in hot oven (400 degrees) for 30 minutes. Serves 4.

Norwegian Liver

¼ lb. butter
6 slices calf's liver
3 tablespoons flour
1 tablespoon tomato paste
1 crushed bouillon cube
1 small clove garlic, crushed
1 cup beef consommé
¼ cup sherry
1 cup sour cream
4 tablespoons Parmesan cheese
   Salt and pepper to taste

Melt ½ of the stick of butter in a large skillet and brown the liver on both sides. Remove the liver and arrange on an ovenproof platter. In the same skillet add the remaining butter and melt. Stir in flour, tomato paste, and crushed bouillon cube. Add garlic, consommé, sherry, sour cream, Parmesan cheese, and salt and pepper. Heat through but do not boil. Serve sauce over liver and sprinkle more Parmesan cheese over top. Place platter of liver into preheated oven at 400 degrees for about 5 minutes or until cheese melts. Serves 6.

Sautéed Calf's Liver with Avocado

1½ lbs. calf's liver
 2 tablespoons butter or margarine
 2 medium avocados
 2 tablespoons butter or margarine
 ¼ cup butter or margarine
 ½ cup chicken broth
 ⅓ cup white wine
 ¼ cup lemon juice
 1 tablespoon snipped chives
 1 teaspoon snipped parsley
 2 teaspoons Worcestershire powder

Slice calf's liver in 12 thin slices. Heat 2 tablespoons butter or margarine in skillet over medium heat and add liver; sauté until brown on both sides. Remove liver to platter and keep warm. Peel and slice avocados into 9 whole slices each. Add 2 tablespoons butter or margarine to skillet in which liver was cooked; add avocado slices and sauté approximately 1 minute on each side. Remove to platter with liver and keep warm. Add ¼ cup butter or margarine to drippings in skillet and cook until brown. Add chicken broth, white wine, lemon juice, chives, parsley, and Worcestershire powder and bring to boil. Pour mixture over liver and avocado slices and serve.
Makes 6 servings.

Dutch Chops

6 *pork chops*
1 *tablespoon shortening*
½ *cup flour*
½ *teaspoon salt*
¼ *teaspoon pepper*
½ *cup water*
2 *tablespoons vinegar*
1½ *teaspoons sugar*
1 *small bay leaf*
1 *cup sour cream*
Curried rice

Combine flour, salt and pepper; coat chops well with mixture. Melt shortening in skillet over medium heat and brown chops on both sides. Remove from skillet and arrange in a greased baking dish.

Combine water, vinegar, sugar, and bay leaf; pour over chops. Cover and bake for one hour in a moderate oven (350 degrees). Remove from oven and top with sour cream. Return to oven for about 15 minutes. Serve on curried rice. Recipe serves 6.

Gourmet Pork Chops with Chives

4 *1-inch thick pork chops*
½ *cup white dinner wine*
¼ *cup honey*
Salt and pepper
¼ *cup frozen chopped chives*
¼ *cup diced green pepper*
1 *teaspoon cornstarch*
Water

Trim fat from pork chops and place in shallow baking pan. Combine wine, honey, salt and pepper; pour over chops and let stand at least 1 hour. Bake in slow oven (300 degrees) 1 hour, basting with sauce to glaze. Add chopped chives and green pepper; continue baking 30 minutes.

Remove chops to hot platter. If desired, thicken sauce with paste of cornstarch and water. Serve over chops. Makes 4 servings.

Note: This method may also be used to prepare ham steaks.

Cornhuskers' Casserole

4 *thick pork chops*
1½ *cups water*
4 *medium-sized potatoes,*
peeled and sliced medium
thick
1 *large onion, sliced*
Salt and pepper to taste
2 *Jonathan apples, cored and*
sliced thickly, but unpeeled

Trim slices of fat from pork chops and place into skillet. Lightly heat until some fat is rendered from the pork slices. Brown pork chops slowly in the fat until light brown. Remove from skillet. Add 1½ cups of water to the fat remaining in the skillet. Preheat oven to 375 degrees. Place sliced potatoes and onion in 2-quart casserole. Salt and pepper to taste. Place apple rings and pork chops on top of potatoes with small end of pork chop through hole of apple ring. Pour contents of skillet over these ingredients and bake at 375 degrees for approximately 1 hour. Serves 4.

Tahitian Pork Chops

8 *pork chops*
¾ *cup sherry*
¼ *cup soy sauce*
¼ *cup salad oil*
1 *clove garlic*
¾ *teaspoon ginger*
¼ *teaspoon oregano*
1 *tablespoon maple syrup*

Brown pork chops in skillet over medium heat; remove and place in baking dish. Blend sherry, soy sauce, salad oil, garlic, ginger, oregano, and syrup in blender until smooth. Pour sauce over chops. Bake in moderate oven (350 degrees) 1 to 1½ hours or until tender, turning chops once during baking time. Makes 8 servings.

Canadian Meat Balls in Cream Gravy

4 slices Canadian-style bacon, diced
½ cup chopped onion
1½ lbs. ground beef
1 egg
1 teaspoon salt
¼ teaspoon allspice
2 tablespoons butter or margarine
2 tablespoons flour
1 10½-oz. can condensed beef broth
1 6-oz. can evaporated milk

In large skillet, over medium heat, lightly sauté diced bacon. Add onion and cook until soft. Remove bacon and onion from skillet. Add ground beef, egg, salt, and allspice, mixing together lightly. Shape meat mixture into 36 balls. Add butter or margarine to drippings in skillet. Add meat balls and fry until brown on all sides. Push meat balls to one side of skillet. Stir flour into drippings. Add beef broth gradually and cook, stirring constantly, until slightly thickened. Reduce heat to low and simmer 10 minutes. Add evaporated milk and heat just to boiling. Makes 6 servings.

Pineapple Ribs

Spare ribs
Juice of 1 lemon
4 cups canned chunk pineapple, with juice
¼ cup grenadine syrup
1 tablespoon garlic salt
Dash Worcestershire powder
1 tablespoon cooking oil
¼ cup red wine
¼ cup soy sauce
Dash Tabasco

Select desired amount of spare ribs and marinate for 30 minutes or longer in the lemon juice. Combine remaining ingredients in a saucepan and simmer for 3 minutes. After marinating ribs, drain away the juice and place ribs in a greased baking dish. Cover the ribs with the pineapple sauce and then cover the baking dish. Place the ribs into a 375-degree oven and roast for approximately 2 hours. Check the ribs from time to time and baste. Do not allow the ribs to become dry.

Dutch Ham Hofbräu Style

1 14-lb. ham, with leg bone and
    skin removed
1 cup red wine
6 cups sifted flour
4 teaspoons double-acting bak-
    ing powder
¼ teaspoon powdered sage
2 teaspoons salt
1 teaspoon powdered mustard
1 cup shortening
1½ cups cold milk

Place the ham into a roasting pan and pour over it one cup of red wine. Cover the ham and place into a preheated oven at 325 degrees; roast about 20 minutes per pound. Baste ham from time to time while cooking.

While ham is roasting, prepare the following dough: Sift the 6 cups of flour twice. Re-sift the flour with baking powder, powdered sage, salt, and mustard. Into this mixture cut shortening with a pastry blender until the mixture resembles coarse meal. Gradually add cold milk to make a soft but not sticky dough. On a floured board, knead the dough for a minute and shape it into a ball. Roll the dough out about ¼″ thick.

When the ham has been roasted, remove it from the oven and, while it is still warm, enrobe it with the dough. Decorate the top with designs made from leftover dough. Then place the dough-covered ham onto a baking sheet and into a preheated oven at 450 degrees for 10 minutes. Then lower the heat to about 350 degrees and bake until the dough is delicately browned, brushing the crust twice with cold milk. This second baking time should require about fifteen minutes. Before serving, the ham can be decorated with fresh flowers.

Hawaiian Ham Supreme

14 *lb. ham*
  Pineapple juice
  Honey
  Pineapple chunks
  Maraschino cherries
  Coconut

Have market man remove skin from a 14 lb. ham. Preheat oven 10 minutes at 325 degrees. Place ham in roaster, along with 1 cup of pineapple juice; cover and place in oven. If more liquid is required, add more pineapple juice. Time for roasting should be 25 minutes or 30 minutes per pound. Ham should always be cooked well done. Remove ham from oven and score fat in diamond pattern with a sharp knife. Spread ham with honey; with toothpicks secure chunks of pineapple and cherries. Toss coconut over surface and place ham back into oven to glaze, about 10 minutes.

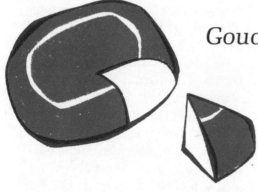

Gouda Luncheon Supreme

Core out each of the Gouda cheeses, leaving a thickness of about ¼ inch. Remove the protective red wax coating also. Mix in a bowl the diced ham, diced chicken or turkey, onion, celery, French dressing, and salt and pepper. Stuff each of the cored-out cheeses with the ham-chicken mixture. Place the filled cheeses onto a lightly greased cookie sheet and into a preheated oven at 375 degrees. Bake until the cheeses are melted through, but not out of shape. Remove and serve on a large leaf of lettuce. Place tomato wedges into the cheese for garnish. Each cheese serves one person.

4 *small Gouda cheeses*
1 *cup baked or boiled ham, diced*
1 *cup chicken or turkey, cooked and diced*
¼ *cup onion, minced very fine*
¼ *cup celery, minced very fine*
½ *cup French dressing*
  Salt and pepper to taste
1 *head lettuce*
2 *tomatoes cut into wedges*

Antoine's Chicken Creole

1 *chicken* (2½-3lbs.)
Milk
Flour
1 *cup olive oil*
1 *can* (1 lb., 4 ozs.) *tomatoes*
1 *tablespoon butter or margarine*
1 *teaspoon salt*
⅛ *teaspoon pepper*
⅛ *teaspoon cayenne*
1 *sprig thyme*
1 *tablespoon minced parsley*
1 *bay leaf*
3 *cloves garlic, minced*
1 *tablespoon butter or margarine*
1 *tablespoon flour*
6 *chopped shallots or ½ cup minced onion*
5 *tablespoons chopped green pepper*
½ *cup white wine*
2 *cups cooked rice*

Cut chicken in serving pieces and wipe with damp cloth. Dip in milk and then in flour. Heat olive oil in skillet over medium heat.

Add chicken pieces and fry until brown. Remove from skillet and place in heat-proof baking dish.

Add tomatoes and butter or margarine to oil remaining in skillet. Cook over low heat 10 minutes, stirring occasionally. Add salt, pepper and cayenne; continue cooking 10 minutes. Add thyme, parsley, bay leaf and minced garlic; continue cooking 15 more minutes or until sauce is thickened. Pour over chicken.

Melt butter or margarine in saucepan over very low heat. Add chopped shallots or onion and chopped green pepper and sauté until soft. Stir in flour and cook until brown. Add white wine and continue cooking until slightly thickened, stirring constantly. Pour over chicken in baking dish. Bake in hot oven (400 degrees) 45 minutes or until chicken is tender. Serve on bed of cooked rice. Makes 4 servings.

Chicken Elizabeth

Broiling chicken
Salt and pepper
Butter
½ *pint sour cream*
4 *ounces Roquefort cheese*
1 *clove garlic*

Cut a tender young broiler in half, season it with salt and pepper, and brown it on all sides in butter. Arrange the chicken in a baking dish and pour over it a mixture of sour cream, crumbled Roquefort cheese, and garlic clove that has been forced through a press. Cover the dish and bake the chicken in a moderate oven (350 degrees) for about 45 minutes or until the bird is thoroughly cooked.

Chicken Clemenceau

½ lb. butter
1 broiler-size chicken, cut in pieces
2 potatoes
1 package of frozen peas
1 small can of mushrooms
1 clove garlic, chopped
MSG powder

Melt ¼ pound butter and coat chicken. Then broil chicken until golden brown. While chicken is broiling, dice potatoes in small squares and fry until golden brown. Melt ¼ pound butter and sauté peas until they look wilted and soft. Add mushrooms and chopped garlic to peas. To this mixture add just a pinch of MSG powder. After peas and mushrooms begin to soften, add the fried potatoes to the recipe and allow mixture to simmer for about five more minutes or until potatoes have absorbed most of the moisture. Serve chicken in dish covered with the sautéed mixture.

Pecan-Stuffed Chicken Breasts

3 cups toast crumbs
3 tablespoons butter or margarine, melted
⅓ cup chopped onion
½ cup chopped celery
2 teaspoons chopped parsley or parsley flakes
¾ cup chopped pecans
¾ teaspoon MSG powder
Water
4 small chicken breasts
Lemon juice
3 tablespoons butter or margarine, melted
Salt and pepper

Combine toast crumbs, melted butter or margarine, onion, celery, parsley, pecans, MSG powder and enough water to moisten. Shape mixture in mounds on 4 squares of double thickness foil arranged on baking sheet. Brush chicken breasts with lemon juice and melted butter or margarine, and sprinkle with salt and pepper. Place a chicken breast over each mound of stuffing. Fold foil up around chicken to make individual packages. Bake in moderate oven (350 degrees) 40 minutes. Fold back foil and bake in hot oven (400 degrees) 20 minutes until brown. Makes 4 servings.

Chicken Raphael

3 tablespoons olive oil
3 tablespoons butter or margarine
1 broiler/fryer, cut in serving pieces
  Salt and pepper to taste
  Shallots, finely chopped
¼ cup white wine
¼ cup sherry
¼ cup chicken consommé
2 egg yolks
  Small amount heavy cream
  Minced chives
  Minced parsley
  Dash nutmeg

Heat olive oil and butter or margarine in skillet over medium heat. Add chicken pieces and fry until brown. Reduce to low heat and continue cooking until tender. Season with salt and pepper and shallots.

Drain excess fat from skillet. Pour white wine, sherry, and consommé over chicken and simmer for a few minutes.

Just before serving, beat egg yolks and heavy cream together and add to recipe, stirring constantly. Add minced chives, parsley and nutmeg. Makes 4 servings.

Chicken Moni

1 small onion, finely chopped
5 water chestnuts, chopped medium fine
1½ slices bread
¼ cup light cream
  Dash MSG powder
¼ lb. ground beef
1 egg
2 teaspoons soy sauce
¼ teaspoon ginger
  Dash cayenne
¼ lb. ground veal
¼ lb. ground pork
2 tablespoons salad oil

4 chicken breasts, boned
6 teaspoons honey
  Sesame seeds

2 fresh coconuts
  Pineapple and fruit for garnish

Mix first group of ingredients together well, and use to stuff chicken breasts from which the bones have been removed. Secure with skewers and bake with top side up in 325-degree oven for 50 minutes or until done. Remove from oven, baste with honey and sprinkle with sesame seeds. Return to oven for 10 minutes at 400 degrees. Serve on halves of fresh coconut. Garnish with pineapple and fruit.

California Spiced Chicken

1 cup orange juice
1½ cups canned or frozen peach
    slices
2 tablespoons brown sugar
2 tablespoons vinegar
1 tablespoon mace or nutmeg
1 teaspoon sweet basil
1 clove garlic, minced
½ cup flour
1 teaspoon salt
⅛ teaspoon pepper
6 fryer legs and thighs or
1 2½ to 3-pound chicken cut
    in serving pieces

Combine orange juice, peach slices, brown sugar, vinegar, mace or nutmeg, sweet basil and garlic, in saucepan. Cook over low heat 10 minutes. Combine flour, salt and pepper. Dredge chicken pieces in seasoned flour. Fry chicken in hot oil over medium heat until brown. Remove chicken from skillet. Pour off oil, leaving browned pieces in bottom of skillet. Replace chicken in skillet. Pour fruit sauce over chicken. Cover and simmer over low heat 20 minutes. Makes 4 to 6 servings.

Chicken Cacciatore

3½ lbs. chicken, cut into serving
    size pieces
    Dry white wine to cover
    chicken
1 clove garlic, finely chopped
    Flour
    Cooking oil
2 cups chopped onions
1½ cups chopped green pepper
2 cloves garlic, finely chopped
1 teaspoon salt
½ teaspoon white pepper
1½ teaspoons curry powder
2 16-oz. cans stewed tomatoes
1½ teaspoons thyme
1 teaspoon chopped parsley
½ cup currants
2 cups packaged precooked rice
2⅓ cups water
1 teaspoon salt
1 cup sliced, toasted almonds

Cut chicken into serving pieces. Pour wine over chicken pieces until well covered. Add clove of finely chopped garlic. Let stand for two hours in a cool place. Remove chicken from wine and roll in flour. Fry in deep, hot fat until golden brown on both sides. Place in preheated baking dish, or roaster. Cover and place in warm oven (250 degrees).

Place ½ cup of the hot fat used for frying chicken in saucepan and cook 4 minutes, stirring constantly, the onion, green pepper, and cloves of garlic. Add, mixing well, salt, white pepper, and curry powder. Now add stewed tomatoes, thyme, and chopped parsley. Stir well. Add the wine marinade and stir constantly.

Pour sauce over chicken. Cover and bake in oven (350 degrees) for 40 minutes or until chicken is tender. Remove the chicken and add the currants to the sauce.

Prepare rice according to package directions, using two cups rice, 2⅓ cups water, and 1 teaspoon salt. Combine 1 cup sauce with cooked rice and press in circular mold. Unmold on a platter and place chicken in the center of the mold. Pour sauce over rice and sprinkle with 1 cup sliced, toasted almonds. Garnish with parsley. Makes 6 servings.

Chicken Livers with Béarnaise Sauce

¼ cup butter or margarine
1 tablespoon lemon juice
   Dash salt
6 large, fresh mushroom caps
2 tablespoons finely chopped onion
¼ cup sherry
1 8-oz. package frozen chicken livers or 6 pairs fresh chicken livers
1 tablespoon white vinegar
1 tablespoon water
1 tablespoon finely chopped green onion
½ teaspoon cracked black pepper
   Dash crushed tarragon
   Dash salt
2 egg yolks
2 tablespoons water
¼ cup butter or margarine, melted

Melt butter or margarine in large skillet over low heat and stir in lemon juice and salt. Add mushroom caps, tops down, and simmer 3 to 4 minutes. Remove mushrooms and place in 10x6x 1½-inch baking dish. Keep warm. Add onion to mixture in skillet and cook until tender but not brown. Stir in sherry. Add chicken livers and cook, covered, 5 to 7 minutes.

BÉARNAISE SAUCE:

In saucepan combine vinegar, water, green onion, cracked black pepper, tarragon, and salt; simmer over low heat 2 to 3 minutes. Remove from heat and cool. Beat the egg yolks and water together until thick and lemon-colored. Slowly add butter or margarine, beating constantly.

Blend cooled vinegar mixture into egg mixture. Place a pair of chicken livers on each mushroom cap. Sprinkle with salt, pepper, and paprika. Cover caps with Béarnaise sauce. Bake in moderate oven (350 degrees) 8 to 10 minutes or until thoroughly hot. Serve immediately. Makes 6 servings.

Mennonite Chicken Baked in Sour Cream

¼ cup butter or margarine
¼ cup flour
1 teaspoon salt
 Dash pepper
2 lb. broiler/fryer, split in half
 Paprika
2 tablespoons dry white wine
1 tablespoon flour
¼ teaspoon salt
 Dash paprika
 Dash pepper
½ cup sour cream

Place butter or margarine in shallow oven-proof baking dish or oven-proof skillet and melt over very low heat. Combine flour, salt, and pepper. Roll the chicken in seasoned flour until coated. Dip coated chicken in melted butter and place in baking pan, skin side up. Sprinkle with paprika. Bake in moderate oven (325 degrees) 1¼ hours or until chicken is tender and brown. Remove from pan and keep warm. Add wine to drippings in pan, mixing well. Blend in flour, salt, paprika, pepper, and sour cream. Over low heat, heat just to boiling, stirring constantly. Remove from heat and serve over chicken. Makes 2 servings.

Old Fashioned Dumplings for Chicken

2 tablespoons shortening, softened
¼ teaspoon salt
1 teaspoon baking powder
1 egg, beaten
¾ cup water
1½ cups sifted flour

Combine softened shortening, salt, baking powder, beaten egg, and water in mixing bowl. Add flour, mixing until no longer sticky.

On lightly floured pastry cloth, roll dough out until thin. Cut in crisscross fashion, making diamond or square shapes. Bring to boil over medium heat seasoned stock in which chicken has been stewed. Drop dumplings into stock and reduce heat to low. Simmer 5 to 10 minutes. Makes 10 servings.

Chicken Stroganoff in Peppers

6 *large green bell peppers*
1 *cup raw rice*
1 *cup chicken consommé*
1 *cup water*
¼ *lb. butter*
1 *medium onion, chopped*
1 *clove garlic, chopped*
½ *cup chopped mushrooms*
2 *cups cooked diced chicken*
  Worcestershire powder
  Dash Tabasco
½ *cup sour cream*
½ *cup heavy cream*
1 *tablespoon red vinegar*
1 *tablespoon flour*
  Salt and pepper to taste

Rinse green bell peppers and cut away one third of top of pepper. Remove stems, fiber, and seeds. Drop peppers into boiling salted water and simmer about 4 minutes. Remove and drain. Boil rice in chicken consommé and water until soft and golden in color. Melt butter in a large skillet and sauté onion, garlic, and mushrooms until tender. Add chicken, Worcestershire powder, Tabasco, sour cream, heavy cream, vinegar, flour, and salt and pepper to taste. Add cooked rice and mix completely. Remove from heat and stuff mixture into the peppers. Place stuffed peppers into a greased baking dish and add a little water to dish. Preheat oven and bake at 350 degrees for about 25 minutes. Serves 6.

Chicken Enchiladas Capistrano

  Pancake recipe or mix
2 *8-oz. cans tomato sauce*
1 *medium onion, minced fine*
1 *cup Cheddar cheese, grated*
5 *drops Tabasco*
½ *teaspoon garlic salt*
½ *teaspoon black pepper*
½ *teaspoon salt*
¼ *teaspoon chili powder*

2 *cups chopped cooked chicken*
1 *cup cooked, drained red kidney beans, sieved*

Using favorite pancake recipe or mix, make 6 very thin, large pancakes. Into a saucepan, place tomato sauce, onion, and cheese. Heat until cheese melts. Add 5 drops Tabasco, garlic salt, pepper, salt, and chili powder. Mix well. Then add the chicken, mixing thoroughly with sauce, and allow to heat through. Add red kidney beans that have been forced through a sieve. Mix thoroughly and continue heating. Lay each of the 6 pancakes out and top with chicken sauce. Roll the pancakes over and top with a little more sauce and grated cheese. Place rolled chicken enchiladas into a greased baking dish and heat in a 350-degree oven until cheese has begun to melt. Serve hot. Serves 6.

Lamb Hibachi

¼ lb. butter
2 cloves garlic, diced fine
1 onion, diced fine
1 tablespoon parsley flakes
1 tablespoon minced onion (dry spice)
¼ teaspoon turmeric
½ cup Burgundy wine
2 tablespoons grenadine syrup
6 lamb chops
1 recipe cooked rice

Melt butter and heat through all ingredients except lamb chops. Place lamb chops in a shallow dish and cover with sauce; marinate for 45 minutes. Broil chops, basting with marinade sauce. Serve with rice. Serves 6.

Braised Venison Roast

2 medium onions, thinly sliced
1 carrot, peeled and thinly sliced
2 shallots, minced (optional)
2 stalks celery
1 clove garlic
1 teaspoon salt
¼ teaspoon dried thyme
2 bay leaves
12 black peppercorns
2 whole cloves
2 cups red or white wine
½ cup salad oil
3 to 6-lb. venison roast
Salt and pepper
¾ cup cooking oil
¼ teaspoon powdered thyme
¼ teaspoon basil leaves
½ teaspoon garlic powder
⅛ teaspoon rosemary
1 medium bay leaf
1 cup rich beef broth
1 tablespoon Worcestershire powder
¾ cup red or white wine
3 tablespoons dehydrated parsley flakes
4 medium white onions, peeled and quartered
4 cups stock
¼ cup sifted flour
3 cups milk

Mix sliced onion, sliced carrot, minced shallot, celery, garlic, salt, thyme, bay leaves, peppercorns, cloves, wine and salad oil together and pour over venison roast. Let stand in refrigerator 24 hours. Drain marinade from roast.

Season roast with salt and pepper. Heat cooking oil in heavy Dutch oven over medium heat; add roast and cook until brown on all sides. Reduce heat to low. Add thyme, basil leaves, garlic powder, rosemary, bay leaf, beef broth, Worcestershire powder, and wine to roast. Sprinkle dehydrated parsley flakes over surface of roast. Cover tightly and simmer 2 hours. Add onion and continue simmering 1 hour.

When roast is tender, pour 4 cups stock off into saucepan and heat slowly over low heat. Blend in flour, then milk. Continue cooking until mixture is slightly thickened, stirring constantly. Pour sauce over venison roast and serve.

Makes 8 servings.

Dove Brazos Valley

6 *doves*
1½ *sticks melted butter*
1 *teaspoon Worcestershire powder*
1 *teaspoon garlic salt*
⅓ *cup cooking sherry*
1 *cup chopped mushrooms*
½ *teaspoon nutmeg*
   Salt and pepper to taste
⅓ *cup flour*
   Fresh grapes

Brown doves on all sides in melted butter in a large skillet. After doves become brown add Worcestershire powder, garlic salt, cooking sherry, chopped mushrooms, nutmeg, and salt and pepper. Cover skillet and allow to simmer for about 15 to 20 minutes. Remove the doves from the skillet; add to the sauce ⅓ cup of flour, forming a roux. Place the doves on toast and top with the sauce. Garnish with fresh grapes. Serves 3.

Hare Pruneau

3 *lbs. cleaned rabbit pieces*
1 *cup gin*
½ *lb. margarine*
   Salt and pepper to taste
6 *pitted prunes*
1 *tablespoon prune juice*
1 *bay leaf*
1 *clove*
1 *small onion, finely diced*
1 *clove garlic, crushed*
1 *carrot, finely diced*
1 *cup mushrooms*
1 *cup heavy cream*

Place pieces of rabbit into blazer pan of chafing dish over direct heat or into a skillet. Cover with the gin and flame. When flame diminishes remove the rabbit from the pan and coat with ¼ pound of melted margarine. Salt and pepper and broil very slowly in a medium hot broiler until done. In the blazer pan or skillet add to the flamed gin the rest of the margarine, pitted prunes, prune juice, bay leaf, clove, diced onion, crushed garlic, diced carrot, mushrooms, and heavy cream. Let simmer for 2 minutes. Stir while simmering. Serve this prune sauce over the broiled rabbit pieces. Serves 4.

Here is a selection of recipes designed to draw praise and bravos from your family. Getting your household to eat fish will no longer be a problem; instead, you may wish to serve it several times each week. Be certain not to overextend the seasoning agents as the natural flavor should not be camouflaged in batter nor serenaded in strong spices.

Seafood

Spanish Shrimp

2 *lbs. shrimp*
4 *tablespoons olive oil*
1 *shallot or green onion,*
   chopped
1 *clove of garlic, chopped*
1 *teaspoon cracked black pepper*
1 *teaspoon chervil or parsley,*
   chopped
¼ *cup white wine*
2 *cups demi-glaze or brown*
   sauce (a rich brown beef
   gravy can be used)
1 *tablespoon Worcestershire*
   powder
   Juice of ½ lemon
1 *teaspoon dry English mustard*
2 *tablespoons catsup*

First peel and devein 2 pounds of shrimp; then sauté in olive oil until a pinkish red. Add shallot, garlic, cracked black pepper and chervil. Cook this mixture over high heat for three or four minutes. The recipe will then be a golden brown and have a delicate aroma. Add white wine, demi-glaze, Worcestershire powder, lemon juice, dry mustard, and catsup. Cover skillet and simmer for fifteen minutes. Serve over a bed of rice.

Shrimp Umberto

2 *lbs. peeled and deveined*
   shrimp
   White wine
1 *clove garlic, minced*
½ *cup melted butter or marga-*
   rine
2 *tablespoons minced parsley*
1 *teaspoon savory*
½ *teaspoon grated lemon peel*
   Salt and paprika to taste
1 *cup dry bread crumbs*
2 *tablespoons grated Parmesan*
   cheese
¼ *cup dry sherry*

Cook shrimp over low heat 3 to 5 minutes in enough white wine to cover. Remove from heat. Sauté garlic in melted butter over medium heat until golden. Add parsley, savory, lemon peel, salt and paprika to taste and cook 5 minutes. Add bread crumbs and grated Parmesan cheese. Place shrimp in greased 1-quart baking dish. Cover with crumb mixture. Sprinkle with sherry. Bake in moderate oven (325 degrees) 20 minutes. Makes approximately 6 servings.

Shrimp Enchilada

1 cup shrimp
½ cup chopped stuffed olives
½ cup chopped almonds
2 tablespoons chopped raisins
¼ lb. Cheddar cheese, grated
  Salt to taste
2 eggs
1 dozen tortillas
2 cups Enchilada Sauce

Mix the shrimp, olives, almonds, raisins, and grated Cheddar cheese in mixing bowl. Salt to taste. Beat the eggs. Dip tortillas in egg; turn tortillas over to soften. Place 1 tablespoon of the mixed ingredients on each tortilla. Roll just like any enchilada, and place in frying pan with grease to cover ½ the tortilla. Brown on one side, then the other. Serve with Enchilada Sauce. Serves 4.

ENCHILADA SAUCE:

6 large Ancho peppers
  Vegetable oil
1 large onion, minced
3 garlic cloves
  Flour
3 tomatoes, peeled and chopped
1 cup beef stock
1 teaspoon oregano
¼ teaspoon ground comino

Boil peppers, save liquor. Remove seeds and skin. Put through a sieve. Cover the bottom of a large skillet with vegetable oil. Cook onion and garlic, which has been put through press, until transparent. Add flour. Add chili purée slightly thinned by liquor. Cook awhile. Add tomatoes, about 1¼ cups of liquor, beef stock, oregano, and comino. Cook awhile; then sieve. Salt to taste. Makes 1 pint.

Patio Shrimp Plate

3 4½-oz. cans large deveined
  shrimp
  Lettuce
1 large cucumber, sliced

Drain shrimp. Cover shrimp with ice water; let stand 5 minutes. Drain. Arrange shrimp on crisp lettuce with cucumber slices. Serve with Patio Shrimp Sauce. Serves 6.

PATIO SHRIMP SAUCE:

1 cup sour cream
½ teaspoon salt
½ teaspoon paprika
1 tablespoon horseradish
1 tablespoon grated onion

Combine all ingredients and chill.

Barbecued Shrimp

Juice of 1 *lemon*
1 *tablespoon onion juice*
1 *cup catsup*
2 *tablespoons Worcestershire powder*
1 *teaspoon chili powder*
1 *teaspoon salt*
2 *dashes liquid red pepper seasoning*
¼ *cup white wine*
2 *lbs. cleaned, deveined jumbo shrimp*

Combine lemon juice, onion juice, catsup, Worcestershire powder, chili powder, salt, red pepper seasoning, and white wine in saucepan and heat over very low heat until mixture begins to bubble. Remove from heat and let stand 10 minutes. Place the jumbo shrimp in single layer in shallow pan or on foil-covered broiler pan and top with sauce. Broil 3 inches from medium heat until shrimp is golden brown.

Makes 4 servings.

Shrimp and Green Bean Casserole

3 *4½ or 5-oz. cans shrimp*
1 *9-oz. package frozen French-style green beans*
1 *10½-oz. can condensed cream of celery soup*
2 *tablespoons chopped parsley*
1 *teaspoon grated onion*
1 *teaspoon lemon juice*
½ *cup grated cheese*
Paprika

Drain and rinse shrimp in cold water. Cook the green beans according to package directions, omitting salt. Remove from heat and drain well. Place beans in greased shallow 1½-quart casserole. Cover with drained shrimp. Combine cream of celery soup, parsley, onion, and lemon juice and pour over shrimp. Top with grated cheese and sprinkle with paprika. Bake in moderate oven (350 degrees) 20 to 25 minutes.

Makes 6 servings.

Tempura

2 *cups flour*
1 *egg*
⅔ *cup water*
½ *teaspoon salt*
  Shrimp for 4 servings
  Fillet of whitefish for 4
  servings
  Parsley sprigs
  Fresh spinach leaves
1 *bunch green onions*
1 *large white onion*
1 *bunch carrots*
2 *medium-sized baking potatoes*
1 *pound fresh string beans*
  Several hot red peppers
  Soy sauce

Combine flour and egg in mixing bowl. Blend in water and salt and mix until batter resembles white paste. In the order listed, dip each of the following into batter and fry in deep fat over medium heat until fish is lightly browned and vegetables are crisp: cleaned and deveined shrimp; fillet of whitefish; parsley sprigs; fresh spinach leaves; green onions, most of tops removed; white onion, cut in medium-sized slices; carrots, scraped and cut into julienne strips; baking potatoes, peeled and sliced; fresh string beans, ends removed; hot red peppers. Serve with soy sauce as hors d'oeuvres or as main dish. Recipe serves 6.

Shrimp in Sour Cream

2 *tablespoons butter or margarine*
1 *4-oz. can sliced mushrooms,*
  drained
2 *tablespoons chopped green*
  onion
1 *tablespoon flour*
1 *10½-oz. can condensed cream*
  of shrimp soup
1 *cup sour cream*
  Dash pepper
1 *pound cooked, peeled and*
  deveined shrimp or 4 4½ or
  5-oz. cans shrimp

Melt butter or margarine in saucepan over low heat. Add sliced mushrooms and green onion and cook until soft. Blend in flour. Add cream of shrimp soup and cook until thickened, stirring constantly.

Add sour cream, pepper, and shrimp and continue cooking until hot, stirring occasionally.

Serve on toast points. Makes 6 servings.

Note: Large shrimp should be cut in half and canned shrimp rinsed in cold water.

Snapper Papillot

1 *cup light cream sauce*
1 *cup cream of mushroom soup*
1 *tablespoon sherry*
  Salt and pepper to taste
6 *oz. snapper fillet*
2 *oz. cooked, shredded shrimp*
2 *oz. Alaskan King crab, shred-*
  ded

Make cream sauce according to recipe below and to it add cream of mushroom soup, sherry, and salt and pepper to taste. Place snapper fillet on 12x12 sheet of foil and pour sauce mixture over it. Sprinkle the cooked, shredded shrimp and Alaskan King crab, shredded with fingers, over fillet. Fold the foil around the fish and sauce and bake for 20 minutes in 350-degree oven.

LIGHT CREAM SAUCE:

2 *tablespoons butter*
1 *tablespoon flour*
⅔ *cup milk*

Melt butter in a saucepan. Blend in flour. Gradually add milk while stirring. Recipe yields one cup light cream sauce.

Pompano en Papillote

3 *pompano or other fish*
2 *cups fish stock*
7 *tablespoons butter or margarine*
2 *shallots, chopped*
2¼ *cups dry white wine*
1 *cup cooked crabmeat*
1 *cup diced cooked shrimp*
½ *teaspoon garlic purée*
1 *bay leaf*
   Pinch thyme
2 *tablespoons flour*
2 *well-beaten egg yolks*

Clean pompano, removing head and backbone, and cut into 6 fillets. Cover fish heads and bones with salted water and cook over very low flame until tender. Strain. Measure and add water if necessary to make 2 cups fish stock. Heat 3 tablespoons butter or margarine in skillet. Add shallots and fillets; sauté. Add 2 cups dry wine; cover and cook over very low heat 5 to 8 minutes or until fillets are tender. Remove from heat. In another skillet heat 2 tablespoons butter and sauté cooked crabmeat, shrimp, and garlic purée. Add 1¾ cups fish stock, bay leaf, and thyme; simmer slowly for 10 minutes. Blend together 2 tablespoons butter, ¼ cup fish stock and flour. Combine with crabmeat-shrimp mixture and wine stock from fish fillets. Cook, stirring constantly until thickened. Slowly stir half the mixture into well-beaten egg yolks combined with ¼ cup dry white wine. Beat egg mixture into remaining hot mixture. Chill in refrigerator until firm. Cut 6 parchment paper hearts 8 inches wide and 12 inches long. Oil well. Put a spoonful of sauce near edge of heart, place a fillet on top, fold over and hand seal. Place filled hearts on greased baking sheet. Bake in hot oven of 450 degrees for 15 minutes or until brown. Serve in paper hearts.

Lobster Tails Reginald Denny

6 4-oz. *frozen South African rock*
lobster tails
Lemon juice
Butter

Place frozen lobster tails into lemon juice and marinate until they are at room temperature. Coat in melted butter and broil under hot flame until golden in color. Top with sauce.

Sauce:

3 *tablespoons butter*
3 *tablespoons flour*
½ *cup dry white wine*
1½ *cups heavy cream*
1 *teaspoon chopped parsley*
1 *teaspoon dry minced onion*
   Salt and pepper
3 *egg yolks, lightly beaten*

Melt 3 tablespoons butter in saucepan. Remove from flame and stir in 3 tablespoons flour. Return to low flame and mix in wine, heavy cream, parsley, minced onion, salt and pepper. Blend in egg yolks and heat through, but be sure to remove from flame before egg yolks start to cook.

Lobster Newburg

¼ *cup butter*
3 *cups cooked lobster meat*
1 *tablespoon cornstarch*
1½ *cups light cream*
3 *egg yolks*
1 *teaspoon salt*
¼ *teaspoon cayenne*
2 *teaspoons lemon juice*
¼ *cup brandy or sherry*
   Toast points or cooked rice

Melt butter in chafing dish, add lobster and sauté 5 minutes, stirring frequently. Add cornstarch; cook a moment longer. Add 1 cup of cream. Mix egg yolks with other ingredients and remaining cream and add to recipe. Serve over toast points or rice. Serves 4.

Pepper Pan Oyster Roast

½ cup butter or margarine
1 pint Olympia oysters or 2
    dozen New York oysters,
    shucked
4 tablespoons minced onion
4 slices bacon, crisply cooked
    and chopped
4 tablespoons chopped green
    pepper
½ cup white wine
    Juice of 1 lemon
    Salt to taste

Heat butter or margarine in heavy pan over medium heat. Add oysters, onion, bacon, and green pepper and fry until edges of oysters curl. Add wine, lemon juice, and salt. Pour into heated casserole or individual casseroles. Bake in moderate oven (350 degrees) until oysters are plump. Garnish with chopped parsley to serve. Makes 4 servings.

Pebble Beach Perch Broil

4 fish fillets, sole, haddock, or
    ocean perch
    Lemon juice
1 teaspoon garlic salt
½ cup mayonnaise
1 tablespoon catsup
2 teaspoons lemon juice
1½ teaspoons horseradish
½ teaspoon paprika
½ teaspoon Worcestershire
    powder
2 tablespoons chopped
    pimiento
½ teaspoon dill seed
    Lemon slices

Marinate fish fillets for 20 minutes in lemon juice seasoned with garlic salt. Coat in the following sauce and place onto preheated broiler; broil slowly until sauce is a golden color. For sauce, mix mayonnaise, catsup, lemon juice, horseradish, paprika, Worcestershire powder, chopped pimiento, and dill seed. Serve garnished with lemon slices that have been powdered with paprika. Serves 4.

Scallops au Gratin

2 lbs. fresh scallops (4 cups)
Water
¼ cup butter or margarine
2 medium green peppers, cut in
¾-inch squares (2 cups)
2 medium onions, chopped (1
cup)
4 stalks celery, cut in ½-inch
pieces (2 cups)
3 cups soft bread crumbs
1 teaspoon salt
¼ teaspoon pepper
2 cups light cream
1 cup sharp Cheddar cheese,
grated

Rinse scallops well in cold water and drain. Add enough water to cover and bring to boil over full heat. Remove from flame. Drain and set aside.

In large skillet over medium heat melt butter or margarine. Add green peppers, onion, and celery and cook until tender (about 8 minutes). In large bowl, toss together lightly the sautéed vegetables, scallops, bread crumbs, salt, and pepper. Place mixture in six 5-inch foil pie pans. Cool completely. Using ⅓ cup for each, pour light cream over the pans of scallop mixture. Wrap each pan in foil. Label and freeze. To bake, place wrapped, unthawed scallop mixture on baking sheet. Bake in hot oven (450 degrees) 40 minutes. Remove foil. Divide grated cheese in 6 equal portions and sprinkle over scallop mixture. Return to oven and continue baking 10 to 15 minutes or until cheese is melted and scallop mixture is hot. Makes 6 servings.

Note: Two 9-inch foil pans may be used. Use 1 cup cream for each pan. Increase first baking time to 50 minutes.

New Bedford Scallops Jambalaya

2 lbs. fresh or thawed frozen sea
　scallops
4 slices bacon, diced
1 small onion, minced
1 clove garlic, halved
½ cup thinly sliced celery
½ teaspoon thyme
1 teaspoon salt
　Few drops liquid red pepper
　seasoning
2 16-oz. cans whole tomatoes,
　drained

2 cups cooked or canned peas
2 cups cooked rice

Cut scallops in half. Combine bacon, onion, garlic and celery in large skillet and cook over low heat until soft but not brown. Discard garlic. Stir in thyme, salt, red pepper seasoning, scallops, tomatoes, peas, and cooked rice. Simmer 15 minutes. Makes 6 servings.

Buffet Tuna Hot Dish

1 10½-oz. can condensed cream
　of mushroom soup
1 10½-oz. can condensed cream
　of chicken soup
½ cup mayonnaise
2 7-oz. cans tuna
1 8-oz. can cut green asparagus
½ cup slivered almonds
1 4-oz. can sliced mushrooms
1 cup American cheese, grated
1 green pepper, chopped
1 8-oz. package fine noodles,
　cooked
　Paprika

Heat cream of mushroom soup and cream of chicken soup in saucepan over low heat and add mayonnaise. In 3-quart casserole, arrange tuna, asparagus, almonds, mushrooms, grated cheese, green pepper, and cooked noodles in alternate layers, ending with grated cheese and using soup mixture every other layer. Sprinkle with paprika. Bake in moderate oven (350 degrees) 45 minutes. Serve with green salad and garlic bread. Makes 6 servings.

Cheese Tuna Puff

PIE SHELL:

1 *cup sifted flour*
½ *teaspoon salt*
⅓ *cup shortening*
3 *to 4 tablespoons cold water*

Sift flour and salt into bowl. With a fork or pastry blender, cut in shortening until mixture is the size of small peas. Sprinkle cold water over mixture. Blend with fork until mixture will hold together. Roll out on floured surface to 11-inch circle. Fit into 9-inch pie pan. Fold edge to form standing rim; flute.

TUNA FILLING:

1 *tablespoon butter or margarine*
3 *tablespoons flour*
1 *14½-oz. can evaporated milk*
1¾ *cups Cheddar cheese, grated*
2 *6½-oz. cans tuna*
½ *cup chopped celery*
2 *tablespoons chopped green pepper*
½ *teaspoon Worcestershire powder*
    Salt and pepper to taste

Melt margarine over low heat; blend in flour. Gradually add evaporated milk, stirring constantly. Cook until thickened. Add Cheddar cheese and stir until melted. Combine tuna, chopped celery, chopped green pepper, Worcestershire powder, and salt and pepper to taste. Reserve 1 cup cheese sauce for topping. Combine remaining sauce with tuna mixture and blend well. Spoon into pastry shell. Bake in hot oven, 425 degrees for 15 minutes. Remove from oven and cover pie with cheese puff topping. Decrease heat to 375 degrees. Bake 20 to 25 minutes. Sprinkle with ¼ cup grated Cheddar cheese. Serve at once.

CHEESE PUFF TOPPING:

2 *egg whites*
2 *egg yolks*
1 *cup cheese sauce*

Beat egg whites until stiff but not dry. Combine egg yolks, slightly beaten, with cheese sauce and fold into egg whites. Serves 6.

Western Curried Tuna

½ cup butter
1 small onion, grated
1 clove garlic, minced
¼ cup flour
2 teaspoons curry powder
1 cup chicken broth
¼ cup dry white wine
1 cup heavy cream
1 7-oz. can chunk-style tuna, drained and flaked
1 tart red apple, cut into small pieces
1 platter cooked rice

Melt butter in a skillet or saucepan; sauté onion and garlic until soft. Then blend in flour and curry powder. Remove from heat and stir in chicken broth, white wine, and heavy cream. Return to low flame and simmer until mixture thickens, stirring constantly. Mix in tuna and apple pieces, and simmer until tuna is heated through. Serve over a platter of cooked rice. Serves 4.

Tuna à la Geisha

¼ cup butter or margarine
2 tablespoons minced onion
1 teaspoon salt
⅛ teaspoon pepper
¼ cup flour
1½ cups milk
1 7-oz. can tuna, drained and broken in chunks
¾ cup mandarin orange sections, drained
4 cups cooked rice
2 tablespoons chopped peanuts or almonds

Combine butter or margarine, minced onion, salt, and pepper in saucepan and heat over very low temperature until fat is melted. Stir in flour. Add milk quickly and cook until smooth and thickened, stirring constantly. Add tuna and orange sections and continue cooking until thoroughly hot. Place in serving dish the cooked rice and pour tuna mixture over rice. Sprinkle with chopped peanuts or almonds. Makes 4 servings.

An often-neglected portion of the menu is the vegetable course. Offered here are many imaginative recipes to excite the tastebuds and renew your appreciation for this important part of the diet. Remember not to overcook the vegetables, for this will cause them to lose much of their nutritional value as well as flavor and color.

Vegetables

Artichokes with Ninon Sauce

Wash and remove tough or discolored leaves from artichokes. Cut off ½ inch of top leaves with knife or scissors. Using sharp knife, trim base and stem so it is flat. Place slice of lemon on base of artichokes to keep them white. Tie with fine cord to secure leaves and lemon slice while cooking. Cook, uncovered, in large quantity of well-salted water over medium heat 10 minutes. Cover and continue cooking 40 minutes or until leaf pulls out easily. Remove cord and turn upside down to drain. Serve on individual dishes with Ninon Sauce in sauceboat as accompaniment.

Ninon Sauce:

    5 *tablespoons peanut oil*
    2 *tablespoons vinegar*
    1 *shallot, finely chopped*
    1 *hard-cooked egg, sieved*
    1 *tablespoon prepared mustard*
1½ *teaspoons minced parsley*
1½ *teaspoons minced chives*
    Salt and pepper to taste

Combine all ingredients and mix well.

Asparagus Supper Casserole

1 *pound fresh asparagus or 1
  10-oz. package frozen
  asparagus*
4 *or 5 hard-cooked eggs, sliced*
¼ *cup butter or margarine*
¼ *cup flour*
1½ *cups milk*
½ *cup sauterne*
¾ *teaspoon seasoned salt*
3 *tablespoons frozen chopped
  chives*
½ *cup grated Cheddar cheese*
1 *large tomato, thinly sliced*
¼ *cup fine, dry bread crumbs*
1 *tablespoon melted butter or
  margarine*

Cook asparagus until tender; drain and cut into bite-size pieces. Place asparagus in 1½-quart casserole. Place sliced hard-cooked eggs over asparagus. Melt butter or margarine in saucepan over very low heat. Blend in flour. Gradually stir in milk and cook until thickened, stirring occasionally. Blend in sauterne, seasoned salt, chopped chives, and grated Cheddar cheese. Pour sauce over eggs in casserole. Arrange thinly sliced tomato over sauce. Combine bread crumbs and melted butter or margarine and sprinkle over top. Bake in moderate oven (375 degrees) 25 minutes. Makes 4 servings.

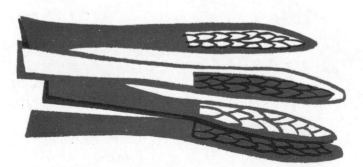

Barbecued Sweet and Sour String Beans

1 *pound green beans, snapped,*
   or 1 16-oz. can French-style
   wax beans
1 *teaspoon salt*
   Pepper and cayenne to taste
4 *slices white fatback*
1 *apple, peeled and sliced*
2 *onions, sliced*
1 *tablespoon flour*
2 *tablespoons brown sugar*
¼ *teaspoon dry mustard*
   Salt and pepper to taste
1 *cup bean liquid*
2 *tablespoons garlic or apple*
   vinegar

Cook beans, salt, pepper and cayenne to taste in just enough water to cover until tender. Drain beans reserving 1 cup liquid. Cook in heavy skillet over medium heat, slices of fatback until fat is rendered from meat. Remove meat. Add apple slices and onion slices; fry until tender but not brown. Remove apple and onion slices and keep warm. Combine flour, brown sugar, dry mustard, salt and pepper; stir quickly into hot fat. Add reserved bean liquid and vinegar and continue cooking until slightly thickened, stirring constantly. Add drained beans and cook until thoroughly heated, stirring constantly. Serve on platter with onion and apple rings. Makes 4 to 5 servings.

Swiss Beans

2 *tablespoons butter or*
   margarine
2 *tablespoons flour*
1 *teaspoon salt*
¼ *teaspoon pepper*
1 *teaspoon sugar*
½ *teaspoon grated onion*
1 *cup sour cream*
4 *cups green beans, sliced*
   lengthwise
2 *cups Kellogg's Special K*
½ *lb. process Swiss cheese,*
   grated

Melt margarine or butter. Blend in flour, salt, pepper, sugar, and grated onion. Add sour cream gradually and cook until thickened, stirring occasionally. Fold in green beans which have been sliced lengthwise. Pour into greased 1½-quart casserole. Combine Kellogg's Special K and grated cheese; sprinkle over beans. Bake in hot oven, 400 degrees, for 20 minutes. Serves 6.

String Beans Biscay

1 tablespoon butter or margarine
2 onions, finely chopped
2 cloves garlic, finely chopped
1 small green pepper, finely
    chopped
1 6-oz. can tomato paste
½ cup dry white wine
¾ pound string beans, snapped
    or cut

½ lb. raw ham, cut in ½-inch
    cubes
Salt, thyme, cayenne, and
    liquid red pepper seasoning
Hard-cooked egg slices
Capers
Sliced Olives

Melt butter in large saucepan over low heat. Add onions, garlic, and green pepper; cook until onions are slightly golden. Add tomato paste and cook 5 minutes. Add white wine, string beans and raw ham. Season to taste with salt, thyme, cayenne and liquid red pepper seasoning. Cover and simmer over low heat 25 to 35 minutes. (Add small amount white wine or water, if necessary.) Garnish with hard-cooked egg slices, capers, and sliced olives. Makes approximately 4 servings.

Laredo Ranch Beans

2 *cups of pinto beans*
8 *cups of water*
½ *lb. salt pork*
2 *onions, finely diced*
1 *bell pepper, finely diced*
1 *medium-sized can tomatoes*
1 *clove garlic, finely diced*
¼ *teaspoon dry mustard*
¼ *teaspoon chili powder*
½ *teaspoon MSG powder*
1 *tablespoon Worcestershire powder*
Salt and pepper to taste

Rinse beans and place into a kettle with the 8 cups of water. Boil slowly for two hours until beans are tender. Remove the floaters (the beans that come to the top of the water) and add salt pork, onions, bell pepper, tomatoes, garlic, mustard, chili powder, MSG powder, Worcestershire powder, and salt and pepper to taste. Boil slowly for about two more hours.

Lima Bonne Femme

3 *cups lima beans, cooked and drained*
2 *tablespoons melted butter*
½ *large onion, diced fine*
½ *pimiento, diced fine*
1 *cup sour cream*
Salt and pepper

Melt butter in skillet. Add onion and pimiento and sauté until soft. Add lima beans and allow to heat through by simmering for about four minutes. Add sour cream and salt and pepper to taste. Recipe can be simmered for two more minutes after the sour cream has been added.

Gingered Belgian Carrots

4 *tablespoons sugar*
1 *can (1 lb., 13-oz.) Belgian-*
   style carrots
½ *teaspoon ground ginger*
   Carrot juice

In heavy skillet, over medium heat, caramelize sugar (cook until melted and of rich brown color) stirring frequently. Drain carrots, reserving liquid. Add carrots to caramelized sugar and shake over heat until carrots are coated with sugar. Dissolve ground ginger in small amount of carrot juice. Add to carrots and shake pan again. Recipe serves 4.

Stuffed Carrots

6 *or 8 large carrots*
2 *hard-boiled eggs, chopped*
1 *tablespoon mayonnaise*
1 *tablespoon celery, finely*
   chopped
1 *tablespoon minced onion*
1 *tablespoon minced pickle*
   Paprika
   Grated Parmesan cheese

Boil carrots whole (unscraped) until tender. Peel, then split down the center. Scoop out core of each carrot half; mash cores with fork in separate bowl. Add chopped eggs, mayonnaise, celery, onion, and pickle; mix well with carrot centers. Stuff carrot boats and sprinkle with paprika and grated Parmesan cheese.

Brussels Sprouts Mattern

2 10½-oz. packages frozen Brussels sprouts
½ cup butter
1 teaspoon Worcestershire powder
2 teaspoons prepared mustard
1 tablespoon chili sauce
  Salt and pepper to taste

Cook Brussels sprouts, covered, in a small amount of boiling salted water for about 15 minutes, or just until tender. Drain and serve immediately with sauce made of remaining ingredients: Melt butter in a small saucepan; add Worcestershire powder, mustard, chili sauce, and salt and pepper to taste; stir until smooth. Pour over the drained Brussels sprouts, or pass in a bowl. Serves 6.

Almond Cauliflower

1 large cauliflower
4 tablespoons butter
½ cup slivered almonds
1 cup fine bread crumbs
1 clove garlic, minced

Steam cauliflower for 20 minutes or until tender. Heat butter in a skillet and sauté other items until almonds are golden and bread crumbs are crisp. Serve over cauliflower. Serves 6.

Scalloped Fresh Corn

3 cups fresh corn, cut
  from cob
½ cup sliced ripe olives
½ to ¾ cup mozzarella cheese,
  diced
¾ teaspoon salt
¼ teaspoon pepper
4½ teaspoons butter or
  margarine

Combine corn, ripe olives, mozzarella cheese, salt and pepper; pour into shallow 1½ to 2-quart baking dish. Dot with butter or margarine. Bake in moderate oven (325 degrees) 25 minutes or until cheese is melted and bubbling. Makes 6 servings.

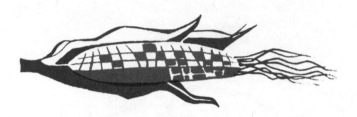

Heavenly Hominy

1 large onion, minced
  Butter
5 cups canned hominy
½ can cream of mushroom soup
1 can cream of celery soup
1 large can Parmesan cheese
1 tablespoon Worcestershire
  powder
  Juice of one lemon
1 small jar pimiento, minced
  Salt, pepper, and paprika to
  taste
  Bread crumbs

Melt butter over low heat; sauté onion. Add hominy and heat through. Add soups; blend in Parmesan cheese, Worcestershire powder, lemon juice, and minced pimiento. Season to taste with salt, pepper, and paprika. Place mixture in oblong casserole, 12x 8x2, and cover with bread crumbs. Bake 45 minutes in 350-degree oven. Recipe serves 4.

Mary Judge's Mexican Peas

1 16-oz. can English peas
½ 10-oz. can Rotel tomatoes
   and green chilies
1 large onion, sliced
   Diced, cooked ham
   Cheese
1 large tomato

Drain liquor from peas into saucepan; add tomato. Cook onion in this mixture; then add desired amount of ham and cheese, and heat until cheese melts. Add peas and heat through. Serves 6.

Eggplant Soufflé

1 large or 2 small eggplants
¼ cup butter or margarine
¼ cup flour
2 cups milk, scalded
1½ cups shredded Cheddar
    cheese
4 eggs, well beaten
½ teaspoon salt
½ teaspoon white pepper
1 cup cracker crumbs
½ cup grated Cheddar cheese

Peel and dice eggplant. Cook in salted water until tender. Drain and mash. Melt butter or margarine in saucepan over very low temperature; stir in flour. Scald milk and stir in, continuing to cook until thickened, stirring occasionally. Remove from heat. Add shredded Cheddar cheese. Cool. Add well-beaten eggs, salt and white pepper. Combine mashed eggplant and cheese sauce. Add cracker crumbs and pour into greased 2-quart casserole. Sprinkle with grated Cheddar cheese.

Bake in moderate oven (350 degrees) 30 minutes or until firm. Makes 8 servings.

Lasagne Verde

1 *large potato, sliced*
½ *9-oz. package frozen green peas*
½ *9-oz. package frozen green
   beans*
1 *8-oz. package wide noodles*
1 *bunch parsley, finely chopped*
1 *clove garlic, finely chopped*
½ *cup grated Romano cheese*
½ *cup olive oil*
½ *cup butter or margarine*
1 *cup sweet cream
   Salt and pepper*

Boil potato in salted water until almost tender. Add frozen green peas and string beans and cook until tender. Drain. Cook noodles according to directions on package; drain. Combine parsley and garlic and mash in pestle. Add Romano cheese, olive oil, butter or margarine, sweet cream, and salt and pepper and mix well. Place layer of noodles in large platter. Add layer of vegetables, top with sauce and sprinkle with grated Romano cheese. Repeat layers until all ingredients are used.

Spinach in Madeira

2 *lbs. fresh spinach*
2 *tablespoons butter or
   margarine*
¼ *cup heavy cream
   Salt and pepper to taste
   Dash nutmeg*
¼ *pound fresh mushrooms,
   thinly sliced*
2 *tablespoons Madeira
   Croutons*

In covered pan, cook spinach over low heat until barely tender, in water clinging to leaves. Drain; put through food chopper, using finest blade. Add butter or margarine and heavy cream, beating well. Add salt, pepper, and nutmeg and set aside, keeping warm.

Sauté mushrooms in butter or margarine over medium heat until tender. Combine spinach and mushrooms, and add Madeira. Heat over low heat until very hot but not boiling. Garnish with croutons fried in butter or margarine. Makes 6 servings.

Fresh Tomato-Cheese Strata

12 *slices white bread*
2 *cups creamed cottage cheese*
1 *teaspoon salt*
1 *teaspoon Worcestershire powder*
¼ *teaspoon oregano, crushed*
⅛ *teaspoon pepper*
6 *eggs*
4 *medium tomatoes, sliced*
1 *tablespoon minced onion*
¼ *teaspoon salt*
⅛ *teaspoon pepper*
1½ *cups milk*
½ *cup grated sharp Cheddar cheese*

Place 6 bread slices on bottom of 12x8x2-inch baking dish. Beat together cottage cheese, salt, Worcestershire powder, oregano, pepper, and 2 of the eggs; spread over bread. Cover cottage cheese mixture with half the sliced tomatoes and sprinkle with minced onion, salt, and pepper. Cover tomatoes with the remaining 6 bread slices. Beat 4 remaining eggs and milk together and carefully pour over bread. Cut the remaining tomato slices in half and arrange around edge of dish in scalloped effect; sprinkle with grated sharp Cheddar cheese. Chill in refrigerator 1 hour. Bake in moderate oven (350 degrees) 50 minutes or until puffed and brown. Makes 6 to 8 servings.

Tomatoes Bombay

6 *tomatoes*
½ *cup raisins*
   Small amount butter or
   margarine
2 *cups cooked rice*
½ *green pepper, diced*
½ *pimiento, diced*
3 *tablespoons olive oil*
   Juice of 1 lemon
½ *teaspoon salt*
½ *teaspoon curry powder*
   Pepper to taste
1 *tablespoon chutney*

Plunge tomatoes into boiling water, then into cold water, and slip skins from them. Cut off tops and reserve. Scoop some pulp from center of tomatoes. Holding each tomato in palm of hand, squeeze gently and turn upside down to remove seeds and juice. Let drain 1 hour and chill in refrigerator. Cook raisins in small amount of butter or margarine over low heat for a few minutes.

Combine rice, green pepper, pimiento, and cooked raisins. In separate bowl combine olive oil, lemon juice, salt, curry powder, pepper to taste and chutney, mixing well. Combine rice mixture and chutney mixture, mixing gently. Fill tomato shells with rice mixture and replace tops. Chill in refrigerator. Serve on lettuce or watercress. Makes 6 servings.

Pennsylvania Tomatoes

6 *large tomatoes (about 3 lbs.)*
½ *cup unsifted flour*
½ *cup butter or margarine*
½ *teaspoon light brown sugar*
1 *teaspoon salt*
¼ *teaspoon pepper*
   Brown sugar
1½ *cups heavy cream*

Cut thin slice from top and bottom of tomatoes, and cut each tomato in 3 crosswise slices. Dip cut sides of slices in flour.

In large skillet over medium heat melt butter or margarine and sauté tomato slices until browned on one side. Sprinkle each uncooked side with ½ teaspoon brown sugar. Turn and sprinkle with salt, pepper and small amount of brown sugar. Sauté until browned. Turn again. Add heavy cream and cook, uncovered, 5 minutes or until tomatoes are tender. Makes 6 servings.

Fireside Stuffed Potatoes

Large, white California potatoes
Bacon, cooked and broken in
small pieces
Cheddar cheese, diced
Chopped onion

Select large white California
potatoes and scrub until thoroughly clean. With an apple corer
drill a hole, starting from the long
end, through the center of the potato to about ¼ inch from the opposite end. With the corer remove
enough pulp from the center of
the potato to form a rather large
cavity. Stuff bacon pieces, diced
Cheddar and chopped onion into
the cavity. Alternate ingredients
until potato is full. Then, with a
plug of the removed potato pulp,
seal the entrance hole. Grease the
potato surface lightly and wrap in
aluminum foil. Bake in preheated
oven (375 degrees) for approximately 45 minutes or until potato
is done.

Patio Potatoes

2½ lbs. potatoes, cooked
 3 cups medium white sauce
 2 cups shredded mild Cheddar
    cheese
 1 4-oz. can peeled green chilies,
    rinsed and cut in pieces
 2 teaspoons salt
 2 cloves garlic, puréed
    Buttered bread crumbs

Peel, slice, or cube cooked potatoes; place in 1½-quart baking
dish. Combine white sauce, shredded Cheddar cheese, green chili
pieces, salt, and puréed garlic in
saucepan. Cook over very low heat
until cheese is melted. Pour cheese
mixture over potatoes. Sprinkle
buttered bread crumbs over top.
Bake in moderate oven (350 degrees) until thoroughly hot and
crumbs are brown.
Makes 6 to 8 servings.

Through the years my fondness for desserts has caused me to gather the best of the sweet-tooth charmers. Keep in mind, since the dessert is the final food presentation of a meal, your guests will most likely form their opinion of you as a food personality by your effectiveness in producing this course.

Desserts

Hawaiian Coconut Ice Box Pie

2 cups sweet milk
2 oz. cornstarch
1 cup sugar
2 tablespoons butter
3 egg yolks, whipped
1 teaspoon vanilla
1 teaspoon coconut extract
1 teaspoon plain gelatin
Cold water
3 egg whites
1 pinch salt
6 tablespoons sugar
1 cup shredded coconut
Whipping cream
9-inch baked pie shell

In top of double boiler bring milk to a boil. Combine cornstarch and sugar and pour into scalding milk. When mixture begins to thicken add butter. After this mixture has thickened add the whipped egg yolks. Lower heat and continue cooking until egg yolks are thoroughly cooked, about 30 minutes. Remove from heat and add vanilla and coconut extract.

Combine plain gelatin in just enough cold water to dissolve. Pour into custard while still warm and mix.

Whip egg whites with sugar and salt. Fold coconut into custard, reserving enough for top of pie; then fold in whipped egg whites. Pour into 9-inch baked pie shell and place in refrigerator to set (45 minutes to an hour). Top with sweetened whipped cream, and sprinkle generously with shredded coconut.

Note: Make certain cream filling is cold and gelatin has started to set before adding meringue.

Imperial Dream Pie

1 *cup toasted, slivered almonds*
1 *cup flaked coconut*
¼ *cup soft butter or margarine*
2 *tablespoons sugar*
1 *cup semi-thawed frozen raspberries and syrup*
1 *envelope unflavored gelatin*
½ *cup dairy sour cream*
1 *tablespoon grated orange rind*
1 *large banana, diced*
2 *cups drained, canned fruit cocktail*
1 *cup heavy cream, whipped*

Grind almonds medium-fine; chop coconut until fine. Combine with margarine and sugar and press evenly over bottom and sides of 9-inch pie pan. Bake in moderate oven (375 degrees) 15 minutes or until lightly browned. Cool.

Drain partially thawed raspberries, reserving syrup. Combine 6 tablespoons of syrup with gelatin; stir over very low heat until gelatin is dissolved. Stir gelatin mixture into raspberries. Add sour cream, grated orange rind, banana, and 1½ cups of the fruit cocktail. Chill mixture in freezer section of refrigerator. Fold in whipped cream. Pile mixture into almond shell. Chill in refrigerator until set. Decorate top with remaining fruit cocktail. Makes 8 servings.

Banana Chocolate Cream Pie

2 *cups milk*
1½ *one-ounce squares unsweetened chocolate*
¾ *cup sugar*
5 *tablespoons flour*
½ *teaspoon salt*
2 *egg yolks, slightly beaten*
1 *tablespoon butter or margarine*
½ *teaspoon vanilla*
1 *9-inch pastry shell or 6 3½-inch tart shells, baked*
3 *ripe (but firm) bananas*
Meringue or sweetened whipped cream (optional)

Combine milk and chocolate in saucepan and cook over very low heat until chocolate is melted, beating until blended. Combine sugar, flour, and salt and stir into chocolate mixture. Cook until thickened, stirring constantly.

Continue cooking 10 minutes, stirring occasionally. Stir chocolate mixture into the slightly beaten egg yolks; cool 1 minute. Add butter and vanilla and cool thoroughly. Place small amount of filling on bottom of baked pie or tart shell. Place banana slices on filling; then add remaining filling. Top with meringue or sweetened whipped cream if desired. Note: Packaged pudding mixes of any flavor may be used for filling. Prepare according to package directions. Cool thoroughly and fill as above.

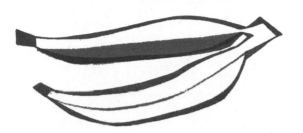

Fresh Banana Refrigerator Pie

2 teaspoons unflavored gelatin
3 tablespoons cold water
⅔ cup sugar
½ cup water
1 tablespoon lemon juice
2 large egg whites
¼ teaspoon salt
1¼ cups heavy cream, whipped
1 teaspoon vanilla
1 tablespoon sugar
1 9-inch pastry shell, baked and cooled
4 medium bananas, sliced lengthwise, in
1 tablespoon lemon juice

Soften gelatin in cold water. Combine sugar, water, and lemon juice in saucepan and cook over medium heat until small amount dropped in cold water forms soft ball. Stir in softened gelatin. Beat egg whites and salt until soft peaks form. Gradually add hot syrup mixture, beating just enough to blend thoroughly. Combine whipped cream, vanilla, and sugar. Fold three-fourths of the whipped cream into egg white mixture. Pour into baked pastry shell. Chill in refrigerator. Just before serving, dip sliced banana sections in lemon juice and arrange on top of pie. Place remaining whipped cream in center of pie.

Chocolate Chiffon Cream Pie

1 *envelope unflavored gelatin*
½ *cup cold water*
2 *squares unsweetened chocolate*
⅔ *cup sugar*
1 *cup milk*
2 *eggs, separated*
¼ *teaspoon salt*
½ *cup heavy cream, plain or whipped*
1 *teaspoon vanilla*
1 *baked pie shell, Brazil-nut, American or almond*

Soften gelatin in cold water. Combine chocolate and half the sugar in top of double boiler. Heat over boiling water until chocolate melts. Beat with rotary beater until smooth. Beat egg yolks. Add milk slowly, stirring continually. Slowly add hot chocolate mixture, stirring until well blended. Return to double boiler. Cook, stirring constantly, about 3 minutes. Add softened gelatin and stir until dissolved. Chill until mixture is consistency of unbeaten egg whites. Add salt to egg whites and beat until stiff but not dry. Gradually beat in remaining ⅓ cup sugar. Fold beaten egg whites and cream into chocolate mixture. Add vanilla. Pour into Brazil-nut piecrust shell or shell of American or almond pastry. Decorate with sliced Brazil nuts and whipped cream.

Ginger Ale Chiffon Pie

1 *envelope unflavored gelatin*
2½ *cups ginger ale*
1 *cup instant dry milk*
⅔ *cup sugar*
4 *egg yolks*
1 *tablespoon butter or*
   margarine
¼ *teaspoon salt*
1 *teaspoon vanilla*
¼ *teaspoon almond extract*
4 *egg whites*
4 *tablespoons sugar*
   Shaved unsweetened
   chocolate
1 *baked 9-inch pastry shell*

Soften gelatin in ½ cup ginger ale. Combine 2 cups ginger ale with instant dry milk, stirring until milk is dissolved. Stir in ⅔ cup sugar. Beat egg yolks in saucepan. Blend in ginger ale–milk mixture. Cook over very low heat until thickened, stirring occasionally (about 12 minutes). Add softened gelatin and continue cooking 2 to 3 minutes, stirring constantly. Add butter or margarine. Remove from heat. Add salt, vanilla and almond extract. Cool. Chill in refrigerator until thickened. Beat vigorously with rotary beater. Stiffly beat 2 egg whites and fold into the chilled mixture. Place into refrigerator once more and chill until thickened. Pour into cold, baked 9-inch pastry shell. Cover top of pie with shaved unsweetened chocolate. Chill once more until firm. Beat 2 egg whites until foamy. Gradually add 4 tablespoons sugar, beating until egg whites are stiff. Spread on pie, being careful to seal meringue onto edge of pastry to prevent shrinkage. Bake in hot oven, 450 degrees, for 4 minutes or until meringue is brown. Remove from oven and decorate top with shaved chocolate. Cool. Chill in refrigerator until served.

Fresh Strawberry Chiffon Pie

1 *tablespoon (1 envelope)*
  unflavored gelatin in
¼ *cup cold water*
3 *egg yolks*
½ *cup sugar*
¼ *teaspoon salt*
¾ *cup milk*
1½ *cups fresh, sliced*
  strawberries
3 *egg whites*
¼ *cup sugar*
1 *9-inch pastry shell, baked and*
  cooled
  Strawberries for garnish
  Whipped cream

Soften gelatin in cold water. Combine egg yolks, sugar, and salt in saucepan. Stir in milk. Cook over very low heat until mixture coats metal spoon. Blend in softened gelatin. Chill in refrigerator until consistency of unbeaten egg whites. Fold in strawberries. Beat egg whites until soft peaks form. Gradually beat in ¼ cup sugar. Fold egg whites into gelatin mixture. Pour into baked 9-inch pastry shell. Chill in refrigerator until firm. Garnish with fresh strawberries and whipped cream.

German Pecan Pie

44 *rich round crackers*
6 *egg whites*
2 *cups sugar*
2 *cups chopped pecans*
1 *teaspoon vanilla*
  Whipped cream
  Grated sweet chocolate

Thoroughly crush crackers and press crumbs onto bottom and sides of two 9-inch greased pie pans. Beat egg whites until foamy. Add sugar gradually and continue beating until soft peaks form. Add pecans and vanilla and pour into crumb shells. Bake in slow oven (275 degrees) 40 minutes. Remove from oven and let cool 2 hours. Top with whipped cream and sprinkle with chocolate. Makes two 9-inch pies.

Skillet Pecan Cake with Kentucky Sauce

4 *cups pecans*
½ *lb. candied cherries*
½ *lb. candied pineapple*
1 *lb. dates, chopped*
1 *cup flour*
1 *cup sugar*
4 *eggs, well beaten*
⅔ *cup commercially prepared*
  sweet and sour sauce
¼ *cup butter or margarine,*
  melted

1 *cup sour cream*
2 *tablespoons confectioners'*
  sugar
¼ *teaspoon grated orange rind*
  Dash bourbon
  Dash orange curaçao
2 *tablespoons orange juice*

Combine pecans, cherries, pineapple and dates in large mixing bowl. Sift flour and sugar together and add to fruit mixture, stirring until coated.

Combine beaten eggs, sweet and sour sauce, and butter or margarine and stir into fruit mixture, mixing well. Place in greased 10-inch skillet or two 8-inch pans. Bake in moderate oven (325 degrees) 2 hours in skillet, 1¼ to 1½ hours in 8-inch pans. Serve with hard sauce or Kentucky Sauce.

KENTUCKY SAUCE:

Combine all ingredients, mixing well. Chill in refrigerator.

Cherry Pound Cake

3 cups sifted flour
2 teaspoons baking powder
1 cup butter (do not use
substitute)
1 pound sifted confectioners'
sugar
5 well-beaten eggs
1 teaspoon vanilla
1 cup milk
½ cup moist flaked coconut
½ cup coarsely chopped nuts
1 bottle (3 or 6-oz.) maraschino
cherries, well drained

Sift together flour and baking powder. Cream butter thoroughly and gradually add sugar, beating well. Add eggs, a small amount at a time, beating well after each addition. Add vanilla. Beginning and ending with dry ingredients, add dry ingredients alternately with milk. Fold in coconut, chopped nuts, and cherries. Pour into greased and floured 10-inch tube pan. Bake in moderate oven (350 degrees) 1 hour. Remove from oven and cool 5 minutes. Remove from pan and finish cooling on cake rack. Dust with confectioners' sugar.

Blueberry Crackle Cake

½ cup shortening
1 cup less 2 tablespoons sugar
1 egg
½ teaspoon salt
½ teaspoon nutmeg
2½ cups flour
4 teaspoons baking powder
1 cup fresh or frozen
blueberries
1¼ cups milk
2 tablespoons sugar
¾ cup butter or margarine
½ cup fresh or frozen
blueberries
Lemon hard sauce

Blend shortening and sugar together until creamy. Add egg, beaten until light, salt and nutmeg. Sift together flour and baking powder. Add 1 cup blueberries to dry ingredients. Alternately fold dry ingredients and milk into egg mixture. Do not beat. Pour into greased pan to depth of 1½ inches. Sprinkle with 2 tablespoons sugar and dot with butter or margarine. Bake in moderate oven (375 degrees) 35 minutes. Serve with extra blueberries and lemon hard sauce.

Christmas Fruit Cake

1½ lbs. mixed candied fruits
½ lb. candied orange peel
¼ lb. candied lemon peel
½ lb. citron
½ lb. white raisins
¼ cup orange juice
¼ cup pineapple juice
1 cup pecans
½ cup blanched almonds
1 cup toasted filberts
   Sifted flour for dusting
1 cup butter
½ cup sugar
½ cup honey
5 eggs
2 cups sifted flour
1 teaspoon salt
1 teaspoon baking powder
1 teaspoon allspice
1 teaspoon powdered cloves

Chop into small pieces all of the candied fruits; mix with raisins. Mix orange juice and pineapple juice and pour over fruit and raisin mixture; allow to stand overnight. Mix pecans, almonds, and filberts (skins will peel off filberts easily after they are toasted). Dust mixed nuts with small amount of flour; then mix with fruit. Cream butter and sugar until fluffy; blend in honey. Add eggs, one at a time, beating after each addition. Be sure this mixture is creamy and smooth. Sift flour, salt, baking powder, allspice, and powdered cloves into a separate bowl. Combine this mixture with the batter and beat until smooth. Add the fruits and nuts to the batter, mixing by hand. Line two 9x5x3 loaf pans with two thicknesses of buttered brown paper. Pour batter into pans and decorate with candied fruits and nuts. Bake cakes 3½ to 4 hours in preheated 275-degree oven. Keep a pan of water in the bottom of the oven while cakes are baking. Cakes should not be served for at least four weeks. They should be wrapped in a cloth that is dampened from time to time with sherry, port or brandy.

Chocolate Cheesecake

Chocolate cookies to make
2 *cups crumbs (about* 34)
½ *teaspoon cinnamon*
½ *cup butter or margarine,*
   melted
¾ *cup sugar*
3 *eggs*
3 *8-oz. packages softened*
   cream cheese
8 *oz. semi-sweet chocolate,*
   melted
2 *tablespoons cocoa*
1 *teaspoon vanilla*
3 *cups sour cream*
¼ *cup butter or margarine,*
   melted
½ *cup heavy cream, whipped*
   Candied violets

Crush chocolate cookies into fine crumbs. Add cinnamon and melted butter or margarine. Press crumb mixture on bottom and sides of greased 9-inch spring-form pan. Chill in refrigerator. Beat sugar and eggs together and gradually add softened cream cheese. Stir in melted chocolate, cocoa, and vanilla. Add sour cream, beating well. Fold in ¼ cup melted butter or margarine, and pour batter into chilled shell. Bake in moderate oven (350 degrees) 45 minutes. Filling will seem quite liquid. Chill in refrigerator until firm. Remove side of pan. Decorate with whipped cream and candied violets.

Rainbow Cake

1 *3-oz. package cherry gelatin*
1 *3-oz. package lime gelatin*
3 *cups boiling water*
1 *cup graham cracker crumbs*
¼ *cup confectioners' sugar*
¼ *cup butter or margarine,*
   melted
1 *3-oz. package lemon*
   gelatin in
¾ *cup canned pineapple juice*
   (do not use fresh or frozen
   pineapple juice)
1 *cup heavy cream, whipped*

In two separate 8x8x2-inch pans place 1 package cherry gelatin and 1 package lime gelatin. Add 1½ cups boiling water to each, stirring

until dissolved. Chill in refrigerator until very firm.

Combine cracker crumbs, confectioners' sugar, and melted butter or margarine. Press crumb mixture on bottom and sides of 13x9x2-inch pan, reserving ¼ cup. Dissolve lemon gelatin in boiling pineapple juice. Chill until consistency of syrup; fold into whipped cream.

Cut cherry and lime flavored gelatin into cubes. Fold into whipped cream mixture. Pour into crumb-lined pan. Sprinkle with reserved crumb mixture. Chill in refrigerator until firm. Cut in squares to serve. Makes 12.

Walnut Prune Cake

1½ cups sifted flour
1 teaspoon soda
½ teaspoon salt
2 eggs
1 cup sugar
⅓ cup prune juice
1½ teaspoons lemon extract
1 cup plumped, pitted chopped prunes
1 cup chopped walnuts
¾ cup salad oil

Sift together flour, soda, and salt. Beat eggs until light and fluffy. Gradually add sugar, beating constantly. Add prune juice and lemon extract.

Combine sifted dry ingredients with egg mixture. Add prunes and walnuts, mixing well. Stir in salad oil.

Pour into greased and floured 9x9x2-inch pan. Bake in moderate oven (350 degrees) 60 to 65 minutes. Remove from oven and cool 5 minutes. Remove from pan and sprinkle with confectioners' sugar. Finish cooling on cake rack.

Giant Prune-Cinnamon Buns

2 13¾-oz. packages hot roll mix
⅓ cup soft butter or margarine
1 cup light brown sugar, firmly packed
1 tablespoon cinnamon
2 cups plumped prunes, pitted and chopped
¾ cup melted butter or margarine
1 cup sugar

Form dough from hot roll mix, according to package directions. Combine butter or margarine, brown sugar, cinnamon, and chopped prunes, mixing well. On lightly floured board roll dough to 14x20-inch rectangle. Spread with prune mixture. Starting at wide edge, roll as for jelly roll. Pinch edges to seal. Cut into 18 or 20 slices. Combine ¾ cup melted butter or margarine and 1 cup sugar; spread on bottom of two greased 13x9-inch baking pans. Place 9 or 10 rolls in each pan. Cover and let rise 35 minutes or until almost double in bulk. Bake in moderate oven (375 degrees) 35 minutes. Remove from oven and turn upside down on large tray. Let stand 1 or 2 minutes and remove pan. Place plumped prune in center of each bun, if desired. Serve warm. Makes 18 to 20.

Lemon Soufflé

1 *pint milk*
½ *cup sugar*
½ *cup butter*
½ *cup flour*
8 *beaten egg yolks*
8 *egg whites*
¼ *cup sugar*
3 *grated lemon rinds*
  Juice of three lemons

In a saucepan add milk and ½ cup sugar. Place over flame and bring to a boil. In second saucepan melt butter and add flour. Mix first and second mixtures together and add beaten egg yolks. With a mixer, whip egg whites until almost stiff; then add ¼ cup sugar, grated lemon rind, and lemon juice. Finish whipping until stiff. Fold into warm mixture and turn into a soufflé dish that has been buttered and coated with sugar. Bake in a preheated oven at 375 degrees for 50 minutes. Serve topped with Lemon Creme Sauce.

LEMON CREME SAUCE:

5 *ounces sugar*
4 *ounces sweet butter*
1 *whole egg*
2 *egg yolks*
1 *grated lemon rind*
  Juice of 2 lemons

Place all ingredients into saucepan and bring to a boil. Serve over Lemon Soufflé.

Pots de Crème

1 *6-oz. package semi-sweet chocolate pieces*
1¼ *cups light cream*
2 *egg yolks*
  Dash salt

In heavy saucepan combine chocolate and cream. Cook over very low heat until blended and smooth, stirring constantly. (Do not allow to boil.) Beat egg yolks and salt until thick and light. Gradually stir in chocolate mixture. Pour into 6 or 7 traditional crème pots or small sherbets, filling ⅔ full. Cover and chill in refrigerator at least 3 hours. Before chilling, mixture may be topped with meringue or whipped cream. Makes 6 to 7 servings.

Baked Pineapple Alaska

The recipe for Baked Pineapple Alaska is not valued as an unusual recipe, but it is one of the few dishes highly compatible with torch cooking. For the novice in torch cooking, this recipe is most useful. After one has achieved complete satisfaction torching Baked Pineapple Alaska, he may then apply the torch to other and more difficult concoctions.

Fresh pineapple
Brick ice cream
Meringue

Select one fresh pineapple for every two persons. Divide pineapple with a sharp knife into two halves. With a spoon, core out some of the heart of each section. Place brick ice cream into the cored-out sections and top with meringue, being careful to seal completely to edges of pineapple. Brown meringue with cooking torch or put pineapple halves into preheated 500-degree oven for about 5 minutes, or until meringue is lightly browned.

For meringue: Combine 5 egg whites with 1 teaspoon sugar and 1 teaspoon vanilla extract and whip until very stiff.

Old Tennessee Woodford Pudding

1 *cup sifted flour*
1 *teaspoon soda*
1 *cup sugar*
½ *cup butter or margarine*
3 *egg yolks*
1 *cup blackberry jam*
½ *cup buttermilk*
3 *well-beaten egg whites*

Sift together flour and soda. Cream together sugar and butter or margarine. Add egg yolks and blackberry jam. Add dry ingredients to creamed mixture alternately with buttermilk. Fold in beaten egg whites and pour into greased 8x8x2-inch pan. Bake in moderate oven (350 degrees) 30 to 35 minutes. Serve topped with whipped cream. Makes approximately 6 servings.

Jamaican Bananas

4 *tablespoons butter*
4 *bananas, skinned and sliced*
  in 1½-inch wedges
2 *tablespoons brown sugar*
2 *tablespoons confectioners'*
  sugar
¼ *cup rum*
1 *cup coconut, shredded*

Melt butter in the blazer pan of a chafing dish directly over heat. Place sliced bananas in butter and brown lightly. Mix in both brown and confectioners' sugar and continue to heat for 4 to 6 minutes. Add rum and flame. When flame has diminished, sprinkle coconut over bananas and serve on dessert plates. This recipe can also be served over vanilla ice cream or plain cake.

Watermelon with Rum

Cut a 3-inch plug from a watermelon and reserve. Pour rum into melon through hole, a small amount at a time, until melon will absorb no more. Fit plug back into melon. Seal cut with tape or butter or margarine. Let stand in cool place overnight or longer. Cut into wedges to serve.

Potpourri

Cheese Blintzes

FILLING:

1 *lb. dry cottage cheese*
2 *eggs, beaten*
1 *tablespoon sugar*
  Pinch cinnamon

Combine all ingredients and mix until of smooth consistency.

CRÊPES OR PANCAKES:

1 *quart milk*
3 *eggs, beaten*
1 *cup sifted flour*
  Sour cream or applesauce

Mix milk, beaten eggs and flour together to form smooth batter. Heat 6-inch skillet over medium temperature until very hot. Wipe inside of skillet with oil, leaving very thin coating. Pour batter into skillet immediately pouring off excess. Fry until light brown. Pull lightly at edges until pancake rolls. Loosen from skillet and place, browned side up, on hot platter or cloth. Repeat until batter is used.

Place a tablespoonful of filling on browned side of each pancake. Fold in edges, envelope fashion, sealing in filling. Pour oil in skillet to half the depth of each blintz. Fry blintzes over medium heat until brown on all sides. Remove from skillet and dry in cloth. Serve with sour cream or applesauce. Fruit fillings may also be used. Makes 15 to 20.

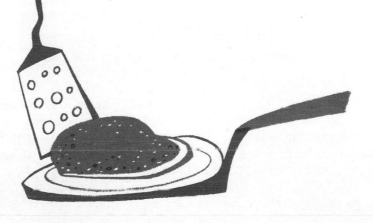

Southern Kitchen's Famous Hush Puppies

1½ cups white corn meal
½ cup sifted flour
1 teaspoon baking powder
¼ teaspoon baking soda
1 teaspoon salt
¼ cup finely chopped green onions, part tops
½ cup crumbled, crisply fried bacon pieces
¾ cup buttermilk or sour milk
1 egg, beaten

Combine corn meal, flour, baking powder, soda, salt, green onions, and fried crumbled bacon. Stir in buttermilk or sour milk and egg.

Let stand 20 to 30 minutes to let batter thicken. Pour salad or cooking oil in deep pan to depth of 2 inches. Heat over medium heat (375 to 400 degrees). Drop batter by heaping teaspoonfuls into hot oil. Fry to a deep rich brown. Drain on absorbent paper. Makes 15 to 18.

Texas Gourmet Dressing

Enough prepared corn bread to fill two 8x12x2 pans
1 pound pecans
3 4-oz. cans mushrooms
8 cups turkey stock
2 onions, diced
1 cup diced celery
Salt and pepper

Crumble corn bread and mix with pecans, mushrooms, turkey stock, diced onions and celery, and salt and pepper to taste. Place into two pans greased with butter; bake in preheated 400-degree oven until brown. This recipe should fill both pans.

Boston Brown Bread

1 cup water
1½ cups raisins
2 tablespoons shortening
½ cup prune juice
1 egg
1 teaspoon vanilla
1 cup sugar
½ teaspoon salt
2 cups flour
¾ cup wheat germ
2 teaspoons baking soda (measure carefully)
½ cup shelled pecans, broken in pieces

In saucepan combine water and raisins and bring to boil. Boil one minute and remove from heat. Blend in shortening. Allow mixture to cool about 10 minutes. Mix in prune juice, egg, and vanilla; blend thoroughly.

Sift together sugar, salt, flour, wheat germ, and baking soda. Combine the two mixtures and mix, **do not beat.** Stir in pecans.

Fill greased baking cans ⅔ full and place into preheated oven (350 degrees). Bake 45 minutes or longer, until crusty. Recipe makes 3 or 4 loaves depending on size of baking cans.

El Sombrero Corn Bread

1½ cups corn meal
1 teaspoon salt
3 teaspoons baking powder
2 eggs, slightly beaten
⅔ cup vegetable oil
1 cup sour cream
1 16-oz. can cream-style corn
3 canned Jalapeño peppers, seeded and chopped
1 cup grated Cheddar cheese

In medium mixing bowl combine corn meal, salt, and baking powder. Add slightly beaten eggs, vegetable oil, and sour cream; stir until just blended. Stir in corn and Jalapeño peppers. Pour half of batter into greased 8x8x2-inch pan. Cover with half of the grated cheese. Repeat with remaining batter and cheese. Bake in moderate oven (350 degrees) 35 to 40 minutes. Cut into squares and serve hot.

Quick Onion Kuchen

2 tablespoons butter or mar-
    garine
4 large onions, sliced
4 slices rye bread
2 eggs, beaten
1 cup sour cream
¼ teaspoon salt
    Pepper to taste
½ teaspoon caraway seed, if
    desired
2 to 4 slices bacon

Heat butter or margarine in skillet over medium heat; add sliced onion and sauté until tender. In greased shallow baking pan, place rye bread slices and cover with sautéed onions. Combine beaten eggs, sour cream, salt, pepper, and caraway seed and pour over onions. Cut bacon slices in half and arrange on top. Bake in moderate oven (325 degrees) 25 minutes or until bacon is crisp. Makes 4 servings.

Cheese Balls

¾ lb. extra sharp Cheddar cheese
3 egg whites
⅓ cup flour
4 dashes Tabasco
    Dash salt
1 teaspoon parsley flakes
    Paprika
    Corn meal
    Hot, melted shortening or oil

Grate Cheddar cheese; beat egg whites until very stiff and add grated cheese. Add flour, Tabasco, salt, parsley flakes, and paprika for color. Roll mixture into small balls and roll in corn meal. Place balls in skillet with about ¼ inch hot, melted shortening or oil. Allow the cheese balls to cook until golden brown, constantly turning with a long fork.

Canadian Cheese Soup

¼ cup butter or margarine
½ cup finely diced onion
½ cup finely diced carrots
½ cup finely diced celery
¼ cup flour
4½ teaspoons cornstarch
1 quart chicken stock
1 quart milk
⅛ teaspoon soda
1 cup process American cheese,
   grated
   Salt and pepper
2 tablespoons finely chopped
   parsley

Melt butter or margarine over medium heat. Add diced onion, carrots, and celery and cook until soft. Blend in flour and cornstarch and cook until bubbly. Blend in chicken stock and milk to make smooth sauce. Add soda and grated cheese; season with salt and pepper. Just before serving, add chopped parsley. Makes 8 servings.

Holiday Sweet Soup

1 cup dried apricots
1 cup dried prunes
1 quart apple cider
2 tablespoons sugar
   Juice of 1 lemon
¼ teaspoon nutmeg
¼ teaspoon cinnamon
   Dash ground cloves
   Pinch salt
6 lemon slices and whole cloves
   for garnish

Wash apricots and prunes and dry. Combine fruit with cider in a kettle and heat to boiling. Lower heat and simmer for 30 minutes or until fruit is tender. Add sugar, lemon juice, spices, and salt. Serve soup chilled or hot and garnish with a lemon slice and a whole clove. Recipe serves 6.

Cream of Asparagus Soup

2 tablespoons butter or margarine
½ cup chopped onion
½ cup chopped celery
2 16-oz. cans green asparagus spears

6 chicken bouillon cubes
4 tablespoons butter or margarine
¼ cup flour
1 cup light cream
Salt and pepper to taste

Melt butter or margarine in saucepan over low heat. Add onion and celery and cook until tender. Drain the 2 cans of asparagus spears, reserving liquid. Cut tips and set aside. Dice stalks and add to cooked vegetables along with asparagus liquid and water to make 5 cups. Add bouillon cubes. Bring to boil and cook 5 minutes. Remove from heat and put through sieve or food mill. Melt 4 tablespoons butter or margarine in saucepan over very low heat and stir in flour. Stir in light cream, continuing to cook until thickened, stirring constantly. Add sieved asparagus mixture, asparagus tips, salt and pepper, and heat to serving temperature. Makes approximately 1½ quarts.

Egg Croquettes

¾ cup chopped fresh or canned
  mushrooms
3 tablespoons butter or margarine
4 tablespoons flour
1 cup milk
½ teaspoon Worcestershire
  powder
  Salt, pepper, and cayenne to
  taste
1 teaspoon minced chives or
  onion
4 hard-cooked eggs, minced
  Fine bread crumbs
1 egg yolk, beaten

Cook mushrooms in butter over medium heat until tender but not browned. Remove mushrooms and save. Stir flour into butter or margarine that remains. Gradually add milk, Worcestershire powder, salt, pepper, and cayenne and cook over very low heat until thick, stirring constantly. Remove from flame. Add cooked mushrooms, minced chives or onion, and minced hard-cooked eggs. Chill in refrigerator.

Form into croquettes. Roll in fine bread crumbs, then roll in beaten egg yolk. Roll again in bread crumbs. Fry in deep hot fat (375–400 degrees) until golden brown. Drain on absorbent paper. Serve plain or with hot sauce. Makes 4 servings

Eggs Parisienne

2 large eggs
1 tablespoon chopped chives
1 tablespoon sour cream
2 teaspoons grated Parmesan
  cheese
¼ teaspoon salt
  Butter or margarine

Beat eggs, chopped chives, sour cream, Parmesan cheese, and salt together until well mixed. Heat butter or margarine in skillet over low temperature. Add egg mixture and cook, stirring constantly, until eggs are set. Makes 1 serving.

Huevos Rancheros

3 tablespoons olive oil
1 large onion, sliced
1 large green pepper, sliced
1 clove garlic, crushed
1 tablespoon flour
3½ cups peeled, cooked tomatoes
   Salt and pepper
   Chili powder
   Cumin
   Oregano
2 tablespoons dry white wine
6 eggs
   Sharp Cheddar cheese, cubed
   Pitted black olives

Heat olive oil in saucepan over low heat. Add onion, green pepper, and garlic and cook 3 minutes. Blend in flour. Add tomatoes and cook, stirring, for a few minutes. Add salt and pepper, chili powder, cumin and oregano to taste. Add wine and cook 5 minutes.

Pour sauce into shallow baking dish. Break eggs into shallow dish, one at a time, and slip into depression in sauce. Between eggs, place cubed Cheddar cheese and black olives. Bake in moderate oven (350 degrees) 12 minutes or until eggs are set. Makes 6 servings.

Roquefort Cream Dressing

½ cup crumbled Roquefort or
   blue cheese
1 3-oz. package cream cheese
½ cup cream
½ cup mayonnaise
1 tablespoon lemon juice
1 tablespoon wine vinegar

Blend the Roquefort or blue cheese with the cream cheese. Gradually blend in the cream; then add the mayonnaise, lemon juice, and vinegar.

Recipe yields 1¼ cups.

Searching out the colorful and historical backgrounds of recipes and ingredients is an enjoyable experience for many people. This section provides outstanding food reports adapted from those published previously in my syndicated newspaper column. These creative editorials stir romance and intrigue into even the most ordinary food preparations.

Syndicated
Newspaper Columns

Hong Kong is a merchant city devoted to buying and selling. Here in this English-administered Chinese metropolis you really can find a bargain. Hong Kong is a duty-free port.

In my opinion, Hong Kong Harbor is the most beautiful in the world. Nightside with the lights flickering along the water's edge and the whole harbor specked with tiny lights from junks and sampans, it is difficult to imagine the frantic activity of the daytime commercial community. Tomorrow the boats will move in and out of the harbor transporting goods and produce, heading for their fishing grounds. Living on these little boats are the boat people of Hong Kong.

In Hong Kong's Aberdeen Bay the boat people will provide you with water-taxi service to the Sea Palace Floating Restaurant. Sampan girls clamor for your fare and skillfully navigate your party to the restaurant. The Sea Palace is itself a riverboat. The decor is Chinese pagoda. Brilliant colors and bright decorations festoon the floating dining room. The restaurant specializes in seafood, which you select when you enter.

Aberdeen

2 tablespoons cornstarch
2 teaspoons soy sauce
3 cups cold chicken
    consommé or chicken broth
1 teaspoon sugar
1 teaspoon garlic powder
    Salt to taste
    Pepper to taste
16 mushrooms, chopped
2 tablespoons margarine
8 eggs
2 green onions, chopped
1 stalk celery, chopped
1 can bean sprouts, drained
    (1 lb., 4 oz. size)
2 cups cooked shrimp, chopped

2 teaspoons soy sauce
1 teaspoon salt
¼ teaspoon pepper
    Peanut oil

In a saucepan dissolve cornstarch in soy sauce and consommé or broth. Add sugar, garlic powder, salt and pepper, and cook over medium heat, stirring constantly until sauce boils and thickens. Keep this sauce warm while preparing the pancakes.

Using a skillet, melt margarine and in it sauté the chopped mushrooms. In a mixing bowl beat eggs

The Sea Palace is a three-decker: lower floor for the crew's living quarters; second floor for games (actually gambling is not legal in Hong Kong so the famous Chinese game mah-jongg is played); then up to the third floor for the gourmet's selection from the menu. Here the menu is not brought to you; you go to the menu. In an area by the entrance are large wicker baskets sectioned off to separate various fishes, crabs, lobsters, and snails from the sea. With the point of a finger to your idea of dining pleasure, the fishboy snaps up your choice and takes it to the cook. You return to your table and await the result of the chef's expertise. Very meticulous cooks, the Chinese devote much time and thought to the preparation of food with skill and dedication. They serve the cooked morsels beautifully and the final happy scene is a unique restaurant complete with dining seascape and delicious gourmet chow.

Egg Foo Yung is a seafood Chinese pancake, an Oriental all-in-one meal. Take your time with this recipe. It requires some chopping and mixing with care, especially as the Sea Palace performs it, but the recipe is easily executed by just following instructions.

Egg Foo Yung

lightly, add the already sautéed mushrooms, green onions, celery, bean sprouts, shrimp, soy sauce, salt and pepper.

Heat a 6-inch skillet over medium heat until nearly smoking. Pour in a thin film of peanut oil, just enough to cover the bottom of the skillet. Continue to heat oil until it looks wavy. Pour ½ cup of the egg mixture into the hot skillet. Fry until brown, turn, and fry until brown on the other side. Repeat until batter is all used. Pour 2 tablespoons sauce over each pancake. Serve remaining sauce in bowl. Makes 4 servings.

When you are setting your festive holiday table with all kinds of traditional goodies around a splendid bowl of eggnog, the most exotic ingredient there will probably be nutmeg. Some of the finest nutmegs come from our own hemisphere, from Grenada in the Windward Islands. Or, your nutmeg may have come from Indonesia, which is almost 12,000 miles away.

Last year we imported 4.5 million pounds of nutmegs from 11 different countries. That's quite a lot of nutmeg when you remember how much lovely aroma you get from just a little sprinkling of this spice. On the other hand, maybe it's not a bit too much when you consider all the things that taste so much more exciting with a dash of this beige-colored spice.

Nutmeg trees are evergreens which "must smell the sea," so tradition says. That means they live on islands or peninsulas. The Moluccas, or, as they have been called, "Nutmeg Islands," were known to the Malays and Javanese for many ages before the advent of Europeans. The spice buyers of ancient Greece and Rome knew as little about the existence of the spice lands of the Far East as they did about the Western Hemisphere. They surely had some kind of vague notion that there must be countries, even beyond India, which produced spices. But, for centuries, the crafty Arab spice traders kept Europe in the dark about spice origins. It must have been about A.D. 600 that nutmegs began making their way to Europe, where they became very popular in the next few centuries.

Numerous explorers and botanists have written about nutmeg. Pierre Pomet, chief druggist to the late King Louis XIV, who described nutmegs in 1725, included a charming note on the climate

Applesauce

1 14-oz. *package gingerbread mix*
1 *cup heavy cream*
2 *tablespoons sugar*
1 *teaspoon ground nutmeg*
½ *cup canned applesauce*
  Red or green maraschino cherries

and life in the Nutmeg Islands. "The climate is so temperate," wrote Pomet, "that the Men live to 120 years of age. They have nothing to do but eat, drink and sleep, and now and then walk about, while the women employ themselves in separating the Brouze from the Nutmeg, drying the Mace and breaking the shell wherein is the nutmeg. This is the chief commodity of the country, and almost all they live by."

The nutmeg tree traveled to the Western Hemisphere in 1843, when the captain of a visiting Dutch ship gave a couple of nutmeg seeds to one of the planters on the island of Grenada. Nutmegs loved the climate and soil of this part of the Caribbean area and produced lustily. Until 1955, about half of the world's nutmegs came from there. Then came Hurricane Janet, destroying about three-fourths of the trees. (You may remember that the recent, very erratic Flora originated in this part of the Caribbean, but it did very little damage to the nutmeg trees.) In another year or two, nutmeg production in Grenada should be very nearly back to normal.

All this while we've been talking about nutmeg without once mentioning mace. These are "sister spices." The nutmeg fruit looks like a small peach and the pulp is edible, though fibrous. Once that's removed there is a handsome red lace-like fiber around the core. The lace is mace, "the pound cake spice." Next comes a thin, unusable shell, and inside this is the whole nutmeg, about the size of a hazelnut. While nutmeg and mace differ somewhat in flavor, either is delightful in a great variety of foods, especially in rich and creamy mixtures.

Gingerbread

Prepare gingerbread as directed on package and bake in 8x8x2-inch pan. Cut into 2-inch squares.

Place cream, sugar and nutmeg in a bowl and beat until cream stands in soft peaks. Fold in applesauce.

Serve over warm gingerbread. Garnish with red or green maraschino cherries. Recipe serves 9.

Only a very narrow strip of sea divides the Rock of Gibraltar and Europe from Morocco and Africa. Old legend has it that the two continents were not divided by the sea in ancient times until Hercules tore them apart with his strong hands. Near Tangier you can still see the famous Rock of Hercules, the exact spot where this feat was supposed to have been accomplished.

Although I strongly believe there is a basis of truth to many old legends, I have grave doubts about this particular one, simply because there is such marked difference between the two sides of that narrow strip of sea. They are obviously two different worlds. Of course, Gibraltar is a highly peculiar place, with its British administration and friendly British policemen, but even on the Spanish side, you still feel conscious that you are in Europe. When you set foot on the other side in Africa, you are whisked back to biblical times where burnoosed figures walk sedately along with overladen mules. There

Arabian Roast Chicken

1 *chicken*
2 *tablespoons honey*
1 *oz. melted butter*
1 *teaspoon rosewater*
½ *oz. pistachio nuts, finely chopped*
½ *oz. crystallized cherries, cut in quarters*
1 *oz. preserved ginger, chopped*

Melt the butter and add it to the honey. Prick the breast and legs of the bird and rub some of the honey and butter well in. Pour more of the honey mixture and the rosewater inside the bird. Roast in the usual way. When done, cut the bird in half, lay it flat on the serving dish and sprinkle it with the 'nuts, cherries and ginger. Recipe serves 2.

are colorful and motley markets full of noise and outlandish spices. You enter restaurants where you are seated on very low benches and served Moroccan couscous by bowing Arabs. Practically all Middle Eastern dishes have an unusual mixture of sweet and savory. Nutmeg and cinnamon are often used in savory dishes, a spice which the Westerner reserves for sweet dishes as a matter of tradition. Otherwise why should we discard apples stuffed with minced chicken, if we consider it quite in order to eat applesauce with pork? We serve turkey with cranberry sauce, so why should we not try to roast a chicken the Arabian way with honey and nuts? Once you start looking at Arabian cooking from this angle, you will find that it affords a refreshingly new scope for cooks with imagination.

The following recipe is an example of simple Arabian cooking that also spells out economy.

with Honey and Nuts

One of the oldest of all continued stories—the "soap opera" of its day—is a collection of tales entitled "One Thousand and One Nights." These stories date from the 14th century and were told by Queen Scheherazade to her husband, the Sultan.

This Sultan obviously needed variety in his life, for he had decreed that none of his brides were to live longer than a day. Came Queen Scheherazade's turn, she was smart enough to start telling the Sultan a long and fascinating story. When she got to the most exciting part of the tale she would announce that the next day would bring another fabulous episode. The Sultan wanted to hear more of the story, so she lived on for 1001 nights.

One of the thrillers which is still popular six centuries later is the story of Sinbad the Sailor, who learned to open the robber cave filled with gold and jewels of all kinds simply by saying, "Open, Sesame!"

Sesame is one of the world's oldest spice and oil seeds. Probably the robbers had chosen "Open, Sesame" as a password because then, as now, ripe sesame seeds fairly pop out of their pods. This popping out of seeds has always been a problem to the sesame seed grower.

Sesame seeds are white and have a glossy, pearly skin. In each seed is a miniature droplet of oil of nut-like sweetness. It has been highly esteemed for thousands of years. In fact, in the British Museum in London there are ancient tablets mentioning sesame. On these, hewn in stone, is the Assyrian story of the creation of the world. In one scene the gods take time out to "eat bread and drink sesame wine."

Since those days sesame seeds have been used as a food in the Near East, the Orient, and Africa. More than 4.5 billion pounds of sesame seeds are grown throughout the world. Much of it is used as a flavorful oil, but millions of pounds are used as whole seeds. We find it in the Near East confection, halvah; in pralines; on loaves of Italian bread, delicately golden. We also meet it in ever-increasing numbers of cocktail crackers, cookies, rolls, and other bread products.

Sesame seeds can be used in many dishes where one might ordinarily use very finely chopped nuts. If they are to be stirred into a mixture, used in a filling or stuffing, showered on salad greens or buttered noodles, they should be toasted. About 20 minutes in a moderate oven, thinly scattered in a baking dish, toasts them pale brown and brings out their best flavor. If they are to be sprinkled on cookies, bread, or rolls, toasting is unnecessary as they will turn golden as the dough bakes.

Sesame seeds are an increasingly popular item as more cooks realize how very easily they can add delicious flavor and richness to their own favorite recipes. Just shake them in, without worrying much about measuring: "the more the better."

Sesame seeds are nourishing. Small wonder they served as a sort of K ration for Greek soldiers many centuries ago. Sesame seeds are high in calcium and vitamin C, with appreciable amounts of lecithin, B-12, and vitamins D and F. However, we use them principally for their delicately good flavor, as, for instance, in the following recipe.

Asparagus with Toasted Sesame Seed Butter

2 tablespoons butter or margarine
1 tablespoon lemon juice
2 tablespoons toasted sesame
seeds
2 pounds cooked asparagus

Melt butter or margarine; add lemon juice and sesame seeds. Pour over cooked asparagus. Serve at once. Recipe serves 6.

Every year Florida growers have to plant more and longer rows of sweet corn to satisfy our yen for this all-American treat. In fact, between November and the end of May, Florida sends up to 700 million ears of fresh sweet corn to our dinner tables. Only the tender, choice, well-developed ears go to fresh market.

The Florida corn industry is so big that it reminds us of Paul Bunyan's cornstalk. (Paul Bunyan's tall tales began to accumulate about 1910 and have been collecting ever since.) Paul Bunyan once planted a single grain of corn which grew so fast and so big that nobody could see the top. His partner, Swede Charlie, climbed up, but couldn't get back down because the stalk grew upward faster than Charlie could slide down. Soon the U.S. Navy complained that the roots of Paul's cornstalk had reached under Lake Huron on one side and under Lake Michigan on the other. They interfered with navigation and the cornstalk must be cut down. Fifty men chopped as hard as they could. When the cornstalk finally gave way and began falling it is said the top whistled through the air two and a half days before it struck the ground miles away.

There are other tall corn tales in American folklore. One man, so the story goes, had very, very rich corn land. One day he planted rows of corn and then hammered a stake into the ground to mark his stopping place. Next morning each seed was full grown, with 10 ears on it, and even the wooden stake could boast 4 ears of corn.

Watch them harvest sweet corn in Florida and you'll think Paul Bunyan is at work. They pick 20 rows at a time. Not only pick, but grade and crate the ears at top speed. Seventy to 100 men and women work beside or on what's called a "mule train." This is a small pack-

Baked Fresh

2 cups fresh corn, cut off the
  cob
1 tablespoon flour
1 tablespoon sugar
1 tablespoon butter or margarine
3 eggs, beaten
1½ teaspoons salt
⅛ teaspoon ground black pepper

1 cup milk
½ cup heavy cream

Combine all ingredients. Turn into buttered 6-cup casserole. Place in pan of hot water. Bake in preheated oven (325 degrees) 1½ hours or until knife inserted in center comes out clean. Recipe serves 6.

ing shed on wheels, which is pulled along slowly by tractor. Watching this crew in motion is almost like watching a ballet. As the ears move along on a belt from grader to packer to crate-closer, not a single motion seems wasted. That's because they're in a huge hurry to get the fresh corn out of the field heat into the icy bath of the hydro-cooler. This quick cooling after harvest and the prompt trip to market under a blanket of shaved ice preserve the delicate sweetness of the corn. This should be a lesson to every homemaker: once purchased, either cook the fresh corn immediately or refrigerate it and cook it as soon as possible.

Sweet corn of good quality has a cob well filled with bright, plump, milky kernels; its "milk" is thick and creamy. Fresh, green husks are a sign of prime quality.

When boiling corn on the cob, drop it into enough boiling water to cover the ears. Add a teaspoon of sugar per quart of water. Cover and cook rapidly, just until set. That means 5 or 6 minutes for tender young corn; about 10 minutes for more mature ears. Serve piping hot with salt, fresh ground black pepper, and butter, or a seasoned butter.

Foil-wrapped corn may be baked either over a charcoal grill or in a preheated oven set at about 425 degrees. To prepare, husk corn and remove silks. Place each ear on a square of aluminum foil. Sprinkle with salt, pepper, and a generous dab of butter or margarine. Wrap securely by making a double lengthwise fold on top of the ear. Turn up the ends of the foil and fold smoothly against the corn. Whether grilled or baked, allow 20 to 25 minutes cooking time. Try the following recipe using fresh corn.

Corn Casserole

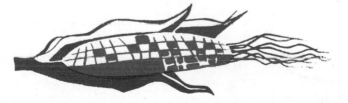

President Johnson was no doubt our most popular salesman of the meat and sauce wedding of flavors we call barbecue. Popular it has always been, but if just perchance there breathed a man in the world who had not heard of this Western taste experience, he surely must have been informed of it via the communications media from the LBJ Ranch fiestas where the great, the near-great, and the soon-to-be-great were most graciously entertained in true Western style.

Really, barbecue is not a food. It is a **method** of cooking meaning, literally, "to roast from snout to tail." We don't often, if ever, have the opportunity to barbecue such a huge piece of meat today, so we concentrate on the smaller cuts, with great emphasis on the sauce. The grandfather of all barbecue sauces is chili; at least, so it was in the beginning. But we have sought out a great many inventions, until

Barbecue

SWEET AND SOUR SPARE RIBS:

This recipe can be cooked in your oven and served inside by the fire, or outside on the patio.

Begin by selecting the desired amount of spare ribs and marinating them for thirty minutes in lemon juice.

Make the sauce as follows:

1 bottle catsup
½ cup white Karo syrup
⅓ cup wine vinegar
1 tablespoon garlic salt
Juice of one lemon
Dash Tabasco
1 teaspoon Worcestershire powder

today there are hundreds of variations of barbecue sauce; everyone has a favorite. This interest in sauce, possibly, is what caused the visitor from the East to remark that "out West they barbecue everything except ice cream."

Barbecuing was introduced to us by the early French explorers. Those Frenchmen lived off the game of the land, cooked and ate outdoors, there being nothing else for them to do in this unexplored, unsettled country of ours. This is probably why barbecue still brings to mind a picture of outdoor dining, and indeed it is very much suited for the great outdoors still.

The Frenchmen were looking for gold, which they didn't find. More likely, the really great discovery was the barbecue which Americans discovered from the French.

Mix together and simmer for 10 to 15 minutes. Drain the lemon juice marinade from the ribs and place ribs in a greased oven dish. Pour the sweet and sour sauce over the ribs and place a cover over the oven dish. Put them into a 375-degree oven and roast for one hour and thirty minutes. Check ribs from time to time and baste with the sauce. Do not allow ribs to become too dry. They should be moist and tender. If they are not as brown as you like them, allow them to cook the last 10 minutes with the cover off.

Incidentally, try serving these as hors d'oeuvres before dinner, really the first course of the meal. But provide only a few per person. It's mighty tempting, pardner, to make a whole meal of them. A big ten-gallon-hat cheer is in order for those early French explorers.

An ancient Chinese cook once said, "Every eating material can be made palatable," and his countrymen have always taken him at his word. Among the products eaten in China are snakes, shark fins, fermented eggs, and birds' nests. Such strange sounding ingredients for recipes as these have detoured many a fine cook away from Chinese food, as it seemed too bizarre to undertake. But it is the Chinese genius for giving flavor and optimum spirit to commonplace vegetables, meat, and fish that has earned them their great culinary fame.

If you examine Chinese recipes you will discover that they are compounded of such familiar foods as chicken, shrimp, pork, eggs, mushrooms, duck, cabbage, and cucumbers. Many Chinese specialties have Western near-counterparts. Egg foo yung, constructed with meat

Beef

or seafood, is quite similar to our omelets. Won ton soup is a clear chicken stock with pork-filled won tons, a kind of Chinese ravioli. Many simple Chinese dishes permit the imaginative cook much latitude. "Chop suey" simply means a mixture. And "sub gum," though it translates as ten different varieties of beauty, actually means a mixture of ten different items, usually green groceries.

With all of their teasing eye appeal and intrinsic flavors, most Chinese dishes do not require a fat purse to effect properly. I would say that the requisite for becoming a good Chinese cook is to possess a strong arm for chopping and a wary eye for timing. Most foodstuffs cooked in the Chinese manner are first minced and julienned, then flame-kissed until tender but not overcooked. Add the following recipe to your lexicon of Chinese foods.

Chop Suey

1½ lbs. beef, diced
¼ cup oil
2 tablespoons soy sauce
2 teaspoons salt
  Freshly ground black pepper
3 cups celery, cut in 1-inch pieces
2 large onions, chopped
1 tablespoon molasses
2 cups beef bouillon
2 cups canned bean sprouts, drained
3 tablespoons cornstarch
¼ cup water
6 cups hot boiled rice

Fry beef in oil over high heat for 3 minutes, stirring constantly. Stir in soy sauce, salt, and pepper. Remove meat and keep hot. To oil remaining in saucepan, add celery, onion, molasses, and bouillon. Bring to a boil and cook for 10 minutes, stirring frequently. Add bean sprouts and cook for 3 minutes. Replace beef. Mix cornstarch and ¼ cup water, and add. Cook until thickened, stirring constantly. Serve with rice. Recipe serves 6.

Preparation of food enjoys first place as America's number one avocation. Movie stars, politicians, teenagers, and businessmen have nudged the housewife and the chef over and joined their ranks, claiming some culinary fame of their own.

When appreciation of fine food reaches such a peak of general interest, we are no longer just eating; we are dining. Today America is dining in a large and fancy way. Supermarkets now have fancy food sections and department stores have joined the parade, featuring such items as rattlesnake meat from Florida, grasshoppers (fried, of course) from Japan, truffles and snails from France, caviar from the Balkans—almost everything which is considered an eatable delicacy in other parts of the world.

Beef

2 lbs. lean beef cubes, diced into
  1-inch squares
½ lb. butter
1 onion, diced
1 cup mushrooms
  Dash Tabasco
1 tablespoon Worcestershire
  powder
½ bell pepper, diced
1 clove garlic, diced
1 tablespoon garlic salt
1 cup sour cream
1 cup heavy cream
3 tablespoons wine vinegar
2 tablespoons flour
  Rice
  Beef consommé
  Water

We are dining in more exclusive, more specialized restaurants, and dining out in ever-increasing numbers, too. Tastes are favoring the international cuisines, emphasizing traditional Old World foods. The art of turning ordinary groceries into haute cuisine is the goal of every true gourmet. Mark Twain once said of writing, "All the words are in the dictionary." We might paraphrase his statement, and, applying it to cooking, say, "All the ingredients are in the supermarket." Ah, but there's the catch: how shall we put them together? We must have a plan, a blueprint, a recipe.

Here's my interpretation, my blueprint, for a traditional Old World favorite, Beef Stroganoff, a recipe which will haunt your hungry moments for weeks to come.

Stroganoff

Sauté beef cubes in butter until brown. After meat begins to brown, add onions, mushrooms, Tabasco, Worcestershire powder, bell pepper, garlic and garlic salt. When these ingredients begin to soften, add sour cream, heavy cream, and wine vinegar. Now add the flour. Let this mixture continue to simmer for one hour or until meat cubes are completely tender. Serve Beef Stroganoff over rice, which has been boiled in one part beef consommé and one part water until golden brown. Garnish. Recipe serves four.

In countries near the Equator very pungently spiced foods are usually served. People who have grown up in India, Brazil or Indonesia offer several explanations for this preference: "The spices which go into the making of a good curry grow best in tropical heat. People usually eat what grows near at hand—we've loved good, nippy spicing since childhood." A native of India tells me, "Our foods just wouldn't taste right without plenty of spice. Eating hot dishes promotes perspiration which helps keep the body cool."

Here in the United States we eat curries and such bravely spiced foods because they are delicious. The curry powder ground and blended in this country is richly aromatic, but mild compared with curry powders packed for India and the Far East.

It's amazing to know that curry powder is no Johnny-come-lately to the American spice shelf. Actually, curry powder has been sold for generations. In a cookbook printed in Philadelphia in 1792, I found a recipe for Curry of Chicken which directs, "Get a bottle of curry powder. Strew it over the chicken when frying. If it is not seasoned highly enough, put in a little cayenne." Other cookbooks more than a century old add more proof that this intriguing bouquet has been known for a very long time.

They were eating curries in India almost 1500 years ago. Curries are mentioned in an Indian tale wherein one of the characters ate "rice dressed in butter, with its full accompaniment of curries." Naturally these early curries wouldn't have been seasoned with curry powder such as we know. In India, even today, the housewife generally grinds or bruises whole spices as they are needed for the day's meals.

Even more important, those ancient curries would have been made

Bombay Turkey

Roasting turkey
Salt and pepper
Curry powder
Salad oil
2 tablespoons minced prepared onion
12 lbs. gray moist pottery clay (approximately)

Select an average-size roasting turkey and season the cavity and outside with salt, pepper, and curry powder; rub the surface lightly with salad oil. Into the cavity place the minced prepared onion. Wrap the turkey securely in foil, placing the shiny surface toward the turkey. Using approximately

without red peppers. "Chilies," the Indians call these pungent peppers, and add them in generous numbers. These originated in the Western Hemisphere and would not have reached India until America was discovered a thousand years later. Today, of course, any curry dish without the snap of red peppers would be unthinkable!

All curry powders are a rich blend of spices, although almost all formulas differ somewhat (some are even well-kept family secrets in India). Cumin, coriander, fenugreek, turmeric, and red pepper are used in varying amounts. In addition, manufacturers may use one or more spices such as cinnamon, allspice, cardamom, cloves, fennel, ginger, yellow mustard, mace, and black or white pepper.

Curry powder is the handiest kind of seasoning for many American standbys. It gives exciting flavor to meats, fish, fowl, vegetables, salad dressings, and soups. This doesn't mean you must try for an Indian-type curried dish. Rather you "appropriate" the national spice of India into your Yankee kitchen and recipe, using just enough to enhance the natural flavors of the food.

For instance, add a teaspoon of curry powder to a can of green pea soup. Or, to a can of cream of mushroom soup and a 7-ounce can of tuna fish to be served over toast or in patty cases. For delicious flavor, cook a cup of rice in 2 cups chicken stock and season with 2 teaspoons curry powder and a tablespoon of instant minced onion. Add a teaspoon of curry powder to the mayonnaise for an egg, seafood, or potato salad.

The following recipe is one of the most exciting I have found for curry. It is delightful at any season of the year and extremely compatible for dinner parties since it has an ostentatious nature.

in Clay

12 pounds of gray moist pottery clay, completely cover the foil-wrapped turkey with a ¼-inch layer of the clay.

Be sure that the bird is completely sealed, leaving no open places, and place—encased in the clay—into an open roasting pan. (Do not cover the roasting pan with a lid.) Place pan into a preheated oven at 400 degrees and cook about 12 to 14 minutes per pound. When roasting time is completed, break the clay away and remove the turkey from the foil.

One of the most difficult recipes to bring off properly is Peking Duck, yet it is at the top of the list as an epicure's delight. A likewise troublesome kitchen adventure is the staging of the Polynesian version of Roast Almond Duck. While these two classic items of cuisine represent the epitome in duck cookery, I rarely ever receive a request for their blueprints. Each year, however, when wild ducks darken our skies and you can hear bursts of gunfire from nearby lakes and marshes, my telephone rings constantly with requests for recipes and suggestions for handling this wild game bird.

There is always some question as to the degree of rareness permissible, but never any argument in favor of well done, and therefore dry, tough, and thus badly done duck. Mallard, canvas back, teal, and the rest of the wild duck brotherhood should hang for at least 24 hours, and preferably for 48 hours, before cooking. If the weather is favorable, the flesh becomes even more tender and the flavor enhanced from the hanging of a week or longer. The oil sacs in the duck's tail should be very judiciously removed during the cleaning

Breast of Wild Duck

2 or 3 *wild ducks*
1 or 2 *chicken or duck livers, chopped*
Hot fat or butter
Salt and pepper
1 *tablespoon chopped shallot*
1 *small bay leaf*
Thyme
¼ *teaspoon rosemary*
½ *teaspoon MSG powder*
5 *peppercorns*
6 *tablespoons red wine*
2 *tablespoons brown sauce*
2 *tablespoons cognac*

Clean wild ducks and truss the legs and wings close to the body. Put the roasting pan in the oven and heat the oven to 450 degrees. Put the ducks in the hot pan and cook them for 12 to 15 minutes, depending upon the weight of the birds. (Remember, wild ducks are never served well done.) Let the ducks stand for about 10 minutes, then remove the breasts, and put them where they will keep warm but not cook. Save all the blood. Chop the remaining carcasses and press in a duck press or, lacking a press, break up the carcasses and put them through a meat grinder, using the coarsest blade, and strain

process. The blood of the wild duck retains the best flavor, so the duck should be wiped with a damp cloth, not washed.

The flavor of wild duck varies from time to time during the year, and always region-wise, because of variation in diet. Some wild ducks eat fish, but the slight fishy taint may be removed by placing a whole peeled lemon or bits of carrot, parsley, and celery in the unstuffed cavity of the bird. A small onion and an apple, or even a strip of bacon, placed in the cavity will help to remove unfriendly tastes. My favorite taste catalyst is juniper berries, either fresh or canned. When a wild duck has excessive weight it should be parboiled slightly, prior to the preparation time, to melt away extraneous fat.

The most plentiful North American water fowl is the mallard duck. This game bird is a fast, far-ranging flyer. A sharp fruit sauce is the most compatible item to serve with mallard.

The following recipe is one that is easy to accomplish and will pass the most difficult taste test.

New Orleans

the juice which is extracted through a fine sieve.

Prepare the following sauce: Sauté 1 or 2 chicken or duck livers, chopped, in hot fat or butter for 2 to 3 minutes, turning them as they cook. They should be rare. Sprinkle them with salt and pepper. In another pan, put chopped shallot, bay leaf, a little thyme, rosemary, MSG powder, peppercorns, and red wine, and cook slowly until the wine is reduced by one-third. Stir in brown sauce and bring again to a boil. Add the cooked livers, mix well, and pass through a fine sieve. Return the sauce to the pan and add, very gradually, the blood saved when the breasts were carved, and the juice from the carcasses, having first skimmed off all the fat. Stir vigorously while reheating, but do not boil or the sauce will curdle. Add cognac. Slice the breasts, arrange the slices on a serving dish, and pour the sauce over them. Garnish with crescents of bread sautéed in butter. Recipe serves 4.

My television program, "The Gourmet," now seen in numerous cities across the country, had its beginning in Hollywood. Each week following the telecast I would accompany the director and other members of the crew for a light repast at the famous Hollywood Brown Derby Restaurant. We usually discussed our glaring mistakes and enjoyed this period of unwinding from the terrible tension. I wouldn't really say that I was afraid of television in those days, I was terrified!

The timing of our little get-together each week at the Derby paralleled the visit of that wonderful lady of show business, the late Gracie Allen. Gracie, along with her husband, George Burns, frequented the Derby just prior to the production of their celebrated network television show. I noticed that Miss Allen never ordered from the menu and always was served the same interesting entremets. She chose to dine lightly before an evening at the studio. Finally, I prevailed upon the captain of service at the Derby to effect the recipe for me. The very first taste haunted my hungry moments for weeks to come. Obviously, I added this superb recipe to my repertoire of fine recipes and have savored and enjoyed it through the years.

I would like to share this delight with you, and this is the blueprint.

Brussels Sprouts

à la Gracie Allen

1½ lbs. fresh Brussels sprouts
Water
Salt
2 cups heavy cream
1 cup Parmesan cheese
White pepper

Peel away the exterior surface leaves of the Brussels sprouts. Place them into boiling water to which just a hint of salt has been added. Simmer the sprouts slowly until barely tender. Be careful not to overcook the vegetable. Drain the water from the Brussels sprouts and place them on a heated serving dish. Place the heavy cream into a double boiler and add the Parmesan cheese. Heat slowly until the cheese has melted. Dash into the sauce a suspicion of white pepper. Top the Brussels sprouts with the sauce and serve hot. Recipe serves 4.

In a little restaurant in Tijuana, Mexico, the Cardini family, its owners and operators, combined a love of fine food with an atmosphere of gourmet wisdom. Here, they created a salad which was to become a hallmark among epicurean recipes. They named it Caesar after the name of their food establishment—Caesar's Restaurant.

The Cardini family has since moved on to Mexico City where they have a fine restaurant, and the Caesar Salad has moved on and up, too. Volumes have been written by various restaurants seeking credit for its origination. But, really, they have only appreciated and appropriated it to the delight of both the Cardinis and gourmets everywhere.

Young Alex Cardini is a good friend of mine. He still champions the colors for his famous food family in Mexico City. Working with him, I have learned to appreciate the simplicity of a good salad, but like many simple things there is much to know and learn, and unlearn, before pure simplicity is turned into great salad-making.

First, due attention must be paid to the green groceries which make up a salad. They should be carefully selected, gently washed and rinsed, and even more carefully **torn** apart. Never cut salad greens. A

Caesar

French salad basket is perfect for drying greens, but a good substitute is a clean, dry towel—place greens inside and gently swing or shake dry without touching them. (When bruised, salad greens deteriorate rapidly, losing their fresh, crispy flavor.) Now place greens into the refrigerator to cool and crisp.

Alex Cardini's cardinal rule for salad-making states: "A salad should never be overdone." Always remember this, too: the dressing is **secondary** to the green leaves. Yes, I know it's the dressing which provides the delicious taste you love. Nevertheless, a dressing should be used sparingly, tossed with the greens—again very gently—to coat all the salad bowl contents, and never used to excess.

Perhaps you have already discovered one or more reasons why your salads do not measure up to those of a fine restaurant. Simple? Yes. But if these rules are abandoned your salads will be taste-starved, chopped-up nothings instead of creative green springtime itself. Try this original recipe for Caesar Salad and note the difference. And vive la différence!

You will need a wooden salad bowl which has been oiled. This wooden, oiled bowl should never be washed with soap; only rinsed and dried.

Salad

Romaine leaves, whole
Salt
Freshly ground black pepper
Olive oil
Parmesan cheese
Croutons
Garlic
Anchovy paste
Eggs
Worcestershire powder
Lime juice

Into the wooden bowl place whole romaine leaves (8 per serving). Sprinkle with salt and freshly ground black pepper, to taste. Coat with olive oil (4 ounces per serving). Sprinkle Parmesan cheese (2½ tablespoons per serving) and lime juice over the romaine. Add to greens croutons (4 per person) that have been seasoned with garlic, Worcestershire powder and anchovy paste. Toss lightly. Break coddled egg (coddled one minute, using 1 per person) onto greens and toss again lightly. Always toss in the same direction.

It seems amazing that caraway seeds about 5,000 years old could have been preserved in the debris left by the primitive lake dwellers of Switzerland. Archaeologists explain it this way: Even things as perishable as seeds can be kept indefinitely if kept either completely wet—submerged—or completely dry. The caraway seeds in Switzerland were preserved in a peat bog. On the other hand, the grains discovered in ancient Egyptian tombs were kept completely dry for many centuries. It is alternate wetting and drying that destroys, archaeologists say.

Caraway seeds left their early home in Asia Minor a very long time ago. The "Medical Papyrus" of Egypt, written more than 3,500 years ago, gives some of the medicinal uses of caraway. Pliny, who lived in Roman banquet days, said about caraway that "it will grow in most places and its seed is in great demand in the kitchen for culinary purposes."

Roman soldiers without doubt dispersed or planted caraway throughout most of the known world. England and Germany seem to have been enjoying caraway for at least 800 years. Each cook had his own notions of seasoning and every householder his favorite spice. Caraway and cumin (which resembles caraway somewhat) were used in cheese, soups, breads, cakes, dainties generally.

The English of Shakespeare's day loved caraway seeds. In one of his plays, Justice Shallow says, "You shall see my orchard, where in an arbour we will eat a pippin [that is, an apple] of last year's graffing,

Caraway Seed

1 8-oz. package noodles
2 tablespoons caraway seeds
2 tablespoons butter or margarine
1 teaspoon salt
¼ teaspoon ground black pepper

with a dish of caraways." It was the custom to bruise the seeds and scatter them on apple wedges.

For the last 100 years, the Netherlands, right across the channel from England, have been growing great amounts of the world's best caraway seeds. The Dutch discovered long ago that the best time to harvest caraway seed is in the dewiest, dampest time of night or early morning. This keeps the ripe seeds from shattering and scattering.

If you've ever wondered what the Dutch do with some of the land they wrest away from the North Sea, you'll be interested to know it's almost ideal for caraway-growing; the caraway plant loves the heavy clay soil of the coastal districts.

The caraway plant is a biennial of the parsley family. If sown one year, it ripens in July the following year. Its flavor is pleasant, slightly sharp, with a sweet undertone.

It's the simplest thing in the world to keep caraway seed on hand. Its keeping qualities compare with pepper, for it is known that caraway seed in good sound condition can be stored 30 years without losing its fresh look and aromatic flavor.

Caraway seed is mostly used whole. It is the No. 1 flavoring in rye bread and is widely used in rolls, biscuits and cakes. Use it as they do in the Netherlands, to flavor cheese dishes. Take a tip from German and Hungarian cooks and scatter it over sauerkraut, new cabbage, soups, meats and stews.

Noodles

Cook noodles according to package directions and drain thoroughly. Heat caraway seeds with butter or margarine and add to noodles. Add salt and black pepper. Toss lightly and serve hot with roast beef, corned beef, ham, pork or sauerbraten. Recipe serves 6.

Columbus discovered Puerto Rico in 1493 and Americans have been rediscovering it ever since that time. The exotic islands of the Caribbean are many and Puerto Rico ranks very high among the top ten. The colorful isle is only 100 miles long and about 35 miles wide, but 'tis enough. With its shining beaches and sunny days, Puerto Rico is a panorama of island life at its best. Leisurely you have time to sun, to shop, to sit, to enjoy and of course, to dine.

Greater San Juan, which you will probably make your headquarters, is a large city, but out on the island there are a variety of scenes which, if you are not too occupied with sunning, shopping, sitting, enjoying and dining, certainly compel you to go adventuring. Dorado Beach, for instance, is about 23 miles to the west of San Juan via

Caribbean

1 10-in. baked pastry shell
1 envelope (1 tablespoon) unflavored gelatin
½ cup cold water
½ cup sugar
2 tablespoons cornstarch
1¾ cups milk
4 beaten egg yolks
1½ 1-oz. squares unsweetened
  chocolate, melted
1 teaspoon vanilla
4 egg whites
¼ teaspoon cream of tartar
½ cup sugar
2 teaspoons rum extract
1 cup heavy cream, whipped
½ 1-oz. square unsweetened
  chocolate, grated

Route 2. Here there is a Hilton and you can count on a comida puertorriqueña—a full-course Puerto Rican dinner.

Beginning at Dorado Beach or at Las Croabas or Ponce, you can island-hop by launch or plane, or you can restaurant-hop (an activity which has more appeal to gourmets) to your heart's content. During such restaurant-hopping, I obtained one of the best pie recipes in the entire world. It is a Black Bottom Pie and never have I tasted another pie of the superb enchantment this recipe affords. It explodes in tastemosphere. I recommend it highly for entertaining. It cannot fail to impress your guests. Make extra copies of this recipe; they will be asking you for it.

Black Bottom Pie

Soften gelatin in cold water. In a saucepan combine sugar and cornstarch. Add milk, stirring until all the milk has been added. Cook over very low heat until mixture thickens. Stir constantly. Stir small amount of hot mixture into the beaten egg yolks. Gradually add egg mixture to remaining hot mixture. Continue cooking 3 minutes. Remove from heat. To 1 cup custard, add melted unsweetened chocolate and vanilla. Mix well and cool. Pour into a 10-inch baked pastry shell and chill in refrigerator.

Dissolve softened gelatin in remaining custard. Cool until mixture begins to thicken.

Beat egg whites and cream of tartar until foamy. Gradually add sugar, beating mixture until it is stiff. Now fold egg whites into cooled custard. Add rum extract.

As soon as chocolate custard has sct, pour in rum custard mixture. Chill until firm. Top with whipped cream. Sprinkle with unsweetened grated chocolate.

I find that sportsmen have a particular proclivity for Catfish Court-bouillon. As a matter of fact, this authoritative member of the sea-food recipe family is savored by all men and seems designed to evoke bravos from them when served at any gathering.

I extend this caution about cooking seafood: Be certain not to overextend the seasoning agents; since most people enjoy the true natural flavor of seafood, it should not be camouflaged in batter or drowned in strong spices.

But there are exceptions. Cooking rules were made to be broken, too, and I'm taking liberties with my own rule now to present to you one of the favored guests at the Captain's Table, Catfish Courtbouil-lon. I could argue my seafood rule and say that, technically, catfish is a river food, but I don't want to frustrate my Louisiana friends who gave me this recipe. There where Ole Man River meets the sea they don't bother about fine distinctions like that. Fish is fish and they concentrate on knowing what to do with it. Well, you can find out for yourself. The proof of Catfish Courtbouillon is in the eating.

Catfish

6 *lbs. of catfish fillets*
2 *tablespoons salt*
1 *tablespoon red pepper*
⅓ *cup cooking oil*
1 *cup chopped onion*
1 *cup chopped celery*
½ *cup chopped bell pepper*
½ *cup chopped green onion tops*
⅓ *cup chopped parsley*
1 *clove garlic*
1 *can tomato sauce*
¾ *cup tomato catsup*
½ *cup water*

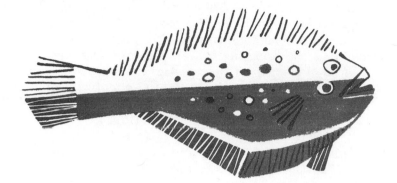

Courtbouillon

Season fillets of catfish with salt and red pepper. Add the cooking oil to the bottom of a heavy metal cooker. Mix together onion, celery, bell pepper, green onion tops, parsley, and garlic. Place a layer of these mixed vegetables on the bottom of the kettle, then a layer of catfish. Repeat the procedure until all of the fish and vegetables are in the kettle. If possible, have a layer of the mixed vegetables on top. Mix the tomato sauce, catsup, and water together and pour evenly over the ingredients in the kettle. Cover the kettle and cook in a 450-degree oven for 1½ hours. Recipe serves six.

So break a rule once, even if it happens to be my own rule. I recommend it. When you bring Catfish Courtbouillon to your "Captain's Table" prepare to receive trophies of praise, as he flexes his taste muscles over it. Results will be the same whether you officiate from the ship's galley or a modern suburban kitchen.

I confess to a great love for hamburgers, a romance that has been going on since childhood. I grew up in a town where a hamburger chef par excellence ruled over the eating-out crowd. Faithful I have been to the hamburger, too. I have ordered them in Paris—have you ever had a hamburger with sauce? I have ordered them in London—have you ever had a hamburger cooked like a small steak and served on a bun? In Hong Kong the hamburger was a large meat ball on a slice of bread, accompanied by a pickle. In Tokyo I requested "the makings" be brought to the table. As the attentive waiter watched me assemble lettuce, tomatoes, bread, meat, mayonnaise, and relish, he sighed and appreciated, "Ah so!" when the masterpiece was finished.

Don't imagine that foreign countries do not offer hamburgers. They do. It's right there on the menu. Every country I have ever visited makes a sincere attempt at producing what they imagine to be an American hamburger. But they just don't quite succeed.

Cheeseburger

½ cup strong coffee

½ cup evaporated milk

4½ teaspoons instant minced onion

2½ lbs. lean ground beef

2 cups soft whole-wheat bread crumbs

2 eggs

2 teaspoons seasoned meat tenderizer

1 teaspoon Worcestershire powder

1 tablespoon prepared mustard

4 slices process American cheese

My experiments in international hamburgers have the suspense of a James Bond saga. I order. What will I get this time? What weapon will they bring for my attack upon this strange concoction? What ingenious side dishes will appear? What kind of meat?

At home and abroad my search for the better, more perfect hamburger continues. Then one fine day I discover my love has a fault!

In the inexorable course of time it comes as it must to all hamburger- and cheeseburger-(to which I had graduated by this time) lovers the knowledge that burgers grow on you.

An ugly word is being bandied about. An ugly number appears on the scale at your morning weighing-in session. Then a doctor, mean person, actually says the ugly word—DIET!

Ah, cheeseburgers, I have loved you, perhaps not wisely, but too well. What to do? Give them up, or go on growing. I analyzed my love. I found I could salvage meat, cheese, the entire fine flavor in another form. Goodbye cheeseburgers. Hello Cheeseburger Pie. Oh, perfect love, without fault or flaw.

Pie

Combine the coffee, milk, and minced onion. Let stand for 10 minutes. Combine the ground beef, bread crumbs, and eggs. Now add the coffee mixture to the meat mixture. Add in meat tenderizer, Worcestershire powder and prepared mustard, mixing each ingredient well into the solid mixture.

Pack into a 10-inch pie pan and place in a 350-degree oven. After baking one hour cut cheese slices diagonally in half and place them around the edges of the pie. Broil 5 or 8 minutes until cheese melts and becomes lightly browned. Serves 8 to 10 people.

The scene is a household in India. A religious ceremony is in progress—in the kitchen! Curries are being blended by the woman gujerati khansama (cook) according to ancient tradition from Hindustani holy books. Cooking in India is a sacred ritual. The formulae for this "salt of the Orient" are legion. Curries are not only one spice, not only one seasoning, but blends of 8, 12, 18, 27; some say as many as 50 possible curry condiments are used in India. So you see there are numberless variations on the main curry theme. Curries range from delicate to authoritative, although a true Indian curry will be pungent, aromatic, and hot! Milder curries are preferred in America, where today there is an extraordinary interest in curried specialties.

At feast time, or banquet time, most of the members of the household are put to work in the kitchen because as many as 20 to 25 separate and different curries will be served at the banquet tables. Different blends are used for fish, or rice, or meats, or vegetables. If the household is well-to-do, particularly if it is a royal household, one

Chicken Curry

gujerati khansama will spend the entire workday grinding condiments in a mortar, following complicated recipes for curry powders.

Excellent curry powders can be bought, but if you have ever thought of blending your own spices, then curry is a challenge worthy of experimentation—fascinating and mysterious as is the India of its origin.

The following condiments are used in curry blends and offer endless variety to achieve that "perfect"—for you—curry magic: Coriander, turmeric, saffron, anise, allspice, cumin, fennel, fenugreek, garlic, kutch-kutch (green ginger), or ginger, white pepper, red pepper, black pepper, bay leaf, sage, mint, paprika, poppy seeds, dill, celery seeds, cinnamon, cloves, mustard, nutmeg, mace, and chilies. Oh yes, and curry leaves! You will note that salt is not included in native condiments lists, but commercial blends contain salt and you may use it if your Western taste so desires.

Pierre

½ cup chopped onion
1 clove garlic, minced
¼ cup salad oil
1 medium tomato, chopped
1 small bay leaf
½ teaspoon cinnamon
3 whole cloves
5 cups cubed uncooked chicken (2½ lbs. boned)
1½ teaspoons salt
1 tablespoon curry powder
½ teaspoon cumin
½ teaspoon coriander
Dash pepper
Pinch powdered saffron
1½ cups water
¼ cup fresh coconut milk

In a large skillet cook onions and garlic in oil until tender but not brown. Add tomato, bay leaf, cinnamon, and cloves; cover and cook 5 minutes. Add cubed chicken; simmer slowly uncovered till juice of chicken has steamed off (about 30 minutes). Stir in salt, curry powder, cumin, coriander, pepper, saffron, and water. Cook slowly for 35 to 40 minutes, or until chicken is tender. Blend in coconut milk. Serve over hot rice. Makes 6 to 8 servings.

The Polynesian food craze that is so popular across the country today had its beginning at Don The Beachcomber's restaurant in Hollywood, California. Don, an almost bankrupt motion picture producer, decided to leave the industry and open a restaurant. Owning a collection of South Pacific Island props and scenery that had provided the color for one of his previous pictures, he decided to decorate a dilapidated old building in the center of Hollywood with these trappings. He prevailed upon a Chinese friend who commanded many fine Cantonese recipes to manage his kitchen. Don's favorite beverages were the rum-based drinks from the Carribbean, and he added a collection of these to his menu for additional character. So with basic Chinese cookery, South Pacific Island decor, and rum-based drinks from the Caribbean, Don The Beachcomber was in business and established the Polynesian food theme. A little later, Don opened a second highly successful restaurant in Honolulu.

While we must give credit to Don The Beachcomber for develop-

Chicken

The original Hawaiian laulau was an individual portion of pork and fish, such as salmon, wrapped in taro and ti leaves and steamed in the underground oven or imu. Here on the mainland certain substitutions and changes must necessarily be made. We use a steam or pressure cooker instead of the island imu, and substitute spinach for taro leaves and cornhusks for ti leaves. I give you my version of a laulau, which is both palatable and easy to prepare.

CHICKEN LAULAUS:

Disjoint enough chickens for the number of people you intend to serve. If you're using fryers, allow ¼ chicken per serving, but two laulaus or servings per person.

Roasters may be cut up proportionately, but can serve from four to six people, depending upon the size of the bird.

Separate the breasts of the chicken, so that a little of the breast meat may be included in each laulau. Brown chicken with flour. Wash spinach and wrap a piece of browned chicken, piece of breast meat, a little finely chopped onion, salt, and pepper in spinach leaves, laying the leaves crosswise and folding them over the portion of chicken. Then cross two cornhusks; lay the spinach-wrapped chicken in the center and pull the ends of the husk over and tie with string. Steam these packages two and a half to three hours in a covered steamer or cook a half to

ing this innovation in food service, its number one ambassador is my good friend, Victor Bergeron (better known as Trader Vic). I first met the very flamboyant Trader Vic in 1954 at his San Francisco restaurant. Since that first meeting I have watched with interest as his reputation has grown to international scope. Starting years ago with one restaurant in Oakland, California, Trader Vic launched a one-man crusade to expose the world to his concepts of Polynesian cookery. His success is obvious, as he now owns and operates fabulous restaurants all over the world. The Trader, an outspoken exponent on American cooking, is often quoted as saying, "We are the most interestingly fed people in the world."

From time to time I receive an exotic package of herbs or condiments from some distant land as a gift from the Trader. He was a guest on my television program, "The Gourmet," and I wish to pass along to you the exotic recipe he negotiated during that hour.

Laulaus

three quarters of an hour in a pressure cooker at 15 pounds pressure. Remove string and serve hot on wooden plates or shells.

CURRY SAUCE:

This curry sauce I'm about to give you is as versatile as it is delicious and there isn't too much curry powder in it. It's wonderful with laulaus, or use it over shrimp, hard-cooked eggs, chicken, or lobster. You'll find a dozen uses for it in years to come.

1 *quart milk, scalded*
1 *fresh coconut, grated*
1½ *tablespoons butter*
1 *large onion, finely chopped*
1 *clove garlic, minced*
1 *finely chopped fresh ginger*

root (may be omitted)
1 *tablespoon curry powder*
½ *teaspoon brown sugar*
2 *tablespoons flour*
Salt to taste

Grate the coconut meat, add to scalded milk, and let stand one hour. Then strain through cheesecloth bag and squeeze until coconut meat is dry. Discard the coconut meat. Melt butter, add chopped onions, garlic, and ginger (if used) and sauté until lightly browned; then add curry powder and sugar. Mix well, add flour, and stir. Gradually add the milk squeezed from the coconut meat, stirring constantly. When ready to serve, add salt to taste. If added too soon, the mixture may curdle.

Chicken Mole is a dish created out of necessity. Legend has it that many years ago in a convent in Puebla, Mexico, the Mother Superior surveyed the stocks of her meager kitchen. Surrounding her, the nuns, anxiously, nervously, awaited orders. The problem? Preparing an appropriate menu for the visiting bishop. The food of the convent was simple fare, but for the bishop, on his tour of duty, the nuns understandably wished to offer something above and beyond usual convent fare.

There existed no "budget" for entertaining—not even entertaining bishops. "We shall simply have to use what we have, and our wits," announced Mother Superior. They went to work hurriedly, searching the cupboards. One nun came forth with tomatoes and onions; another with raisins and almonds; still another with spices . . . cinnamon . . . cloves . . . garlic . . . red peppers. As the Mother Superior looked upon the materials assembled before her, a light came into her eyes. "Chickens—we always have the chickens—and the tortillas. It is enough!"

She set them to work. Sisters divided the duties—one cooking the

Chicken

1 5-lb. chicken, disjointed
3 cups water
  Salt to taste
6 tablespoons shortening
1 medium onion, minced
1 clove garlic, crushed
2 tablespoons flour
3 8-oz. cans tomato sauce
1 cup chicken broth
12 seedless raisins
12 blanched almonds, shredded
1 tablespoon sesame seeds
¼ cup chili powder
1 teaspoon cinnamon
⅛ teaspoon cloves
  Salt to taste
  Tortillas

chicken; another preparing tomato sauce; another chopping raisins, almonds, onions; and still another grinding the red peppers on the metate, then grinding in the cinnamon, and the cloves, and the garlic. Tortillas any of them could make—blindfolded!

The Mother Superior went away to attend to other duties relating to the visit of the bishop. When she returned to the kitchen, the nuns had finished their work, except for the spice-grinding nun, who was still grinding, grinding on the metate. In Spanish, moler means "to grind," so they called the dish Chicken Mole.

Having blended Chicken Mole with the zeal of necessity, plus spiritual mission, the nuns presented the dish to the Bishop, who, no doubt, enjoyed it. They say that word of mouth is the best advertising, and so it must have been in Mexico, because wherever the bishop went he extolled the talents of the cooking nuns of the convent in Puebla and their Chicken Mole—so much so that in time it became the national dish of Mexico.

This is my favorite recipe for Chicken Mole.

Mole

In a large saucepan, place the disjointed chicken, salted to taste, in about 3 cups of water. Cook over medium heat for 1 hour, or until very tender. Remove from heat. Cool in the broth; then remove meat from bones. In a large skillet, melt shortening over low heat; add onions, garlic and flour. Cook until yellow; then add tomato sauce and chicken broth. Allow to thicken. Now add the raisins, almonds, sesame seeds, chili powder, cinnamon, and cloves. Salt once again and cook for 5 to 10 minutes.

One hour before serving time, place pieces of boned chicken onto tortillas. Form into rolls. Place in an oblong baking dish and pour Mole sauce over the chicken-tortilla rolls. Bake in a moderate oven, about 375 degrees, until thoroughly heated. Serve hot. Makes 6 servings.

When traveling about the country, I am often asked what contribution the State of Texas has made to the exceptional food repertoire of America. My answer just naturally turns the thoughts of Lone
Star gourmets to the time when the first winter winds blow down the
Texas plains, or the first chill raindrops find their way into our Texas
autumn: Chili. This phase of Texas food preparation is unexcelled
anywhere in the world.

Texas-style chili is not like any other. And although I can recommend some of the best of the Mexican food found in different parts
of the nation, the finest Mexican cuisine is still found where it had
its origin, in Texas.

If you have been to Mexico you were, perhaps, surprised when you
sampled their native Mexican food. It is very different from Texas-

Chili

2 *lbs. ground round steak*
1 *lb. pork cut into small cubes*
2 *cloves garlic, chopped fine*
1 *large onion, diced fine*
4 *tablespoons shortening or*
  bacon drippings
3 *tablespoons chili powder*
1 *tablespoon flour*
1 *large can tomatoes*
2 *bay leaves*
1 *teaspoon oregano*
1 *teaspoon salt*
2 *teaspoons cumin*
½ *teaspoon coriander*
1 *small block bittersweet*
  chocolate

Mexican food. Contrary to popular opinion, the real Mexican cookery, as we know it today, did not find its way into the chapters of famous cookbooks by route of Mexico, but rather Texas. But, of course, the influence of old Mexico is unmistakable.

Texas beef and Mexican seasonings are what this marriage of ingredients and flavors combines. (Chili is really a pepper plant.) Add a couple or three, with beans, native vegetables, a Texas-size culinary imagination, and you have what the ranchers and cowboys call "a bowl of red."

Here is my favorite recipe for Chili Con Carne. The astringency of most Mexican foods can be subtly subdued by just a hint of chocolate.

con Carne

Place fat into large skillet, and over low flame brown the ground round, pork, garlic, and onions. When the meat is brown and the onions and garlic are soft, add the chili powder, blended with the flour. Press the tomatoes through a fine sieve and add them to the recipe. Break up the bay leaves and add to the mixture, along with oregano, salt, cumin seed, coriander, and chocolate. Simmer slowly for 2 hours or longer. For a thinner chili sauce, add water or tomato juice. Serve garnished with ripe olives. Recipe makes about one quart.

Ancient maps are fascinating to study. Even the most primitive people had crude maps scratched on pieces of bark or rocks. Some maps, centuries old, showed the world as round; others showed it rectangular. One of the oldest, most interesting maps was drawn by Cosmas Indicopleustes. This map dates from A.D. 535, after Cosmas returned from a voyage to India.

The East was always shown at the top of these old maps instead of the North, as on modern maps. Indicopleustes lettered across the top, The East: "the earth beyond the Ocean where men dwelt before the flood." In this part of the earth beyond the Ocean he indicated the terrestrial paradise.

In this terrestrial paradise grew cinnamon and other fragrant spices, they believed in medieval times. Precious gems and precious spices— all were carried out of paradise by the rivers which supposedly flowed out of the Garden of Eden. Fishermen would stretch their nets and

Cinnamon Chocolate

2 eggs
¾ cup sugar
¼ cup cocoa
¼ teaspoon salt
⅛ teaspoon ground cinnamon
¼ cup cold milk
1½ cups hot milk
1 cup hot, cooked rice
1 teaspoon pure vanilla extract
Whipped cream for garnish

Beat eggs slightly. Combine sugar, cocoa, salt, and cinnamon and gradually beat into eggs. Stir in cold milk. Add hot milk and rice. Cook until thickened, stirring constantly. Stir in vanilla. Serve warm and top with whipped cream. Recipe serves 6.

later find them filled with "cinnamon, ginger, rhubarb, cloves, and other such good things."

In an ancient Chinese legend, cinnamon—the variety called Cassia cinnamon—grew in a Chinese paradise. The Cassia cinnamon tree was a beautiful tree. It grew high up in a beautiful garden in the Tibetan mountains at the source of the Yellow River. Strangely enough, this would be about where Europeans would expect to find their paradise. According to legend, anyone who entered this Chinese paradise and ate of the fruit of the cinnamon tree would gain immortality and live happily ever after. While I have doubts concerning this legend, I am certain we will all eat more happily if we incorporate the optimum flavor of cinnamon in more of our recipes.

The following recipe reflects the empathy of cinnamon with a simple dessert.

Rice Pudding

Are you a fan of clam chowder? If you are, I know from past experience that you are going to be decidedly in favor of one of these recipes and decidedly against the other. Public food opinion usually divides right down the middle like the preference for one or the other of the two major political parties.

It is not so simple a matter as New York's casting its votes for Manhattan Chowder, and New England's casting its block of votes for New England (sometimes called Maine) Chowder. A Democrat from California may vote for New England Clam Chowder, and a Republican from Connecticut may vote for Manhattan. Since there is no way to measure support for one or the other (someone should really do a national survey on this!) I play no favorites: I give two recipes. Since I am of the "both-of-them-are-good-school," that makes me an Independent of the Gourmet Party.

What both recipes have in common is clams, and also potatoes

Clam

MANHATTAN CLAM CHOWDER:

6 *strips bacon*
4 *medium onions, diced*
4 *carrots, finely diced*
1 *small stalk celery*
2 *tablespoons chopped fresh parsley*
1 *pint clams (2 cans minced clams may be used, 10½-oz. size)*
1 *12-oz. can tomatoes*
  Salt and pepper to taste (suggest cracked black pepper)
1 *bay leaf*
2 *teaspoons thyme*
1 *tablespoon Worcestershire powder*
3 *medium potatoes, finely diced*

Cut bacon into small pieces and fry in a large kettle until brown, but not crisp. Add diced onions and sauté until soft. Next add finely diced carrots, celery, and chopped parsley. Simmer slowly for about 4 minutes while stirring. Drain clams and tomatoes, placing the liquid into a measuring container. Add enough water to make about 1½ quarts of liquid. Add tomatoes and liquid to the pot and bring to a boil. Season with salt and pepper, bay leaf, thyme, and Worcestershire powder. Reduce heat and simmer for about 45 minutes. Add finely diced potatoes and simmer for 20 minutes more. Last, add the clams and simmer gently for 10 more minutes. Recipe makes about 3 quarts.

and onions. There the similarity ends. Manhattan has tomatoes and New England doesn't; New England has milk and Manhattan doesn't. The clams may come from the same ocean but our forefathers were highly individual and did with clams what they pleased.

A chowder is not technically a soup, nor is it a stew. It is somewhere in between, related in recipe format to bouillabaisse and gumbo. The name comes from France where the fishermen along the coast cooked some of their catch in a large chaudière, or cauldron; somewhere along the way the early Americans developed their own chaudière and it got to be called chowder. Eschewing other fishes of the sea, they cast their votes for clams.

Chowder is a meal in itself and can be, should be, for special occasions.

Happy chowder-time, good living and Bon Appetit!

Chowder

NEW ENGLAND CLAM CHOWDER:

3 dozen soft-shell clams, shucked
2 ounces salt pork
1 cup sliced onion
½ cup sliced leeks
6 cups diced potatoes
2 small bay leaves, crumbled
1 teaspoon salt
Dash black pepper
3 cups water
Clam liquor
4 cups milk, scalded
2 cups light cream, scalded
3 tablespoons butter
2 tablespoons flour

Drain clams, reserving liquor. Keeping separate, finely chop hard part of clams, coarsely chop soft part. Sauté diced salt pork in deep kettle until golden brown. Add finely chopped clams, sliced onion, sliced leeks, diced potatoes, crumbled bay leaves, salt, pepper, and 3 cups of water. Add enough water to clam liquor to make 3 cups liquid. Add to mixture with remaining ingredients of coarsely chopped clams, scalded milk, scalded light cream and butter blended with flour. Continue cooking over low heat for 20 minutes. Serves 6.

Creole cooking, gourmets all agree, is a different tastemaking idea —entirely and uniquely different. Creole cookery is an evolution of history. Beginning with the Frenchman's demand for first-class cooks, the natives (who were of French descent themselves) added their own touch of artistry, and the French gourmets approved. From the American Indians came the formerly secret uses of filé, the basis for the Louisiana gumbo with its distinctive taste contribution. The Spaniards were still to add their likes, imparting a touch of Old Spain to the recipes. The resulting happy mélange of techniques and flavors is truly one-of-a-kind cookery.

So it is with the dessert category of Louisiana cooking. Creole cooking excels with another native product—molasses. Skill with molasses has provided us with a different kind of dessert taste. Molasses is the juice from the sugar cane from which some of the sugar has been removed by extraction. It is concentrated by boiling, but even in boiling none of its vitamins and minerals are destroyed, and it is, therefore, a very nutritious food product.

Creole

MOLASSES PECAN PIE:

1 9-in. unbaked pie shell
¼ cup butter
½ cup granulated sugar
3 eggs, unbeaten
¾ cup molasses
Juice of a lemon
1 cup pecan halves

Line 9-inch pie pan with pastry. Cream butter and sugar together. Add the unbeaten eggs. Now add molasses. Add the lemon juice. Beat. Add pecan halves. Mix well. Pour into pie shell. Bake in 450-degree oven for 10 minutes. Reduce temperature to 350 degrees, and bake for 30 additional minutes.

First, understand that there are different kinds of molasses. The difference depends upon the amount of sugar that has been removed from the sugar cane juice. What is called **first molasses** is the product of the first process of the extraction of this sugar. **Second molasses** is the further diluting of the juice with a reboiling process to extract still more sugar. **Third molasses** is again diluted with more water which extracts more sugar. **Fourth molasses**—better known in the South as **blackstrap molasses**—from which all the sugar has been removed which can be removed. The interesting thing is that this blackstrap still contains a goodly amount of sugar, and even after complete processing, more vitamins and minerals remain in the highly concentrated syrup. This blackstrap the early Creoles considered a powerful medicine. Molasses adds flavor authority to any recipe, plus nutrition of a very high order.

Dessert Cookery

BUTTERED MOLASSES
CANDY PULL:

2 *cups sugar*
1 *cup molasses*
½ *cup water*
¼ *teaspoon cream of tartar*
    Butter, amount about the size
    of half of an egg

Combine sugar, molasses, and water in a heavy saucepan and bring to a boil. After mixture begins to boil, add cream of tartar. When boiled enough to thicken, turn heat off, but before removing from the heat, add butter. When cooled begin to pull like taffy. Do not butter hands while pulling.

Let's take a page from the cookbook of France for a fancy holiday recipe. This versatile recipe you can serve as a dessert, or as a holiday breakfast, or make a perfect brunch for entertaining.

Crêpes are light, small pancakes with a filling which are rolled up into a compact serving package. The most famous, I am sure, of the crêpes is crêpes suzette. These crêpes were named for an actress who played in the Comédie Française about 1900. The role she played had a direct connection with the recipe named for her. Her part in the play was that of a maid, and she had to serve the crêpes to a group of characters meeting for an intimate supper.

But the actors in this play were gourmets, and the crêpes which were sent into the theater as props were cold, of course. Since their discriminating taste buds simply would not tolerate such unappetizing fare as cold crêpes, the actors decided to make a deal with the chef to devise some way of getting hot crêpes to them.

The chef, Joseph by name, responded with pure inspiration—pre-

Crêpes d'Orange

1 cup sifted flour
6 tablespoons confectioners'
   sugar
½ teaspoon salt
1 cup milk
2 eggs
   Cointreau

pare the crêpes beforehand, but reheat them at the table on stage by flaming them. Voilà! A new recipe and a new flair in French cooking had been born. Of course, he appropriately named them for the actress who played the part of the maid and served the crêpes. But the demands of the gourmet actors were really responsible for this recipe, as so often happens when people are not satisfied with less than the best.

To this day crêpes suzette are served at the table and flamed before the interested eyes of the diners. And so you may do with Crêpes d'Orange if you wish. You too can prepare these petite pancakes in advance, then bring them to the table with the sauce all ready, combine them there and flame them. For a large party they can be made up as eaten. Just be sure you have enough batter to keep the crêpes coming to the table; seconds, thirds and even fourths will be demanded.

(French Pancakes)

Sift flour, confectioners' sugar, and salt together. Add milk and stir until perfectly smooth. Add eggs and beat thoroughly. Pour batter from pitcher or large spoon onto lightly greased hot griddle. When pancakes are puffed and full of bubbles (after 1 or 2 minutes), turn and cook about 1 minute on second side. Spread crêpes with Orange Hard Sauce and roll them up. Pour Cointreau over crêpes and flame.

ORANGE HARD SAUCE:

½ cup butter
1 package superfine (XXX) sugar
    Grated rind of 3 oranges
½ teaspoon salt
    Juice of 3 oranges

Combine butter, sugar, orange rind, and salt. Beat well. Add orange juice gradually and blend thoroughly.

When Macbeth's three witches met "in thunder, lightning, or in rain" it's likely they carried dill seeds with them, for in days gone by, dill was considered big magic. With dill seeds and the right incantation, a smart witch could make an enemy's cake fall, take the curl out of her hair, or give the family cat a fit of sneezes.

If the victim had foresight she would have her own supply of dill seeds to brew a beaker of anti-magic, a medieval anti-missile missile. With dill seeds, too, one could cure hiccoughs and headaches, relieve itching, indigestion, and insomnia. In fact, the word "dill" is thought to have come from a Norwegian word meaning to quiet or soothe.

Dill seed is the dried fruit of a tall handsome plant of the parsley family. Its leaves, called "dill weed" by the spice industry, come from this same annual.

Dilled Clam and

2 8-oz. bottles clam juice
2 teaspoons dill seed
2 packages unflavored gelatin
2¼ cups canned tomato juice
¾ teaspoon instant onion powder
1 10-oz. package frozen mixed vegetables or peas, cooked and chilled

Dill seed is mainly sold in whole form; dill weed is shredded. The most famous use of dill seed is as flavoring for cucumber pickles. It is excellent as well in meat marinades and sauces, fish and chicken, creamy sauces and salads, cole slaw, potato salad, macaroni salad, and such vegetables as sauerkraut, green cabbage, and green beans.

Dill is native to Europe and has been used as a seasoning for many centuries. Dill is grown in this country and much is imported from India.

The aroma of dill seed is very good with either clam or tomato and makes an appetizing salad.

Tomato Aspic

Combine one bottle of the clam juice and dill seed in a small saucepan. Bring to boiling point; reduce heat and simmer 10 minutes. Meanwhile, soften gelatin in ½ cup of the tomato juice. Strain dill seeds from hot clam juice. Add hot clam juice to gelatin; stir until dissolved. Add remaining bottle of clam juice, tomato juice and onion powder to gelatin mixture. Chill until consistency resembles unbeaten egg whites. Fold in mixed vegetables. Spoon into 1½ quart mold. Chill until firm; unmold. Serve on lettuce leaves, if desired. Recipe serves 6.

Bracing, nippy air and the crackle of leaves signal the fall of the year and turn a shooting man's heart to thoughts of the great outdoors and a meticulous search for a very delectable little bird—the dove. A small bird, the dove—but many hunters think it all the more challenging to the sportsman and one of the highest-class pleasures of the table. A dove dinner, cooked to a hunting man's discriminating taste, is a gourmet food concerto.

Many years ago I began testing recipes and sampling foods around the world. Surveying people's tastes for certain flavors and combinations of flavors, noting what they most enjoyed and the recipes most often and consistently requested from my television show, "The

Doves

    8 doves, cleaned and dressed
    ⅔ cup brandy
    1 cup butter (or margarine)
    1 tablespoon Worcestershire
      powder
    1 teaspoon garlic salt
    ½ cup chopped truffles
    ½ teaspoon nutmeg
    ½ cup sliced carrots
    1 cup yellow or green seedless
      grapes
      Salt to taste
      Pepper to taste
    ⅓ cup flour
      Toast

Gourmet," I encountered the plain fact that Americans across the country are cautious about eating game and won't include it in their menus. Except for the sportsman, who understands game and takes precautions to keep it fresh and properly dressed, most cooks—even those with the best cooking credentials—avoid it. A great shame— they don't know what they're missing. However, dove is a bird you need have absolutely no worry about eating. You can serve it with safety, and if you use Dove Epicurean as your recipe you will eat it with exclamations of praise. It is a wedding of flavors—tender little birds accompanied with a delicate, haunting sauce.

Epicurean

Place doves into brandy and let stand 30 minutes. Melt butter in a skillet, slowly, over low heat. Add doves to melted butter and cook slowly until lightly browned.

Add Worcestershire powder, garlic salt, truffles, nutmeg, carrots, grapes, salt and pepper to the dictates of your own taste. Cook, covered, over low heat 15 to 20 minutes.

Remove doves. Add flour to skillet mixture, stirring constantly, until thickened. Place doves onto slices of toast. Cover with the sauce in the skillet. Garnish with parsley. This recipe serves 4 sports-men-epicureans.

When I do cooking demonstrations throughout the country, I often tell my audience about two ingredients which are essential to the successful outcome of any recipe, yet never appear in the list of ingredients. Both are paramount in importance and without them no one can hope to become a great cook. They are love and patience.

I know of no better, no more appropriate time than the Christmas season to begin including love and patience in our recipe list. The dinner you serve on Christmas day is a gift of love to your family. In the hurry of preparing for the big day you may forget this, but nevertheless it is true.

If you want to depart from the routine and serve your family a delicious dish for Christmas (or any time), I heartily recommend to you Duck L'Orange with Bigarade Sauce.

Sometimes it requires an act of courage to attempt something new and change the time-honored menu of Christmas. Often it requires an act of faith, too—faith in the credentials of the giver of the recipe. So trust me a little, and strike out in a new direction this Christmas. Begin a new tradition. If you have an adventurous gourmet spirit, if you like duck, if someone dear to you has a penchant for duck, this is the holiday recipe for you. So, love, patience, courage, and faith—these four—form the background for our recipe.

Duck l'Orange

1 small, young duck
Celery, cut in large pieces
Carrots, peeled
Onions, peeled
Orange shells
Curaçao or Grand Marnier liqueur
½ cup brown sugar
⅓ cup lemon juice
½ cup orange juice
½ cup Burgundy
2 cups chicken stock
1 tablespoon margarine, melted
1 tablespoon butter, melted
1½ teaspoons flour
Salt to taste
Pepper to taste
Orange slices

Place the young duck in an open roasting pan with celery, carrots, onions, and orange shells. Roast in a moderate oven (325 degrees) 55 minutes. Remove from the oven and drain off excess fat. Place duck on large piece of foil and pour Curaçao or Grand Marnier liqueur over the duck. Close foil to

Now for the more visible ingredients of Duck l'Orange with Bigarade Sauce. First you find a duck! We are talking about domestic duck which you find in most markets now, possibly fresh, but probably frozen. The growing season for domestic ducks is from early April to late November. These will be young, summer ducks, just what our recipe calls for. (A year-old duck is the best table-fare prospect, but few growers keep them that long.) Baby ducklings breathe and then they begin to eat, and eat, and eat. Their appetites are insatiable. Someone has estimated that it takes about 30 pounds of feed to get a duckling ready for market. So, understandably, ducklings are in the market for sale at the age of 3 to 4 months.

Long Island ducks are preferred, Long Island being the great domestic duck-producing area of our country. This duck is white-feathered; and dressed, the duckling should be plump; the flesh should be almost transparent so that it appears light colored and fresh.

After finding the duck, you will need the other ingredients in the list below in order to produce a winning new traditional recipe for your family. (Courage and faith you have already shown. Please don't forget love and patience!)

with Bigarade Sauce

keep hot. Sprinkle the brown sugar over the vegetables in the roasting pan. Return to oven until sugar melts and vegetables look glazed. Remove. Add lemon juice, orange juice, Burgundy and chicken stock to the vegetables and cook over a low heat about 25 minutes.

Combine margarine, butter and flour in a saucepan. Bring to a boil, but do not brown. Remove from heat and cool. Strain the liquid mixture. Add to the flour mixture and cook over low heat for 10 minutes, stirring constantly. Now add salt and pepper to taste, and Curaçao or Grand Marnier liqueur to taste.

Carve the duck into 8 pieces. Arrange on a platter and garnish with orange slices. Pour the sauce over all. Makes 4 large servings.

India survives fifty centuries of civilization. Since the sixteenth century when Europeans disembarked on Indian soil, fiction and non-fiction, movies and documentaries, communications media of all forms, including word-of-mouth, have been trying to unravel the mystery that is India. Mysterious to the Western man and his Western mind, India lures the traveler and the experiencer of life in great numbers.

Hinduism, the predominant religion, is a philosophy and a way of life that does not reject any other belief, and yet seems to outlast them all by absorbing them all.

Nowhere can this be illustrated better than in the dietary habits and food taboos. Every caste has some kind of food which is forbidden. But they are not always the same foods. Brahmans, the highest caste in India, are vegetarians (curiously, you find many other castes, not Brahman, emulating the high caste by appropriating their vegetarian regimen). Some Indians will not eat pork, others will not touch beef. Some groups of believers are convinced that a man takes on the same characteristics of the animal food he eats.

East Meets West Curry of

Stewing hen (3–4 lbs.)
3 stalks (single) celery, untrimmed
1 large onion, peeled
1 green pepper, seeded
2 cloves garlic
4 juniper berries
6 peppercorns
6 whole cloves
1 cup white wine
Salt and pepper to taste

2 cups water
½ cup white wine
1 teaspoon whole cloves
2 bay leaves
1 single celery stalk, untrimmed

1 onion, peeled
2 drops liquid red pepper seasoning
1½ teaspoons salt
1 pound shrimp, shelled and deveined

Cooked ham (½–¾ lb.)

4½ teaspoons peanut oil
2 onions, coarsely chopped
½ green pepper, chopped
4 stalks (single) celery, sliced
1 cup coconut milk
2 cups chicken stock
1 heaping tablespoon peanut butter
1 cup sour cream

As in other torrid climates, in India there is a belief that hot-as-fire, pungent food stimulates the bodily functions of people subject to intense heat, and thereby counteracts the lack-of-energy slow-down of the inhabitants. The Indians' cure for this malaise is curry. Curry is our generic name for the mixture of many different spices, herbs, and seasonings called masala by the Indians. The flavor of curry dishes is all in the masala. So important is the mixing of curry that every young maiden is given a mortar and pestle as a wedding gift even though she may be marrying into a wealthy household with many servants. Any girl must be adept at mixing and grinding masalas.

These curries are all different; some mild, some hot, some only for meats, others only for vegetables. But still, there is a certain alikeness, at least to the Western taste. The milder curry flavor is the most popular in America.

I cannot say which caste, or castes, might be able to partake of the following recipe at dinner. As you will see, it has three different meats, but I think you will enjoy this intriguing mélange of curried morsels. Recipe serves 8.

Chicken, Ham, and Shrimp

3 *garlic cloves, crushed*
1 *teaspoon sugar*
1½ *teaspoons each: turmeric, cinnamon, cumin, coriander*
½ *teaspoon each: chili pepper, ginger, mace*
1 *tablespoon lemon juice*

Remove lumps of fat and fat skin from chicken and cover with water in a large kettle. Cook over low heat until the chicken is tender. To the cooking water, add celery stalks, large onion, green pepper, garlic cloves, juniper berries, peppercorns, whole cloves, 1 cup of white wine, and salt and pepper to taste. When chicken is tender, remove it from the broth. Cool. Remove skin and bones and cut into cubes and strips. Strain the broth. Cool; then skim off fat. Store in refrigerator until needed.

In a saucepan combine 2 cups water, ½ cup white wine, cloves, bay leaves, celery stalk, onion, red pepper seasoning, and salt. Cook over medium heat until boiling. Add the shrimp and bring to a boil again. Cook for 5 minutes. Remove from heat and drain shrimp.

Cut ham into bite-size pieces. In a saucepan heat peanut oil

EAST MEETS WEST CURRY (cont.)

over medium heat. Add, and sauté until soft, onion, green pepper, celery stalks. Add coconut milk, chicken stock, peanut butter, and sour cream. Blend. Add crushed garlic cloves, sugar, turmeric, cinnamon, cumin, coriander, chili pepper, ginger, mace, and lemon juice. Blend well.

Add chicken, shrimp, and ham. Cover and simmer over low heat for 30 minutes. Serve over steamed rice or mix with toasted rice. (To make toasted rice: In a large skillet, to which a small amount of oil has been added toast slightly the amount of rice you wish to serve. Mix with above curry sauce, using just enough to lightly moisten the toasted rice.)

This curry, properly served, should be accompanied by at least six side dishes, which Indians call *sambals*. The following are suitable sambals which you may wish to use: sliced or chopped onion, crisp sliced cucumber, chopped candied ginger, slivered sweet pickles, sliced bananas, chutneys, toasted sesame seed, hot cucumber relish, plain or toasted coconut, melon balls, seedless raisins, any variety of nuts, crisp bacon bits, mandarin orange sections, or sliced mushrooms. Recipe serves 8.

People, horses, and rabbits have been crunching carrots since pre-history. They came originally from that part of the Near East which is known as "the fertile crescent." Here, many varieties of carrots have been found. The presence of numerous varieties of a plant in one area is generally accepted as proof that this is its original home. We know that carrots were grown in the gardens of Charlemagne at the beginning of the ninth century. From there they traveled to England and Germany. Carrots became very popular quickly. The young ladies of the Hebrides, off the coast of Scotland, served carrot chunks as we might candy, taking them to dances as crunchy snacks. In England, women wore carrot tops fashioned into wreaths in their hair.

Carrots are a famous source of vitamin A, the best source in the whole vegetable kingdom. The beautiful deep orange color comes from the presence of carotene, a "pro-vitamin," or freely translated, a "before vitamin." Carotene is changed to essential vitamin A by the body.

I suggest you serve the following recipe for your family's health and enjoyment.

Orange-Glazed Fresh Carrots

¼ cup butter or margarine
3 tablespoons fresh orange juice
1½ tablespoons sugar
6 whole cloves
¼ teaspoon salt
10 medium-sized fresh carrots (about 5 cups), sliced and cooked
Chopped fresh parsley

Combine butter, orange juice, sugar, cloves, and salt in a saucepan. Cook until butter is melted and sauce is hot. Remove cloves and pour mixture over hot carrots, cooked only until crisp-tender. Garnish with fresh parsley. Recipe yields 6 servings.

Considerable confusion exists among many Americans as to the correct differentiation among Japanese, Chinese, and Polynesian foods. It is generally accepted that the total world of Oriental food represents little variation. Most aficionados of the kitchen combine crisp bamboo shoots, water chestnuts, julienne pork strips, and a whisper of soy sauce, lightly sauté this medley in a blazer pan and serve it under the nomenclature most appealing to them—Chinese, Japanese, or Polynesian.

Apart from these common ingredients, there is actually very little similarity in these three forms of Oriental presentations. The astute gourmet recognizes that Chinese fare was our original concept in Oriental foods. Japanese recipes have picked up many Western char-

Egg

FILLING:

1 *lb. celery, shredded or finely cut*
1 *lb. bean sprouts*
  Boiling water
⅓ *cup cooking oil*
½ *cup chopped green onions*
2 *cloves garlic, crushed*
¼ *lb. water chestnuts, finely cut*
¼ *lb. bamboo shoots, finely cut*
6 *ounces cooked shrimp, pork, or chicken, finely cut*
  Salt and pepper to taste
1 *tablespoon MSG powder*
3 *tablespoons soy sauce*

Fill saucepan to level of ½ inch with boiling water. Add celery and bean sprouts and cook 5 minutes over low heat. Drain well. Heat cooking oil in large skillet over medium heat; add green onions and fry 30 seconds with crushed garlic cloves. Add drained celery and bean sprouts, water chestnuts, bamboo shoots, cooked shrimp, pork, or chicken, salt and pepper, MSG powder and soy sauce, mixing well. Remove from flame. Drain and cool.

acteristics but still reflect, for the most part, the character of Japanese people. Most Polynesian specialties are hitchhikers to Chinese techniques, but likewise have absorbed from other lands.

There is actually no broad classification for Chinese food, but rather, eight separate and distinct provincial systems constitute what is termed Chinese cuisine. The most popular provincial Chinese food in the Western world is Cantonese. Most American-Chinese restaurants serve these lightly-seared delicacies, which also form the foundation for Polynesian and Japanese table servings.

Probably the most popular item among Oriental foods served in this country is Egg Rolls. You will want to add this fine Oriental recipe to your repertoire.

Rolls

EGG WRAPPERS:

- 2 *cups flour*
- ¾ *cup cornstarch*
- ½ *teaspoon salt*
- 3 *eggs*
- 3 *tablespoons cooking oil*
- 2 *cups water (approximately)*

Sift together flour, cornstarch, and salt. Beat eggs and cooking oil together until smooth. Add dry ingredients to egg mixture alternately with water. Beat well. (Batter should be thin enough to fall from spoon in drops. Add more water, if necessary.)

Heat oiled, 6-inch skillet over very low heat. Pour in batter to cover bottom. When bottom of egg wrapper is firm, pour off excess batter. Continue cooking until thoroughly dried. Fry on one side only. Quickly turn skillet over to remove wrapper. Continue in same manner until all batter is used. In center of each wrapper, place spoonful of filling. Roll up, tucking in ends. Brush edge of wrapper with beaten egg to seal roll. Chill in refrigerator. Just before serving, heat oil, 2 inches deep, in large skillet over medium heat. Fry egg rolls on one side 15 minutes or until golden brown. Turn and fry until brown on other side. Drain on absorbent paper.

In the heart of the film capital of the world there is a unique establishment—the Farmer's Market. If you have visited Los Angeles, I'm quite sure you have also visited the fabulous Farmer's Market. Food booths, gift shops, produce markets, specialty stores where you may purchase meat, cheeses, nuts, candy, fruits, groceries make it an eater's paradise!

International dining patio might be the appropriate term, because you may choose from Turkish, Chinese, French, Italian food specialties; seafood, barbecue, ice creams, candies, pies, hamburgers, and other possibilities too numerous to sample on one vacation, even if you go there every day.

California is a salad-eating state and Californians are very salad-

Farmer's Market

Select with care the freshest, best looking green groceries you can find:

1 *head romaine lettuce*
1 *head iceberg lettuce*
3 *tomatoes*
4 *hard-boiled eggs*
1 *16-oz. can English peas*
   (*drained*)

Shred romaine and iceberg lettuce. Section tomatoes and hard-boiled eggs and place in with lettuce. Place English peas into recipe and toss with the following dressing.

conscious. I have seen many film stars at the Market strolling from food stall to food stall hungrily eyeing the luscious offerings and then automatically turning to the salad bar. Here they have a good, nutritious luncheon—tasty and satisfying, but still one that allows them to hold the line on calories which cameras are so expert at detecting and emphasizing. The stars have their glamor image to consider, of course, but to do it with a Farmer's Market Salad is no sacrifice.

When you have made your selection you find a table under a colorful umbrella and dine where you can enjoy the open air and warmth of California living. With the recipe that follows, you can be almost anywhere and still savor a Farmer's Market Salad.

Salad

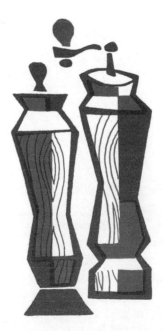

FARMER'S MARKET
SALAD DRESSING:

2 tablespoons chopped green
   onions
1 garlic clove, crushed
¼ cup chopped parsley
1 cup mayonnaise
   Salt to taste
1 tablespoon lemon juice
¼ cup vinegar
¼ cup (2 oz.) blue cheese,
   crumbled
½ cup thick sour cream
   Pepper, freshly ground

Combine all ingredients well. Chill. Makes 2¼ cups.

Mexican food is fun food, a change-of-pace taste. There seems to be something of the fiesta in all their dishes for they are snappy, aromatic, tasteful, and their Spanish names impart an exotic charm to the menu. When served with Mexican pottery, bright native accoutrements, piñatas, and all the easily obtainable decorative pieces, you can transport your guests into a world of Latin enchantment, all for a very economical cost. Mexican food is, in fact, probably less expensive to prepare and serve to large groups than any other.

It is among the Indians that these basic Mexican foods were invented. They are still the regular diet of the people on the land and in the tiny villages, where the corn is cultivated and masa—the dough of tortillas—is prepared from it on the stone metate. Corn is to Mexico what wheat is to America—the staff of life—and in past days the god of corn was worshiped for the whole nation was dependent on it for life. When Cortez arrived not only were they growing corn, but also potatoes, tomatoes, squashes, avocadoes, papayas, pineapples, vanilla beans, and peanuts. None of these foods were known to the Spanish at the time.

Fiesta

3 lbs. chuck roast
1 large onion
2 to 3 tablespoons water
  Salt
1 tablespoon Mole spice
2 tablespoons taco spices
  Vegetable oil
  Tortillas
  Shredded lettuce
  Diced tomatoes
  Hot Sauce

Trim chuck roast and cut into 2-inch cubes. Place meat cubes, onion, and water in pressure saucepan. Add salt, Mole spice, and taco spices. Cover saucepan, adjust cover, and place over full heat. Allow steam to escape according to manufacturer's directions. Cook at 15 pounds pressure for 30 minutes. Remove from heat and reduce pressure immediately.

From this collision of two worlds the Spanish took the new foods home, and thereby lies the misconception of many that Mexican and Spanish foods are alike. They are no more the same than American and English foods.

The **hotness** of Mexican food can be controlled in your own kitchen, although many aficionados of this cuisine like it hot. The chilies (peppers to Norteamericanos), come in many sizes, colors, and tastes—but they are all hot. The Latins claim wonderful things for the chilies, ranging all the way from the belief that they "air-condition" the body (by making the inside hotter than the outside!), to prevention of dangerous fevers—even malaria; from aiding digestion by stimulating gastric juices to intensifying romance!

The following recipe is really the Mexican's sandwich. The taco is easy to prepare, delicious, inexpensive, adaptable to all manner of dining. No genuine Mexican meal will be complete without tacos.

Tacos

Remove meat and onion, and put through food chopper. Add broth from cooker until meat is moist and no longer crumbly. Add additional salt and taco spices to taste.

Heat vegetable oil in a heavy skillet. Place a heaping spoon of meat mixture in center of soft tortilla. Fold tortilla and fry in hot fat until golden brown on each side.

Drain on paper towel. Serve with bowl of shredded lettuce, diced tomatoes and hot sauce.

Whoever heard of a new vegetable in this day and age? You may think you have found a new one on your produce counter when you see your first pole bean.

It will be very familiar to some people, but a complete stranger to many others. Basically, it is the same vegetable as the one we call a snap bean. But, a snap bean grows on bushes while the pole bean grows up stakes and attains a much larger size.

The growing of this crop is a relatively new specialty of Florida. Much of the production is situated in Dade County, not far from the jet runways of Miami Airport. Many centuries ago these beans were being grown by American Indians, who much preferred climbing beans—"beans walking," they called them. They liked to plant them near their corn, the stalks of which could then serve as bean poles. In the very efficient growing of pole beans in Dade County, sesbania sticks are set in a circle to make a sort of tepee (about 12,000 sesbania sticks are required per acre). Once the bean vines start rambling up these supporting sticks nearly all mechanical gadgets be-

Fresh Pole Beans

  4 *large onions, peeled*
1½ *lbs. pole beans*
  2 *teaspoons salt*
  3 *tablespoons butter or*
    margarine
 ¼ *teaspoon ground white pepper*
 ¼ *cup toasted slivered almonds*
    Fresh parsley sprigs

come useless. One mule at a time can make his way between these rows, but pulling only a small cultivator. (Even though a mule like this works hard for a living, once his day's work is done he has only to step into his private truck to commute home to his barn and dinner.)

So even though pole beans must be picked by hand, the fleshy, opera-length pods are almost twice as large as those of bush beans, and it doesn't take long to gather a hamper full. There are still other benefits. Not only do these beans afford a greater number of pickings than the bush varieties, but because pole bean vines are much taller than the bushes of bush beans, there is room for two or three times the yield per acre.

I wish to offer the following recipe for your taste pleasure featuring fresh pole beans but if you are unable to locate them in your local supermarket, you can substitute fresh snap beans.

in Onion Cups

Halve onions crosswise. Hollow out by removing 4 or 5 layers from center of each half. Chop centers or place in a tightly sealed glass jar and refrigerate for use in another recipe. Remove ends of beans and cut into 1-inch pieces. In large saucepan cook beans and onion halves in one inch boiling water with 1½ teaspoons salt, uncovered, for 5 minutes. Cover and continue to boil another 10 minutes or until vegetables are tender. With a slotted spoon, remove onion cups and place in greased, heat-proof dish in a slow oven about 300 degrees to keep hot. Drain beans and return to saucepan. Add butter or margarine, remaining salt, ground white pepper and 2 tablespoons of the almonds. Mix lightly and heat thoroughly. To serve, fill onion halves with the bean mixture and top with the rest of the almonds. Garnish platter with parsley sprigs. Recipe serves 8.

There never has developed a strictly American style of cooking; not, that is, compared with the French way of cooking, or the Chinese, or the Italian. This is because America has taken all of the foods of other nations into its kitchen. They say we are a nation of immigrants; so, as in a colossal tasting bee we sample from every country's cuisine which has immigrated to this nation with its people.

Such is the story of the most popular food flavor in the United States—chocolate. Every year we import 650 million pounds of the cacao bean, from which chocolate is made, and we consume more chocolate than any other nation in the world. We consider it as American as Valley Forge, hardly stopping to think that it is an immigrant food.

It is interesting to trace the evolution of chocolate on its way to us. Columbus had to discover the New World. The Spanish ex-

German Chocolate

½ pound marshmallows
¾ cup milk
¼ teaspoon salt
½ bar German's sweet chocolate
1 teaspoon vanilla
½ pint whipping cream
1 9-in. baked pie shell

plorers had to go to Mexico, there discovering the cacao tree and its raw beans, which the Indians used for brewing a strange new beverage. Cortez had to return, with the secret brew, to Spain, where the new "chocolat" became immediately popular. Its fame spread throughout the continent; then on to America. And all the while, had we but known it, just across our own borders the Mexicans had been cooking with chocolate for centuries. They call it "the food for the gods."

German Chocolate Pie is a pie "for the gods." This is the most popular recipe ever featured on my television show, "The Gourmet." The recipe is not complicated—just delectable. It is not extremely unusual—just a combination of flavors that makes it a winner. It has a touch of the everyday and a touch of the gourmet.

Pie

Combine marshmallows, milk, salt, and German's sweet chocolate in top of a double boiler. When melted and completely blended, set aside and let cool. Add vanilla. Now whip the cream and fold it into the chocolate mixture and pour the mixture into baked pie shell. Place in your refrigerator.

Both pie and crust will taste better if removed from the refrigerator about 20 minutes before serving.

If you wish, you may top German Chocolate Pie with more whipped cream. This is strictly optional, however, as it is deliciously rich without a topping.

Everyone likes this pie. When you serve it you will see why it is the most popular of my recipes; why many years after its debut I still receive requests for additional copies.

John Jacob Astor once remarked that "a man with a million dollars is as well off as a man who is rich!" Well, those must have been the "good old days" people are always talking about. But today anyone of us can enjoy food which only the high and the mighty **could** afford in days gone by.

People often complain to me that they cannot afford to serve gourmet-type food, because it is too expensive. I won't argue about the cost of prime rib or lobster flown from Maine, but I will suggest that you stop and look around the next time you are shopping in your supermarket.

I believe the misunderstanding comes from a misconception of what gourmet food is. Gourmethood depends upon what is **done to the food,** not upon the groceries themselves. A recipe which boasts a

Gourmet

CHARLOTTE RUSSE ECONOMI:

1 *box frozen strawberries*
1½ *pints sour cream*
Brown sugar

Place frozen strawberries, thawed and drained, into a baking dish. Cover strawberries with 1½ pints sour cream. Cover this mixture thoroughly with brown sugar. Place into a preheated oven at 350 degrees and bake until bubbling (20 to 25 minutes). Serve in dessert glasses, either hot or cold.

TRADER DOUG:

1 *fresh pineapple*
Honey

Divide fresh pineapple into four sections, slicing lengthwise and leaving leafy tops. With a sharp knife loosen fruit from the peel, score into chunks. Brush honey over the pineapple. Place under hot broiler heat just long enough to glaze the fruit. Serve with small forks. Four servings per pineapple.

Charlotte Russe Economi is a

flair for seasoning and serving, creativity, rightness to the occasion, tender attention to the component parts, and execution of small details lifts the ordinary into the extraordinary.

So I insist that you can enjoy gourmet food at no more expense than using your wits to gourmet advantage. It is attitude, feeling, appreciation of food, a willingness to experiment, and not the fatness of the purse which is important.

When a recipe with the qualities described above meets a household chef with the qualities of mind and hand just mentioned, culinary miracles come forth.

To prove my point I'm giving you, not one, but two dessert recipes which I consider gourmet quality; yet they are not budget-busters.

Desserts

short-cut version of the famous French dessert, and Trader Doug is an exotic Polynesian offering. One has only two ingredients, the other only three. Still, each is delicious in taste, impressive in looks, and economical. John Jacob himself would have relished either one with billionaire gusto!

Though the Greeks seem to have had a god or a goddess for everything there is a phrase well-known throughout the world, "the French have a word for it," and by comparison, it may be said that "the Greeks have a god, or goddess, for it." Mythological gods abound in Greece. Amid Athens' modern traffic patterns, little English Fords drive past the unforgettable, and almost unbelievable, Acropolis with its Parthenon, which was the temple of Athena, by the Temple of Zeus. Streets are often named for gods, and businesses reside side by side with the temples of the ancients. Likewise, you will find the Rent-A-Car office opposite the Temple of Jupiter. On first hearing this, it gives one pause, but it is a good picture of today's Greece. The very, very old and the new thrive together harmoniously.

In spite of the multitude of gods and goddesses, I have never been able to find evidence of a goddess of gourmet cooking. The ancient Athenians were obviously more interested in art, literature, and ideas, in thinking and lengthy discourses, than in spending more time in

Grecian

1 *can grape leaves*
1 *lb. ground beef*
1 *cup cooked rice, underdone*
½ *cup green onions, finely chopped*
½ *cup chopped parsley*
2 *tablespoons butter or margarine, melted*
1½ *teaspoons salt*
½ *teaspoon fresh ground black pepper*
½ *teaspoon cinnamon*
   Juice of ½ lemon
2 *cups beef broth*
2 *tablespoons tomato catsup*

A can of grape leaves will contain about 50 to 60. Reserve 10 to 15 leaves to line the bottom of cooking pan. Use the remainder for wrapping around the meat stuffing. Pour hot water over the grape leaves when they are removed from the can. Drain and spread on a towel to dry. Remove rough stems.

To mix the stuffing: Blend together ground beef, rice, onions, parsley, and butter. Add seasonings: salt, pepper, and cinnamon. Mix lightly.

the kitchen creating gourmet menus. The native dishes are good, satisfying, hearty fare, but elegance of menu and décor are rarities in Greece. If you are traveling in Greece and you already like Greek food you are in luck, for when you can dine in a little taverna at the foot of the hill of the Acropolis, who could ask for more elegance?

Fruits are plentiful and good in Greece; fish is fresh from the Mediterranean; vegetables are large, wholesome and tasty. Grape leaves are much used in preparation of a national favorite called Dolmades. These are tasty little tidbits of meat and seasonings enveloped in grape leaves. They can be, and **are** great hors d'oeuvres. They can also be a whole meal, the main event. They can be a side dish with a larger meat course. Dolmades are a favorite of tourists, and a recipe easily duplicated once you are home again. One thing: find a specialty (or Greek) food store where you can buy grape leaves, canned, ready for the making of Dolmades.

Dolmades

Place a tablespoon of the meat stuffing in the center of a grape leaf. Fold left and right ends toward the middle, then roll like a sausage. When all the stuffing is used, prepare your cooking pan by lining bottom with leaves. Then place little envelopes of meat mixture all around, stacking them on top of each other until all are in the pan. Pour over the leaves a mixture of lemon juice, broth, and tomato catsup. Cover pan and cook on low heat for an hour. If Dolmades are not very

tender, cook for an additional 15 to 20 minutes.

The Greeks like to serve yogurt with this dish. Sometimes it is served with a lemon slice. To obtain a tart flavor, squeeze juice over Dolmades. This should serve about 8 people.

The place to find native Greek food, and fun, at its best, is in the taverna. These are (usually) small bistro-like eateries where the Greeks like to congregate to enjoy their favorite foods, each other, and themselves. Hospitable, gracious, and thoroughly likable (and they like Americans, too!), these people love to be entertained while they dine. There must be a belief that ear-pounding music aids the appetite, because the strains of "Zorba, the Greek," "Never On Sunday," and native folk songs bring the roof down, perhaps the beginning of acute deafness. And then there is the bouzouki dance (also seen in "Never On Sunday") wherein they break pottery and other assorted tableware.

Greek Taverna

2 medium-sized eggplants
1½ sticks butter
3½ teaspoons salt
1½ cups onions, chopped
1½ lbs. ground lamb, lean
2 tablespoons tomato catsup
⅓ cup dry red wine
½ teaspoon black pepper, freshly ground
¼ teaspoon cinnamon
¼ cup chopped parsley
3 tablespoons flour
2 cups hot milk
1 cup cottage cheese, drained and dry
2 eggs, beaten
⅛ teaspoon nutmeg
¾ cup soda crackers, finely crumbled into meal
¾ cup Parmesan cheese, grated

Peel eggplant, and cut into thin slices. Brown in melted butter (using about 4 tablespoonsful). Brown eggplant on both sides. Remove and season with 1 teaspoon of salt.

In the same skillet, melt 4 more tablespoons of butter, and sauté the onions for about 7 minutes, until soft. Add the lamb and cook for 15 minutes, stirring often. Add tomato catsup, wine, pepper, cinnamon, parsley, and 1½ teaspoons of the salt. Cook over low heat until nearly dry, making sure all ingredients are well blended. Cool and sample for seasoning. Add more salt and pepper to taste, if necessary.

Take the remaining butter,

Some tavernas feature only one or two specialty items, but most offer a large variety of Greek dishes. Unless the menu has a very limited repertoire, you will find Moussaka. Moussaka combines two of Greece's more plentiful and popular foods, lamb and eggplant. Beloved by the natives, this classic Greek cuisine is heartily liked by most visitors who sample it. It has authority, and it is a nutritious and pleasant new taste experience. This recipe features Moussaka à la casserole in the Old World tradition.

Moussaka

place in a saucepan, and melt. Stir in flour and the remaining 1 teaspoon of salt. Stir in milk, constantly agitating ingredients. Bring to point of boiling and cook an additional 6 or 7 minutes before removing from the heat. Allow to cool for a few minutes; then add cottage cheese, eggs, and nutmeg.

Grease an 8x12-inch baking dish, and dust lightly with flour. Cover the bottom of the baking dish with eggplant slices; then add a layer of lamb mixture and sprinkle with cracker meal and Parmesan cheese. Repeat layers of eggplant, lamb mixture, cracker meal, and Parmesan cheese, ending with eggplant for the top layer. Pour sauce over the top, and bake in a preheated 375 degree oven for 1 hour, or until the top is custard-firm and golden-colored. Let cool to warm before serving. Serve by cutting into large squares. This recipe will serve 6 generously.

The man in France to equal our Mr. Webster, of the dictionary Websters, that is, is Monsieur Larousse. In his word bible of the French language he identifies haute cuisine as "high-class cooking." Haute cuisine is the best, the very highest class cooking in and from France. That the French are renowned for their cooking is no secret, of course. Other countries borrow from them, but this has never diminished their cooking quality, nor their reputation.

The very language of France adds its blessing to their famous dishes. When you see on a menu "Les fromages variés," you must be impressed. But what is it? It is what the French call "cheese board" or what we call "assorted cheeses." Or this menu item—"le pigeonneau rôti avec le riz sauvage americain." How about that? "Roast squab with wild rice."

But don't let an imposing name keep you from enjoying haute cuisine for here are gourmetdom's richest rewards.

Haute Cuisine

FRENCH ONION SOUP
ESCOFFIER:

¼ lb. butter
2½ lbs. onions, sliced
1 quart beef stock
1 quart chicken stock
2 tablespoons Worcestershire powder
1 bay leaf

1½ teaspoons celery salt
1 teaspoon black pepper or 12 peppercorns, crushed
Salt to taste
Croutons
1 cup Parmesan cheese

Historic Les Halles market district of Paris (unfortunately torn down now) was traditionally the proper place to find the world's truly great recipes for French Onion Soup. This market district came to life at midnight and until about six in the morning was the busiest section in all Paris. Beginning at midnight, small sidewalk cafes commence serving their specialty—French Onion Soup. This recipe for French Onion Soup Escoffier, given to me by the maître d' of Am Fried de Cochon, is haute cuisine, yet simple to prepare and so versatile it is one recipe where you may safely improvise. For example, if you happen to have the remains of some turkey stock in the refrigerator, you may add it to your recipe with good results. I believe a recipe should be prepared exactly as given for the first time, however. Then if any alterations are desired, you may experiment. Also, every recipe followed precisely **should** always get the same culinary results.

Heat butter in heavy kettle. Add sliced onions and brown well, stirring constantly. Add beef and chicken stock, Worcestershire powder, bay leaf, celery salt, and pepper. Allow to simmer for 40 minutes. Remove bay leaf, and salt to taste. Serve soup at once in heated tureen. Float croutons and sprinkle generously with cheese.

Toujours la haute cuisine. And Bon Appetit!

The art of genuine gourmet cooking begins with the mastering of sauces. No less an authority than the greatest gourmet-chef who ever lived—Escoffier—said so himself. He declared also that if a culinary craftsman could command five basic French sauces, then he was pretty much in business as a chef.

During Escoffier's lifetime a master chef had to be inventive and resourceful. Negotiations of these fundamental sauces—espagnole, velouté, béchamel, tomato, and hollandaise—spelled the difference between a mundane food and one that brought exclamations of praise. Often sauces disguised slightly spoiled foods, camouflaging them with a flavor more agreeable than the food they covered. Refrigeration was not available, and other methods of preservation were not dependable.

Hollandaise

¼ lb. butter (*divided into three parts*)
4 *egg yolks*
2 *teaspoons lemon juice*
Dash of white pepper
Salt

Place one part of the butter into the top part of a glass double boiler over water. (I think it is best to use a glass double boiler for this sauce. Aluminum may discolor it.) Allow the butter to melt slowly, and add egg yolks. Keep heat low. Stir with a **wooden spoon** until creamy; then add the second part of the butter and stir.

(Do not allow the water in the double boiler to boil.) After the second part of the butter is melted and blended into recipe, add the third part. Continue to stir until well mixed; then add lemon juice, salt, and pepper. Remove from flame and stir. Hollandaise sauce should not be served hot, but rather just warm.

There are several points to be especially careful about for a successful sauce. Egg yolks, which are the base of the sauce, can be overcooked quite quickly, which causes curdling. To prevent this trouble, make sure the sauce does not get

These sauces were developed for specific groups of foods, such as meats, fish, fowl, vegetables, etc. As the French chefs' reputations and repertoires expanded, hundreds of variations of these five basic sauces appeared on the gourmet's plate.

Mayonnaise, for instance, was a sauce developed especially for fish. Today we use it for everything else, and its origin has been all but forgotten.

Let's try one of these sauces—a popular one on the American scene, but one which many cooks shy away from and, therefore, deny themselves of its delicious ability to enhance vegetables. Actualizing hollandaise is not difficult, but it does require wholehearted, undivided attention and care in following of directions. The "feel" for when it is coming along right will not be long in coming to you.

Sauce

too hot. If the sauce starts to curdle, stop stirring and remove immediately from the heat. Cool it in a pan of cold water, and stir it gently to reconstitute smoothness. The sauce will "hold"—stay as it should be served—for about 30 minutes if you will place the top part of the double boiler in a shallow pan of warm water. However, it is a sauce best savored when served at once.

Try this recipe for Hollandaise Sauce and serve it as follows for an ideal dish.

BROCCOLI BENEDICT:

Toast
Sliced fried ham
Drained, cooked broccoli

Arrange toast on a plate. Then on the toast place one slice of fried ham. Place drained, cooked broccoli on the ham; then top with Hollandaise Sauce.

Sauce-making will have a marvelous renaissance in your kitchen when you try Broccoli Benedict.

Setting a pretty table with foods too good to resist is one way to encourage the breakfast habit in your family. Get into the breakfast habit by cooking new and special honey-sweetened foods.

Honey is a wholesome food that the ancient Greeks called the "nectar of the gods." Best of all for us, it contains fewer calories than does sugar, which makes it a wonderful topping on toast, grapefruit, strawberries, bananas, hot or cold cereals, as well as a fine ingredient for baked goods. Try out a few of these honey ideas during the week, and see if your family doesn't decide breakfast is well worth getting up for in the morning.

Whether your family is large or small, buffet service might be just the answer to the early morning rush. Set out glasses of juice, bread for the toaster, cereals and milk; then let everyone help himself. The youngsters will especially enjoy Honey Milk Punch, and it will help to send them off well prepared for a busy day at school. You'll need 1½ cups of banana purée, made by putting bananas through a sieve;

Honey Crisp

2 cups sifted all-purpose flour
3 teaspoons baking powder
½ teaspoon salt
¼ cup sugar
¼ cup shortening
1 egg
⅔ cup milk

TOPPING:

3 tablespoons soft butter
½ cup honey
¾ cup shredded coconut
¾ cup cereal flakes

to the purée add ⅓ cup orange juice, 6 tablespoons honey, a pinch of salt, and ¼ teaspoon almond extract. Mix well. Just before the youngsters are due downstairs, add the mixture to a quart of cold milk and beat with an egg beater. Garnish with whipped cream and serve immediately. These ingredients will constitute about 6 servings.

Many breakfast dishes can easily be prepared the evening before, leaving you freer the next day to give family members an assist in finding books and briefcases before they dash off.

Honey is the wonder ingredient that helps to keep made-ahead rolls and coffee cakes moist so that they taste rich and fresh to the last bite.

Prepare our recipe for Honey Crisp Coffee Cake in the afternoon or evening. Cool, and cover well; then heat and serve in the morning. Its special topping of honey, deliciously browned, is too tasty to resist. Knowing that it's waiting for breakfast will inspire the pokiest member of the tribe to hurry to the breakfast table.

Coffee Cake

Sift dry ingredients into a bowl. Cut in shortening. Add egg and milk, stirring only until all flour is moistened. Spread batter in greased 9-inch square pan. Cover with topping, made by combining soft butter, honey, shredded coconut, and cereal flakes. Bake in moderately hot oven (400 degrees) 25 to 30 minutes. Serve warm. Recipe yields 9 to 12 servings.

Annually in San Francisco's Chinatown, after three weeks of preparation by a brigade of cooks, and incorporating most of the stocks of the Chinese markets the famous by-invitation-only Chinese Sportsmen's Banquet takes place. Guests are San Francisco's finest sports figures and they and the financiers, business and professional men, society bigwigs, and others who come to honor them place high value on an invitation for this honorable event.

If you have ever had a full course Chinese dinner you know how many different foods are offered one after another. But a Chinese banquet! It would take linguistic skill in all the Chinese dialects at once to describe the exotic eye-smell-taste experience of that evening in Chinatown. In a many-splendored bite-by-bite ceremony each of the exquisite food delicacies is expectantly sampled. Fortunately, it is not improper to ask for another bite of a particularly taste-pleasing item. At one banquet I was struck by the fact that several men asked for a second portion of a dish the main ingredient of which was peas,

Hong Kong

½ lb. bacon, sliced
1 onion, finely diced
½ green pepper, finely diced

almost exactly like our well-known English green peas. Peas are definitely not a man's favorite vegetable by any stretch of the culinary imagination. I wondered about this small miracle until the Hong Kong Sauté Peas arrived in front of me. Then I knew! Now I wanted this recipe, but how to get it?

The Chinese never give away their ancient, honorable, and treasured cooking secrets, and have, in fact, developed a confounding way of politely refusing to do so. Suddenly, third, fourth, and fifth generation American-Chinese can cook only in their ancestral tongue. They will give you the instructions in **Chinese!**

But my dinner companion for the evening was a gentleman on the San Francisco staff of the FBI. I asked **him** to ask **them.** There is something very authoritative about those three letters F, B, I. Here is the recipe for Hong Kong Sauté Peas, and in Americanese.

I have simplified the recipe into standard ingredients and sizes but follow directions just so.

Sauté Peas

1 *small can of mushrooms, sliced*
1 *tablespoon garlic salt*
6 *drops of Tabasco*
1 *teaspoon Worcestershire powder*
1 *teaspoon MSG powder*
1 *large can English green peas with liquid in the can*

Place bacon slices into skillet and fry until softly and lightly browned. Remove bacon, leaving the bacon fat. Place onion, bell pepper, and mushrooms into the bacon fat. Sauté until items begin to soften.

Add garlic salt, Tabasco, Worcestershire powder, and MSG powder, and simmer slowly for three more minutes. Now add the English green peas, with the liquid in the can. Cover skillet and simmer slowly until peas have a wilted look. Hong Kong Sauté Peas are ready to serve. They should be moist, but should not have excessive liquid.

In the northeast corner of the state of Texas there is a county famous for its stew—Hopkins County. Everyone came to town to the county seat on Saturday for shopping and sociality. Soon it became a custom for each family to bring a victual or two to contribute to the big cast-iron kettle set up at the courthouse square for a genuine Hopkins County Stew. In those days an oldtimer would start a hardwood and hot coal fire early in the morning. As the county folk began to arrive the first thing that went into the huge kettle that had been placed on top of the fire was bacon—a few slices to begin the sizzling goodness. Then came chickens (plentiful in the county), squirrel, quail, perhaps beef or pork. Then the potatoes and onions, beans, or peas, and corn, tomatoes, and proper seasonings.

An extra-long-handled ladle kept the stew moving around for hours and hours. Self-appointed Hopkins County Stew experts volunteered

Hopkins County

1 2-lb. chicken
1 bay leaf
  Pinch thyme
2 sprigs celery tops
6 sprigs parsley
  Salt and pepper to taste
2 cups diced potatoes
1 cup frozen cut green beans
¼ lb. butter (or margarine)
2 medium onions, chopped fine
3 small pods garlic, minced
1 16-oz. can tomatoes
1 cup whole kernel corn
1 cup frozen peas
12 whole onions

for this job. Then, by late afternoon a picnic—Hopkins County style —was well under way. The giant cauldron (20 to 30 gallons) made enough stew to feed them all. And a very, very good stew it was too.

This is still a wonderful way to entertain. Perfect for outside "feeding"—and if the weather plays tricks this stew can be accomplished inside. You need a large iron kettle, and a long-handled ladle. Inform guests to bring something for the party stew. As they arrive ask them to prepare and donate their offerings to the chuckling kettle. Cooking is part of the fun, and oddly enough, this nearly always turns out to be a wonderful stew. To prevent too many cooks from spoiling the broth, the host or hostess should be in charge of stirring, and adjusting seasonings.

I have "modernized" this recipe so you may reproduce it in advance if you wish to do it all yourself.

Stew

Cover chicken with water in a large kettle. Add salt and pepper, and begin cooking over low heat. Prepare a bouquet garni by placing in a loosely woven cloth 1 bay leaf, thyme, 2 sprigs celery tops, sprigs of parsley, salt and pepper. Secure spices by tying package with string. Submerge into water where bouquet garni imparts a spicy flavor and leaves a suspicion of taste when chicken is done. Bring chicken to a boil and cook until tender. Remove chicken from broth. Bone, and dice chicken. Remove bouquet garni, and reserve the broth.

Cook potatoes and green beans together until tender. Fry the chopped onions and garlic in butter or margarine until brown. Add tomatoes. Cook 5 minutes. Now add this to chicken broth. Add corn, frozen peas, 12 whole onions, cooked potatoes and green beans. Return the diced chicken to broth. Stir well; bring to boil; reduce heat to simmer and cook 40 minutes longer.

Serve in individual iron pots, heated well.

"What am I going to do with it?" This lament of the hunter's wife I hear every year. How to cook the game he brings in? While I, myself, am no hunter—the last deer hunt I "attended" someone calculated my score—15 soft drink bottles, 22 beer cans, and the bark off seven trees—and suggested that I content myself with adding to the compendium of cookery of wild creatures and give up "attending" deer hunts.

Cheer up, wives. I have come to your rescue with a recipe for venison, and some advice both marital and culinary regarding same. Also, gentlemen, you will find I do not play favorites. I have advice for you, too. Since the game-to-be-prepared, of necessity, comes before the recipe for preparing it, I will advise the gentlemen first.

Game is definitely a man's dish. Proudly he deposits his hunting prize at the doorstep of the old homestead, so to speak, and leaves the lady of the house to cope with cooking and serving it. Moreover,

Hunter's

A 5-lb. venison roast
2 cups cognac
¼ cup melted butter
¼ cup olive oil
1 clove garlic, chopped fine
3 tablespoons finely chopped parsley
Salt and pepper to taste
3 tablespoons cognac
1 cup red currant jelly
1 teaspoon horseradish
Steamed onions for garnish

If roast is lean and somewhat dry, lard it through with a little pork fat or butter. It may be roasted in oiled paper to supplement fat content. Venison roast should be marinated for 6 hours in cognac. Refrigerate while marinating.

Mix melted butter and olive oil in a skillet and heat. Sauté garlic and parsley until soft and add roast for browning. Brown quickly on

if he can manage to bring the deer in on hoof to display to the little woman, he does. Now this in itself is enough to kill her appetite for game—forever. She can barely force herself to envision how she could cook the poor thing. So, gentlemen, always bring your deer meat home as meat—cut up, wrapped in neat little packages. Further, if you ever expect to see the rewards of your hunting skill on the evening dinner table, never, ever, ever give any details of the hunt. I don't know exactly why, but a deer is a very dear animal to the gals.

O.K. So the game is neatly wrapped, labeled and languishing in the freezer. Sad state of affairs. My advice to you, ladies, is cook that game! Nothing is more pleasing to a man. This treat to his ego is second only to the thrill of shooting and hunting. Give your full attention to preparing Hunter's Venison. Cook it with care and as well as you can. Then invite his friends over to experience the taste of really well-cooked venison.

Venison

both sides over high heat and place into roast pan. Roast in a moderate oven until tender. (A longer roasting period is necessary for older venison.) Using skillet that roast was browned in, add the 3 tablespoons cognac and deglaze over flame. Mix in red currant jelly and horseradish and blend. Serve this sauce over the venison roast and garnish with steamed onions. Serves 6.

Escoffier, the King of Cooks and the Cook of Kings, once said that no one could hope to become a really great cook unless he had a "passionate love of garlic." The great Escoffier used garlic with artistic and subtle discretion, and he taught his many disciples to do the same.

But next door to the famous Frenchman the Italian chefs loved garlic even more passionately than Escoffier and his staff. Italians know how to cook with garlic! Furthermore, when the other basics of Italian cuisine—pasta, tomato, and olive oil—are combined with garlic, a blend with an intrinsic Italian aura is created.

This marriage of flavors is productive of many "children." The addition of a variety of in-law, cousin, aunt and uncle ingredients to the

Italian

SAUCE:

¼ cup olive oil
1 large chopped onion
1 chopped clove of garlic
¾ lb. ground beef
¼ lb. ground pork
1 large can peeled tomatoes
2 small cans tomato paste
2 cups water
1 cup chopped, cooked mushrooms

FILLING:

4 ozs. mozzarella cheese, diced
4 soft scrambled eggs
1 lb. ricotta cheese (or cottage
cheese)
1 teaspoon chopped parsley
Salt to taste
Pepper to taste
1 pound tufoli
Parmesan cheese

basic four-ingredient formula accounts for the infinite selection of dishes which await you in any Italian restaurant, home or cookbook. Just as in the human family, none are exactly the same; still all bear the stamp Italia.

Tufoli is a lesser-known but interesting member of the pastas. It has a tube-like shape, for it is a pasta shell for stuffing. It can be purchased in many supermarkets, and in any specialty food store.

This recipe is divided into two ingredient lists—one for the sauce and one for the stuffing. There are three sections of instructions: one for the sauce; one for the stuffing; and one for cooking and preparation of the Tufoli.

Tufoli Imbottite

To make the sauce, first heat oil in saucepan; add onion and garlic and sauté until golden brown; add meat and stir until brown. Add tomatoes, paste, and water. Season to taste with salt and pepper. Simmer this mixture for 3 hours (the longer it cooks the better the flavor). Now add the mushrooms.

While the sauce is simmering, prepare the filling. Blend mozzarella cheese with warm scrambled eggs (this will melt the cheese); add the ricotta (or cottage cheese), parsley, and salt and pepper to taste. Beat with fork until light and fluffy (or mix with hands as in making meat balls).

Cook one pound of tufoli in a large pot of boiling water for 15 minutes. Drain. Run cold water over them to prevent sticking and to cool for handling. Stuff them with the already-prepared filling. Cover the bottom of a baking pan with the sauce. Line the stuffed tufoli in this; then add more sauce. Repeat this process until all tufoli are used. Cover and put into a 350-degree oven for about 30 to 40 minutes. Serve hot with Parmesan cheese and extra meat sauce. Recipe serves 6.

Painting, composing poems, sculpting statues, singing are all forms of artistic expression we recognize, but they are not the only means of creative expression. I believe cooking is an art, and, of the many foods which our imaginations can conjure up for taste-teasing, cakes rate high in the cooking art world. Cakes are associated with special occasions—birthdays, anniversaries, and seasonal holidays. Almost any reason for celebrating calls for a cake. An abundance of loving, caring, and giving goes into the making of a cake. Is there a man or woman or child who is not pleased and flattered when a cake is baked especially for them?

It's a pity, then, that creative cake-baking is not practiced more today. The recipe given here is a do-it-yourself-from-start-to-finish cake. When you purchase, measure, and mix all of the items according to the Jet Prune Cake blueprint, you will reward yourself and your family with a cake that is individual, delicious, and, I hope, a new taste which you will want to make a permanent resident of your "best cake recipes" file.

Jet

4 *cups sifted cake flour*
2 *teaspoons soda*
3 *cups sugar*
6 *eggs*
2 *cups vegetable oil*
2 *cups buttermilk*
2 *teaspoons nutmeg*
2 *teaspoons cinnamon*
1 *teaspoon salt*
2 *cups chopped cooked prunes*

ICING:

   Whites of 3½ eggs
4 *cups confectioners' sugar*
3 *cups soft butter*
1 *teaspoon vanilla*
1 *teaspoon lemon extract*
   Dash of salt
½ *cup chopped nuts, optional*

There are only two types of cakes: butter cakes and sponge cakes. Butter cakes are those made with butter, shortening, or oil, while the family of sponge cakes depends upon egg whites for leavening. The Jet Prune Cake is a butter-family cake, although the recipe calls for oil, not butter.

I have only a few ironclad rules for baking a good cake. (1) Use the very best ingredients: any cake is only as good as the items you put into it. (2) Measure **exactly** according to the recipe, and make certain also that you use the method described in the recipe. (3) Any cake which will be frosted should be cooled first. Here is where many frostings, which were intended to be the crowning glory of the cake, are ruined. (4) Use the equipment recommended in the recipe.

Incidentally, this is called Jet Prune Cake because it is so quick and easy—you simply combine all the ingredients and mix them together. It's delicious, too, with a light texture many prune cakes do not have.

Prune Cake

Sift cake flour, soda and sugar together. Beat eggs for one minute. Add remaining ingredients, including dry ingredients, and beat 3 minutes. Pour into 3 greased, floured 9-inch pans. Bake in moderate, 350-degree oven, 35 to 40 minutes. For the icing, beat egg whites until stiff, adding confectioners' sugar gradually during the process; then add shortening, vanilla extract, and lemon extract. Add salt. Mix thoroughly. If desired, sprinkle top of iced cake with chopped nuts.

Anyone who has read the epics of the ancient Greek, Homer, or loves the tales of Greek mythology may know about that fabulous herb, moly. (Moly rhymes with holy.) This herb has never been identified exactly, but has been regarded historically as "a sort of garlic" with occult powers. Odysseus, who spent years trying to get home after the Trojan War, would never have returned to Penelope if it hadn't been for the moly which the God, Hermes, had given him.

Remember that Queen Calypso induced him to bite into the apple of immortality which should have killed Odysseus—but he ate the yellow flowered garlic at the same time, so Calypso could do him no harm.

Odysseus met all manner of charming, but deadly females. There was Queen Circe, who turned men into pigs just for fun. The white goddess, Ino, who disguised herself as a mermaid, tried to pull him down to her deep sea tavern. He escaped, too, from the Island of Sirens and the Island of Dogs. None of these wicked beauties were able to harm Odysseus because he kept gnawing away at the garlic-like moly.

To the Romans garlic was not only a cure-all, but a source of great strength. Supposedly it made men brave, so soldiers were supplied with garlic to make them fearless.

Kidney Bean

2 cups (1-lb. can) red kidney beans, drained
1 7-oz. can chunk-type tuna fish, drained
¼ cup sliced cucumbers
6 anchovy fillets, quartered
¼ cup mayonnaise
1 teaspoon vinegar
1½ teaspoons salt
1½ teaspoons basil leaves
¼ teaspoon instant minced garlic
¼ teaspoon ground black pepper
  Head of lettuce
6 tomato wedges

Combine all ingredients except lettuce and tomato wedges. Mix slightly to prevent breaking tuna chunks. Chill one hour. Serve on lettuce and garnish with wedge of tomato. Serve as a main dish salad. Recipe serves 6.

Garlic lost none of its reputation in medieval times, either. It was supposed to be a cure for snake bite, dog bite, and the blues. It was dropped into a sick child's stocking as a "cure" for whooping cough. In 16th century Paris, people ate garlic-flavored butter in the spring to insure good health for the rest of the year. Even today, there are parts of the world where youngsters wear a necklace of garlic as a talisman to ward off evil.

Now that we have all kinds of miracle medicines we can put the world's garlic crop to its best use: in good cooking. Of course, garlic has been used as a seasoning for many centuries and in many lands. It seems to have originated around the Eastern Mediterranean. Passing caravans eventually carried it in all directions. It was taken to China and other eastern lands at a very early date. Garlic was not native to the Americas, but Spanish, Portuguese, and French explorers were probably the ones who brought the garlic bulb to this part of the world where it thrives so well.

Instant minced garlic is ideal in all kinds of cooked dishes, although it flavors cold mixtures such as French dressing beautifully if it's allowed to stay in the mixture for about an hour or more. The following recipe is one I feel best exemplifies the true character of instant minced garlic.

Tuna Salad

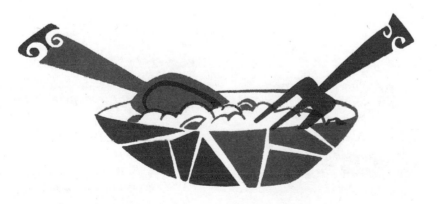

"Flair" is one of the many expressive words we've borrowed from the French. Originally, it meant to sniff the air or follow your nose in order to find out what was "cooking" or going on. Today, "flair" means "an instinct that leads to success in following it."

Or, we might say that a cook is gifted when she has a flair with seasonings, or reaches for one of her dehydrated garlic products for seasoning a meat, fish or fowl or salad dressing. Instinctively she "just knows," as she follows her nose, that garlic will give her creation a tantalizing aroma. When members of the family come in and sniff to see what smells so tempting, we're truly back to the original French use of "flair."

When we're talking about garlic, another French word applies, and that's "soupçon" (pronounced "soups on"). This means "suspicion," and that's how garlic is best used in most cases—just a drifting of aroma; now-you-smell-it, now-you-don't. The easiest and most certain way of regulating garlic aroma and flavor is to use modern dehydrated garlic products: instant minced, powder, or salt. Easy to measure, they assure consistent results.

Just how much is a "suspicion" of garlic? It depends almost entirely on who is cooking what and for whom. As a general rule, however, approximately ¼ teaspoon of instant minced or powdered garlic should give tempting flavor to 6 servings of food. Up this to ½ tea-

Lamb

¼ cup (½ stick) butter or
    margarine
¼ cup all-purpose flour
1 cup milk
1 teaspoon instant minced
    onion
1½ teaspoons salt
¼ teaspoon instant garlic
    powder
¼ teaspoon ground black
    pepper

spoon if using garlic salt, since part of the mixture in this case is plain table salt. When taking a recipe from an old cookbook calling for raw garlic, replace a large clove of garlic with ¼ teaspoon instant minced garlic or garlic powder. If dehydrated garlic products are new to your kitchen, start by using even smaller amounts: stir ⅛ teaspoon minced or powdered garlic into six portions; then taste. If more is needed to make an impression, add it.

Garlic is a very ancient flavoring and medicine. Records show that it was enjoyed by workmen building the Egyptian pyramids six thousand years ago. The Israelites became acquainted with garlic during their stay in Egypt. The Greeks loved garlic; the Romans of Caesar's day did not. However, their descendants, modern Italians, do, and they use garlic in some of their most famous dishes. Garlic seems to have been taken to China about 140 B.C., and its use spread throughout most of Asia and the Far East.

Garlic grows most lustily in warm climates, and so it is not too surprising to learn that the garlic fields of California supply nearly all the garlic dehydrated today.

Every day good cooks are finding new uses for dehydrated garlic products. Here, for instance, is a new recipe for a marvelous garlic-scented dish.

Croquettes

3 cups ground cooked lamb
Flour
1 egg, beaten slightly
1 tablespoon milk
Dry bread crumbs
Salad oil or shortening

Melt butter in a saucepan; blend in flour. Remove from heat and stir in 1 cup milk and onion. Cook until very thick, stirring constantly. Add seasonings and lamb. Mix well. Chill. Shape into croquettes. Roll in flour. Dip into beaten egg mixed with the 1 tablespoon milk and then into bread crumbs. Chill again. Fry in deep fat (375 degrees) 3 to 5 minutes or until golden brown. Drain on absorbent paper. Serve hot.

Recipe yields 12 croquettes or 6 portions.

I believe it was Walter Winchell who said that America should have two Thanksgivings—one for the Atlantic Ocean and one for the Pacific Ocean. He was referring to our natural defenses in a war, of course, but for the epicure two Thanksgivings would be very appropriate because these two vast oceans provide seafare of every conceivable variety.

Because of the appearance of the crab, I fear he has been neglected —by misunderstanding mostly—of the delicate, delectable taste treasure he hides within himself.

While demonstrating food at the World's Fair in New York some years ago, I visited the State of Maryland exhibit, and their outdoor dining featured fresh crab from the Maryland coast. When the whole, cooked crab was served to one woman, she was aghast at the thought of attacking this thing for its food. "I thought they came in cans!" she exclaimed, refusing to touch it.

Fortunately for the convenience of all of us, crab is canned, frozen, and pasteurized, although real fanciers of the crustacean say that fresh crab is the only way to go.

Landlubber Crab Sauce

For the landlubber, here is a short-short course on crab marketed in America:

Blue Crabs: Mostly from Chesapeake Bay, but found along the Atlantic and Gulf from Massachusetts to Texas. Dungeness Crabs: Found along the Pacific from Alaska to Mexico. Fresh, cooked meat picked from body and claws is marketed as one grade. Also available whole, fresh, and frozen. Rock Crabs: Come from New England areas and are similar to Dungeness, but smaller, less abundant. King Crab: Caught in the Bering Sea off Alaska. Average size of big male, marketed, is 11 pounds. Prime meat of King Crab is in the claws, legs, and shoulders; only these parts are used; available fresh or frozen.

This recipe, Landlubber Crab Sauce, is a zippy sauce and magically transforms spaghetti into something above and beyond the ordinary.

with Spaghetti

1 lb. crab meat, fresh, frozen, or pasteurized, or 3 cans (6½– 7½ oz. each)
½ cup chopped onion
½ cup chopped celery
2 cloves garlic, finely chopped
2 tablespoons chopped parsley
¼ cup butter or margarine, melted
1 cup canned tomatoes
1 8-oz. can tomato sauce
¼ teaspoon salt
½ teaspoon paprika
Dash pepper
3 cups cooked spaghetti
Grated Parmesan cheese

Thaw crab meat if frozen. Drain crab meat. Remove any remaining shell or cartilage. Cut crab meat into ½-inch pieces. Cook onion, celery, garlic, and parsley in butter until tender. Add tomatoes, tomato sauce, and seasonings. Simmer for 20 minutes, stirring occasionally. Add crab meat; heat.

Serve over spaghetti. Garnish with Parmesan cheese sprinkled over the top. Recipe serves six.

Each year I conduct numerous Cooking Schools across America. These sessions afford me a splendid opportunity to study table habits in the different areas. Naturally, questions arise regarding some trapping used in various recipes. I have learned that more confusion exists about types of lettuce than any other recipe aggrandizement.

There are five different types of lettuce, but it is iceberg—head lettuce—which is, by far, the most important on the produce counter. It is especially adapted to mass production in western fields. It is so familiar it needs no description. Have you ever wondered why this firm iceberg lettuce is always free of sand or similar foreign matter? It's one of nature's tricks. When a little head lettuce plant begins to grow, it starts by curling several of its larger leaves up and over the space which will shortly be filled by other growing leaves. This forms a sort of porch which wards off blowing sand and dust. In other words, the lettuce head fills out when inner leaves grow up from the stem below.

The butterhead is the second type of lettuce. It, too, is a head, but loosely formed of leaves which are very tender so that they have a

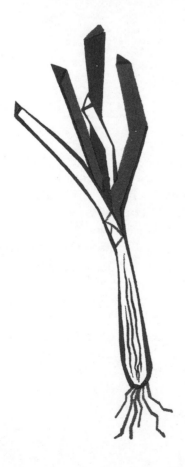

Lettuce

⅓ cup top milk or light cream
3 tablespoons cider vinegar
¾ teaspoon sugar
¾ teaspoon salt
⅛ teaspoon ground black pepper
1 medium head lettuce
1 cup chopped green onions
  (scallions)

sort of satin-smooth or "buttery feeling." "Big Boston" and "White Boston" are the most common varieties. Bibb is a miniature butterhead, about twice the size of a tulip. It is much prized by the trenchant gourmet. Its flavor has been described as "distinctively lettuce with a touch of cultivated dandelion."

Cos or romaine is almost always available, too, on produce counters. This is a long head of lettuce. The leaves are stiff and perhaps a bit coarse, but always sweet and of good quality.

Leaf or bunching lettuce is characterized by loose leaves which never form a head. It is well suited to greenhouse lettuce culture and is the most easily grown in the home garden since it endures somewhat more heat than varieties grown commercially.

The fifth type of lettuce has an enlarged stem and no head. It may, occasionally, be encountered under the name of "celtuce."

Lettuce is not only good eating, but it is good for us. Lettuce, especially the greener types, provides useful amounts of vitamins A and C, iron, and other vitamins and minerals. It gives us desirable roughage for good digestion. With all of these values, it is very low in calories.

in Cream

Combine the first five ingredients and set aside. Wash and dry lettuce, tear into bite-sized pieces, and place in a salad bowl. Add green onions and cream mixture. Toss lightly and serve as a salad course. Recipe serves 6.

My television viewers often accuse me of making them fat, getting them off their diets, tempting them beyond human ability to withstand rich and delicious foods. I plead guilty to taste-tempting my video audience, but innocent of getting them off their diets—that, dear readers, is your own decision.

As battles rage on about this diet and that diet I do, however, find myself very much in sympathy with those who must restrict their diets and miss so much palate-pleasing. As La Rochefoucauld said, "Preserving the health by too strict a regimen is a wearisome malady." Some diets I have seen are more to be feared than the disease!

A favorite story of mine concerns a man who suddenly became deaf. He took himself to a medical clinic to find out why. After examination by several doctors, his hearing apparatus was pronounced normal, so he was turned over to the staff psychiatrist, who promptly diagnosed his trouble as psychosomatic. "I have cured many people of this. It is caused by overstimulation of the nervous system," said the good doctor. "I have found gambling, drinking, women, and highly seasoned, rich foods are the causes."

"So, what do I do about it?" asked the patient.

Liver

1½ lbs. calf's liver sliced into thin pieces
½ pound butter
4 red onions, finely diced
1 4-oz. can mushrooms, drained
½ cup red wine
Salt and pepper to taste

Melt the butter in blazer pan of chafing dish over direct heat. Add onions and mushrooms. Sauté these items until soft. Add wine and salt and pepper to taste. Over these onions and mushrooms place slices of liver. Cover blazer pan with lid and allow to simmer until liver is done. The liver will become white in color when completely cooked. Serve on heated plates.

"Obviously, you will need to give up gambling, drinking, women, and highly seasoned, rich foods."

"Are you kidding, doc?" yelled the patient. "Just for a little hearing!"

That's the plight of the dieter for figure fashion or for health—are you kidding, doc? Just for a little slimness, or health? While it is true that many gourmet foods are loaded with calories, cholesterol, carbohydrate units, or whatever it is popular to watch and count nowadays, it is also true that many equally good recipes are to be found which are not. This recipe will prove that you can have gourmet food with healthfully pure ingredients, low calorie count, and definitely optimum flavor.

This recipe, in my opinion the ultimate in liver preparation, is an original by the famous actor of radio, television, and films, J. Carrol Naish. He demonstrated his chafing dish prowess when he was a guest on my television show in Los Angeles, "The Hollywood Gourmet."

Naish

Even in the sophisticated United States people wear or carry charms. Four-leaf clovers, wishbones, rabbits' feet are for good luck. Five-leaf clovers and two-dollar bills are avoided as bad luck. Throughout the centuries, basil has served as a symbol of both love and hate. In Italy, basil is often called Kiss-Me-Nicholas. Any girl who'd like to be kissed gets herself a sprig of basil. Roman girls make it easy for a bashful beau to propose. If the young man accepts a little bunch of basil from his girl, it's the same thing as asking her to be his wife. On the Island of Crete, basil is grown as a houseplant and signifies "love washed with tears."

How did the word "basil" originate? There have always been two theories. One has it as the root of the Greek word for royalty or king, basileus.

The opposition thought basil came from the word basilisk, a mythical serpent or dragon who could turn people to stone by looking at them. That, no doubt, is how basil got to be a symbol of hatred and abuse. In Greece, when people sowed basil seeds, they took pains to say the most awful things about it; this was to make it grow lustily.

For many years basil has been a symbol of good cooking. Back in the days of Shakespeare an herbalist declared, "A smell of basil is good for the heart and head . . . and maketh a man merrie and glad."

Meat Loaf

- 1 lb. ground beef
- 1 egg, lightly beaten
- 1 teaspoon salt
- 1/8 teaspoon ground black pepper
- 2 8-oz. cans tomato sauce
- 1/2 cup dry bread crumbs
- 2 tablespoons grated Parmesan cheese
- 2 tablespoons olive oil
- 4 teaspoons basil leaves
- 2 teaspoons instant minced onion

Basil is an herb of the mint family. Some dictionaries indicate that "basil" should rhyme with "dazzle." There are some 60 varieties of basil, but here in the United States we like sweet basil the best. Its shiny leaves are a kind of golden green and the entire surface of the leaf is spotted with tiny "wells" filled with an exquisitely fragrant oil. The fields in which basil grows have a heavenly scent, especially when someone brushes up against a basil plant.

If your mouth waters at the mention of pizza, spaghetti or lasagne, it's obvious that you love the subtle aroma of the basil which belongs in each of these famous Italian creations. This herb speaks Italian and, as good cooks left the old country to find new homes in America, they brought basil with them, as one of their most indispensable seasonings.

Basil is marvelous in all kinds of tomato or cheese concoctions, too. Sprinkle basil on tomato halves before broiling them.

Basil teams delightfully with the flavor of green beans, zucchini, chard, new potatoes, and green peas. Try a teaspoonful of dried basil per six servings of vegetables, adding it toward the end of the cooking period.

A half-teaspoon of basil gives delicate aroma to one cup of oil-and-vinegar dressing for green salads, especially if tomatoes and cucumbers are included. Let it stand one hour before using.

Pizza

¼ teaspoon instant garlic powder
5 to 6 thin slices mozzarella
    cheese

Combine ground beef, lightly beaten egg, salt, and pepper in mixing bowl and mix well, being careful not to overmix. Pat into the bottom and sides of a 9-inch pie plate. Set aside.

In separate mixing bowl combine tomato sauce, bread crumbs, Parmesan cheese, olive oil, basil leaves, instant minced onion, and garlic powder. Spoon into meat shell. Bake in a preheated moderate oven (375 degrees) 30 minutes. Top with slices of mozzarella cheese and return to oven for 5 minutes or until cheese is melted. Let Meat Loaf Pizza rest 5 minutes before cutting into pie-shaped wedges. Recipe serves 6.

For the hostess, or host, who wants to bring to the dining table a beautiful food fantasy, a pièce de résistance, a supreme delight, Melon Chicken is just what the gourmet ordered.

Melon Chicken is a Polynesian method of cooking, and it comes to us from Hawaii. In every country there are basic food preparation procedures which are handed down from generation to generation, and which seem quite unusual to us today. We find these tried and true recipes cannot be fundamentally changed with any appreciable improvement, but they can be adapted to our available supply of green groceries, or seasonings, and also to our way of cooking. This is the reason I recommend preparation in the way of the originators of Melon Chicken, but recommend you cook it in your modern, controlled oven, even though the natives cook it in a pit of hot coals. This way we get the exotic effect, the same superb taste and colorful

Melon

1 oval-shaped watermelon
   (approximately 25 lbs.)
1 baking-sized hen
   Salt and pepper
   Selected canned sweet fruits
   (such as pineapple, peaches,
   apricots, cherries, oranges)
½ cup soy sauce
   Minced onion (optional)
½ cup powdered almonds

With a very sharp knife, slice the melon lengthwise—end to end —in halves, and with a large spoon core out enough of the red melon meat and seeds to form a cavity that will hold the chicken. Core melon from both halves, leaving about an inch and a half or two inches of the ripe red fruit.

Season cavity of chicken with salt and pepper and place a few pieces of the sweet canned fruit in the cavity. Brush a light coat of soy sauce over the outside surface of the chicken and place about one tablespoon of soy sauce into the cavity. A few pieces of minced

eye appeal, and you won't have to dig up your backyard to cook native style.

A great wave of interest in Polynesian foods has developed. Surely seamen, adventurers, and world travelers tasted foods like these many years ago on these enchanted isles. But news of such as this never reached the mainland. After World War II when our servicemen came sailing home, they told of some delectable dishes served them in Hawaii and other Polynesian islands. Also the restaurant boom was on; the travel boom was on; Polynesia just had to part with some native secrets of cooking. It was love at first bite for Americans.

Those of us not fortunate enough to live on a tropical isle where exotic ingredients grow around the cook will have to assemble the following to create (by imitation) a mainland Melon Chicken.

Chicken

onion may be added, if desired. Sprinkle a half cup of pulverized or crushed almond powder over the surface of the chicken. Place chicken into the cored-out section of one of the melon halves and cover with the other melon half. Secure the halves together with small metal skewers, and place the melon on a baking sheet or shallow pan. Place into a preheated oven at 400 degrees. Roast at this temperature for 2 hours, then lower the temperature to 300 degrees and continue roasting for approximately 5 hours.

Some time ago I read of an Armenian cook who declared that he knew 100,000 ways of preparing eggplant. He was surely boasting; he probably didn't have more than 1,000 eggplant recipes.

One of the most famous eggplant recipes from the Near East is a Turkish concoction, Imam Baaldi. This means, in Turkish, "The Priest"—or Imam—"has fainted." This is a stuffed eggplant which is flavored with lots of garlic and olive oil, baked slowly and served cold. The story goes that this particular Imam was so excited by the aroma of the dish as it was being carried toward him that he fainted from impatience!

Eggplant is one of the oldest of all cultivated vegetables. Plant historians believe that this vegetable originated either in tropical India or in the warmer parts of China. For many centuries it was known only in southeastern Asia. Gradually it made its way West by caravan to the Arabian peninsula and the lands of northern Africa. The ancient Greeks and Romans must not have known eggplant for they had no name for it.

When Arabs overcame much of southern Europe they brought along their taste for eggplant. The Spanish and Italians learned to love them. When Spanish explorers and conquistadors reached the New World, they in turn transported eggplant to the Caribbean

Mexicano

    1 large (2 lbs.) eggplant
    6 tablespoons butter or
      margarine
   ¼ teaspoon finely minced garlic
   ½ cup diced celery
   ½ cup coarsely shredded carrots
   ¼ cup chopped onion
   ½ teaspoon salt
   ¾ teaspoon chili powder
   ½ teaspoon oregano leaves
   ⅓ cup sliced stuffed olives
    1 cup toasted croutons
   ½ cup chopped tomatoes

Islands and the Central and South American mainland. Records show, for instance, that eggplant was grown in Brazil before 1650. It's a very popular vegetable throughout Latin America and the Caribbean. In Jamaica, eggplants are called "garden eggs," which is a good name for them.

There are many varieties of eggplant although we may see only the big purple ones on our produce counters. There have appeared, however, yellow, white, ash-gray, and brown eggplants. Big and little, round, oblong, pear-shaped, and cucumber-shaped. When eggplants first reached northern Europe, they were planted among oriental plants. That's what happened to the first tomatoes, too. This isn't so surprising, because a couple of centuries ago people used to eat flowers such as violets, rose petals, marigolds, and similar posies.

We can now obtain in our supermarkets fresh eggplant throughout the year, with Florida, California, and Mexico the principal suppliers. Eggplant is often served as a substitute for meat; in fact, eggplant is often called "vegetable beef steak." Men always seem to love it especially.

Unlike the Armenian cook mentioned earlier, I have only forty or fifty excellent eggplant recipes in my own repertoire, but the following is certainly one of the best.

Stuffed Eggplant

Cut a lengthwise slice from one side of the eggplant. Parboil 25 minutes. Cool. Using a grapefruit knife, scoop out pulp to within ¼ inch of the skin and cut into cubes. Melt butter or margarine in a medium-size skillet. Add garlic, celery, carrots, and onion, and cook until onions are transparent. Blend in seasonings, diced eggplant, and remaining ingredients. Spoon the mixture into the eggplant shell. Place in a buttered baking dish and bake in a preheated 400-degree oven for 20 minutes. Recipe serves 6.

Six hundred years ago an irate preacher, reformer John Wycliffe, exclaimed that his parishioners were so inattentive that he might as well tear up his sermons to cover mustard pots! Strong words—and two good insights into life in the Middle Ages. One is that paper was so scarce and people so illiterate they often used valuable documents as common wrappers.

The good minister's outburst also tells us how commonplace and important the spice mustard seed was those many years ago. Mustard, one of the most ancient of spices, is mentioned in the Bible, in ancient Greek and Roman writing, and then later throughout Europe. Mustard came originally from Europe and southwestern Asia. It was used medicinally by the most famous physicians of antiquity, and it was in great demand as a seasoning for meat and fish, being used either whole or ground. It wasn't until the early 18th century, however, that ground mustard became available. Before that time the seeds had to be crushed just before each use.

Mustard

MUSTARD-BAKED EGGS:

¼ lb. sharp Cheddar cheese, shredded
4 eggs
6 tablespoons light cream
1 teaspoon powdered mustard
Dash cayenne pepper
½ teaspoon salt
2 tablespoons butter or margarine

Sprinkle shredded cheese over bottom of buttered 9-inch pie plate. Break eggs over cheese, being careful not to break the yolks. Combine light cream, powdered mustard, cayenne pepper and salt and pour over eggs. Dot with butter or margarine. Bake in preheated moderate oven (350 degrees) 15 to 20 minutes or until eggs are set. Recipe serves 4.

Powdered mustard is also called "ground mustard" or "mustard flour." There are two main varieties: one, a whitish-yellow seed; the other, a brown-black mustard seed. This brown-black seed is also called "Oriental mustard."

Mustard—powdered mustard—is different from all other spices in this one respect: as long as ground mustard remains dry it gives off no aroma whatsoever. You might say its flavor is "locked in." Liquids like cold water (not hot), vinegar, grape juice, or lemon release the flavor in 10 to 15 minutes. Use equal measures of powdered mustard and vinegar/or lemon juice with salt to taste. This makes the very lively mustard which is so delicious on all kinds of meats, cheese, fish, etc. Make just the amount which is needed for each meal, however, for the flavor fades rapidly. This is especially true in an open container at room temperature. In England they prepare it this way, but use the light mustard seeds. The mustard served with egg rolls in Chinese restaurants is made about the same way except that Oriental mustard is used.

Recipes

ENGLISH RABBIT CANAPÉS:

- 6 *slices bread*
- 3 *tablespoons butter or margarine*
- ¼ *lb. (1 cup) sharp American cheese, grated*
- ⅛ *teaspoon black pepper*
- ¼ *teaspoon powdered mustard*
- 4 *teaspoons cooking sherry Parsley flakes*

Cut bread in 1½-inch squares. Sauté one side in butter or margarine and toast other side. Combine grated cheese, black pepper, powdered mustard, and cooking sherry. Spread over toasted sides of bread. Broil about one minute, until cheese is melted and golden brown. Serve hot, garnished with parsley flakes. Recipe makes 24 canapés.

In Germany at Christmastime you will be wised "Fröhliche Weihnachten"; in Italy the greeting will be "Buon Natale"; and in Brazil they will salute you with "Feliz Natal." Around the world, languages differ but the meaning is the same. So it is with Christmas feasting: the national favorites differ from country to country.

The Swedish love their lutfisk at the traditional "God Jul" celebration, while the French think goose is best for a "Joyeux Noël." In Jolly Old England it is prime rib which is the order of the Christmas holiday and in which the British take an understandably warm pride.

Old English

Prime rib or standing rib (½ pound per serving)
Rock salt
2 *tablespoons Worcestershire powder*

Select choice prime rib or standing rib. Season the meat with Worcestershire powder, rubbing the powder into the meat. Into a large, heavy pan such as the bottom section of a roaster, pour rock salt until a layer of it completely covers the bottom surface of the container. Lightly dampen the rock salt with water until the salt is just moist. Place the prime rib onto the salt in a standing rib position. Then cover the prime rib completely with rock salt and again repeat the procedure of

Last year I decided to let turkey be the star of the dining table for Thanksgiving, but for Christmas—Old English Prime Rib! The cooking method described in the following recipe was discovered by the English long before the appearance of thermostatically controlled ovens. They found that by employing rock salt (comparable to our ice cream rock salt) they could seal in the vital juices of the meat, thus retaining flavor and nutrition—and weight, which means money, as well. I have found through many years of using this unique procedure that there is almost 100 percent elimination of shrinkage.

Prime Rib
(cooked in rock salt)

dampening all of the salt very lightly with water. Without a cover for the roaster, place the salt-covered meat into a preheated 500-degree oven.

Allow the prime rib to roast for 12 minutes per pound. When cooking time is completed, remove the roast from the oven. The rock salt will be extremely hard and must be carefully broken away from the prime rib. Gently strike the surface of the salt with a wooden mallet until cracks appear. Then pull the salt sections away from the meat and brush any remaining salt particles from the roast.

This process, which does not impart a salt flavor to the meat, traps the vital flavor juices and insures the very minimum of shrinkage.

If you are not tradition-bound to serve turkey at Christmastime, I am sure you will be a Prime-Rib-for-Christmas booster once you taste this delicious meat. And, to be sure, it is good any time of the year.

This recipe is as unmistakably and traditionally English as the "separate tables" custom. Sitting at my "separate table" with my family at the Selsdon Park Hotel in Sussex one grey November day, I enjoyed English Trifle and became an immediate champion of this recipe.

The Selsdon Park was once a great English mansion. It is still a great English mansion, but now also a resident hotel. Still very much as it was in the days of the aristocracy, it is surrounded by vast lawns, tennis courts, riding paths, and completing the picture, a vintage Rolls Royce awaiting you at the entrance for your drive to the local rail station and a train to London's Victoria Station.

In our room the down mattresses into which you sink about a foot, invited late sleeping. Indescribably luxurious heavy tapestry drapes surrounded the turret-like windows and I fully expected Sherlock Holmes and Dr. Watson to step from behind them at any time in search of Professor Moriarity.

I wanted to live in the English countryside for a while to observe the true English way of life and, at the same time, flex my taste muscles over English food. Contrary to the myth that English cooking is dull and undeserving of praise, I have found no better food

Old English

1 *tablespoon cornstarch*
2 *cups eggnog*
6 *ladyfingers*
½ *cup raspberry jam*
6 *teaspoons sherry (1 teaspoon to each ramekin)*
½ *cup heavy cream*
6 *teaspoons slivered, blanched almonds*

anywhere. One of my most treasured and popular recipes is Old English Prime Rib. I defy anyone to produce a better recipe. On this sojourn in Britain I accumulated many fine recipes including this one —English Trifle.

The "separate table" custom in England is an attempt to preserve privacy and to give prestige to each guest. In a changing world having your own table in the dining room is a changeless security. For a visitor to a strange country, the maître d'hotel's instruction to the waiter, "Show Mr. Wade to his table," makes one feel welcome and at home.

In contrast to the continuous service in American hotels, meals are served only at specified times, which makes a mealtime anticipated and more formal. Downtown London hotels have service anytime, but heaven forbid that the English country dining room should be turned into a coffee shop! I, for one, wouldn't like it.

Here at the Selsdon Park Hotel I met wonderful people, and wonderful foods. English Trifle (pronounced try-ful) was one of them. The recipe is easy to accomplish and dresses up a special dinner or a holiday entertainment with a proper finale.

Trifle

Combine cornstarch and eggnog. Cook over medium heat until mixture thickens and boils (about 5 minutes), stirring constantly. Remove from heat. Cool, and stir. Chill in refrigerator for one hour.

Split ladyfingers lengthwise and spread them with raspberry jam. Place two ladyfinger halves in each of six ramekins with the jam side up. Sprinkle with sherry, one teaspoon for each ramekin. Let stand for a few minutes. Spoon the cooled custard into the ramekins. Whip the heavy cream until stiff. Fill a pastry bag, fitted with a fancy tip, with the whipped cream. Pipe rosettes of cream around the edges of each ramekin and pipe one rosette in the center of each. Now sprinkle with slivered, blanched almonds. Chill in the refrigerator for 30 minutes or until ready to serve. Makes 6 servings.

El Presidente Hotel in Barcelona offers among the best food experiences I have ever had, in a life filled with great food experiences. Barcelona is lucky also—at least the diners there are lucky—to be on the Mediterranean where the seafood is fresh and first-class. Most of the traditional Spanish recipes are seafood favorites, or contain seafood, as for instance, the paella which is really a rice dish but combined with vegetables, fish, meat, and seasonings. Paella at El Presidente is highly recommended.

But the Oysters in Sherry you won't want to miss. In Spain you are offered sherry (the national drink) everywhere, to drink and as an ingredient in most recipes, at least recipes in the haute cuisine of Spain. All meals begin and end with it if you do in Spain as the Spanish do.

Spanish style dining is a whole evening's occupation. Starting late, at 9:30 (pushed to 8:30 in cities for tourists), the menu begins leisurely, is served leisurely, ends leisurely. At 11:30 you may still be awaiting your dessert, but not because of poor service. Quite the contrary; the service is extraordinarily good. This is just the Spanish way of dining. Don't fight it, enjoy it.

Oysters

24 selected oysters
Salt and pepper to taste
Flour
Butter

½ cup fresh lemon juice
1 cup steak sauce
2 tablespoons Worcestershire powder
2 1-oz. jiggers sherry
3 tablespoons water
2 tablespoons flour

The Basques and the Catalans are the cultured cooks of Spain, and Barcelona is the stronghold of the Catalans. On the outskirts of Barcelona—away from El Presidente—you have to do a little detective work to find a good, typically Spanish restaurant. You could run out of time before you find one. The tasca (a tavern that serves food) is usually a good bet. An odd thing about most of these is that they have floors covered with shrimp shells, making a kind of messy-looking place, though the Spanish think not. "The more shells, the better the food," they say.

It's no good asking hotel personnel about restaurants. English-speaking is not necessarily English-understanding, neither is Spanish-speaking the same as Spanish-understanding. This is another reason for recommending El Presidente dining. Everyone knows where it is and how to get there.

As I have said, Spain's main claim to food fame is seafood, and proof of this is that all the nationally famous recipes are from coastal communities. Centuries of experience and experimenting have taught them just how to cook seafood for exclamations of praise from both natives and tourists.

in Sherry Barcelona

Salt and pepper oysters. Dredge in flour and grill on lightly buttered griddle on top of range until crisp and browned on both sides. Do not broil in oven. If no griddle is available, use heavy skillet on top of range. Sprinkle oysters with butter or cooking oil while grilling. Do this on both sides; it browns and crisps them. Heat lemon juice, steak sauce, Worcestershire powder and sherry in saucepan over low heat. Do not allow to come to boil. Blend flour and water and stir into sauce to thicken. Correct sauce seasoning to taste by addition of steak sauce if too thin or sherry if too thick.

Poets have written lovingly and dramatically about the beverage called coffee. John Milton: "One sip of this will bathe the drooping spirits in delight beyond the bliss of dreams." Francis Bacon: "This drink comforteth the brain and heart and helpeth digestion." Alexander Pope: "Coffee—which makes the politician wise, And see through all things with his half-shut eyes." An ancient Arab poet: "O Coffee, Thou dost dispel all cares. . . . Coffee is our gold. . . . Wherever it is served, one enjoys the society of the noblest and most generous men." Both Balzac and Voltaire were great coffee drinkers. The latter remarked that no doubt coffee was a deadly poison, but that it acted quite slowly. Since he lived to be 84 years old, he suffered little from the "poison" he loved. Our own Robert Frost wrote wittily, "If there is one thing more exasperating than a wife who can make good coffee and won't, then that's a wife who cannot make good coffee and will."

There are few pleasures in life more satisfying than a good cup of coffee. The great equalizer, coffee brings comfort and warm cheer

Peach Tart

¼ cup butter or margarine
¼ cup confectioners' sugar
1 cup sifted flour
1 tablespoon cornstarch
2 tablespoons sugar
¼ teaspoon mace
½ cup orange juice
½ cup currant jelly, melted
8 large fresh peaches
Whipping cream

to peasants and kings, to poets and diplomats, soldiers and house-wives.

Did you know that there are 440 million cups of coffee drunk each day in the United States? (I don't know who or when someone sneaked around counting all of these cups, but this is the statistical count for an American coffee day.) However, think not that the U.S. has a corner on the coffee-drinking market. The Arabs have everyone beat with their 20 to 30 cups a day of "gahwa." However, the Arab coffee cup is never full until the time comes to take leave of coffee-house or host. A full cup to the Arab means literally, "Finish this cup, then leave."

Of course, every country has a favorite coffee mate. In France it is "cafe" and crèpes suzette. In Sweden it is "Kaffee" and Lussekake. In China it is "kia-fey" and diem sum (delicacies which touch the heart). But in Vienna the favorite companions for the cups of magic brew are fruit tarts. Peach Tart Viennese is a beautiful dessert to match the aromatic, steaming cup of greatness called coffee.

Viennese

Cream butter and confectioners' sugar (adding sugar gradually and creaming constantly); then add flour, mixing to form soft dough. Pat on bottom and sides of a 12-inch pizza pan. Bake in a 350-degree oven for 20 minutes.

Combine cornstarch, sugar, mace and orange juice in a sauce pan. Cook over very low heat until thick and clear, stirring constantly. Stir in melted currant jelly. Allow to cool slightly. While glaze is cooling, peel, slice and arrange peaches in a single layer in the baked pie shell. Spoon the glaze evenly over the peaches. Chill in refrigerator. Garnish with whipped cream before serving. Serves 6–8 people.

The business world tells us that the giving of "that something extra" is the difference between a successful business and a mediocre one. The sciences and the arts prove to us that attention to details is the mark of genius.

The story is told that a friend of Michelangelo once called upon him at his studio. Finding Michelangelo working upon the very same statue the friend had seen him executing months before, he commented, "You have been idle since the last time I saw you, my friend."

"Oh, no," said the great genius. Whereupon he pointed out that he had worked over this feature to soften it, brought out vitality in this muscle, polished this part, toned down another part.

"Yes, but are not these only trifles?" asked the visitor. "It may be so," replied Michelangelo, "but remember that trifles make perfection, and perfection is no trifle."

Perfect Rice

1 tablespoon butter
1 small onion, finely chopped
2 green lettuce leaves, shredded
⅓ cup sliced mushrooms
1 large tomato, peeled, seeded and chopped
¾ cup white rice
1½ cups hot chicken broth
¾ teaspoon salt
Dash of pepper
1 pimiento, diced
2 tablespoons raisins, sautéed in a little butter
2 tablespoons slivered, toasted almonds
Paprika

If you aspire to be a perfect cook, or even an improved one, then you must by all means pay attention to the small details—the trifles.

I once was supervising the testing of some recipe when one of the cooks laughed at one of the ingredients. I asked what seemed so funny, and she replied that the recipe called for one tablespoon of water and it just struck her as funny, and what difference could one tablespoon of water make anyway?

I explained: In that **particular** recipe it was used to crispen the onions, dilute the tomato sauce, and as a liquid base to blend the seasonings together, all of which permeated the meat in proper viscosity, thereby harmonizing the flavors.

As a perfect recipe for rice, I recommend Perfect Rice Gourmet.

Gourmet

Melt the butter in a saucepan and add the onions. Cook until onions are soft, but not yet brown. Add the shredded lettuce, sliced mushrooms, tomato, and rice. Mix together well and add the hot chicken broth. Salt and pepper, and bring to a boil. Cover and cook over low heat for 20 minutes. Remove from fire and separate the grains of rice by tossing with a long-tined kitchen fork.

Add the diced pimiento and sautéed raisins. Toss again and serve sprinkled with paprika and slivered, toasted almonds.

Please don't let culinary cowardice take control and eliminate any ingredient from this recipe, even though one or two may seem unusual with rice. Believe me, it is salubrious.

"Small world, isn't it?" Traveling by jet, we can enjoy a fresh, juicy papaya in Manila for breakfast, jet on to Hong Kong for a lunch of Pressed Almond Duck, while dinner awaits in Tokyo, featuring the popular Sukiyaki.

Modern communication makes possible a knowledge of foreign foods and exact formulas for duplicating them which once was possible only for an expert chef. Modern transportation makes possible the actual experiencing of concoctions with a foreign flavor that once were only heard about or read about in books. All of this has come about since World War II.

The history of foods develops with the history of nations. With conquest, intermarriage, redivided borders, famine, the waxing and waning of empires, and the spirit of adventure, people have naturally migrated to new areas. Newcomers bring new food ideas. Oldtimers teach the newcomers their food secrets. Hybrids are thus born.

Piccadilly

6 English muffin halves
1 cup Italian tomato sauce
6 slices mozzarella cheese
6 slices Canadian bacon
1 small can sliced mushrooms
2 tablespoons Parmesan cheese
  Dash of oregano

ITALIAN TOMATO SAUCE:

1 16-oz. can tomatoes
4 tablespoons olive oil
  Salt and pepper
  Dash sweet basil
  Oregano

We have a modern-day example of this in the phenomenal growth of pizza in international popularity. Since World War II when soldiers returned from Italy, and tourists visited Italy, and Italians migrated to other countries, hardly a nation can be found without a pizza parlor. Hundreds of different "flavors" of pizza are offered to Americans. Pizza invaded England too, but the Englishmen fought back by giving pizza a permutation of their own, using English muffins instead of crust, and putting the British seal of approval on the little pizzas by renaming them Piccadilly Pizza after Piccadilly Circus in London—the swinging city.

Thus, another hybrid was born. Pizza was imported from Italy to England. I have imported the Piccadilly Pizza from London to America. I definitely recommend that you add these little gems to your repertoire of pizza recipes.

Pizza

Place tomatoes in a saucepan, add olive oil, salt and pepper to taste. Add a dash of sweet basil and oregano. Simmer slowly until sauce thickens. Set sauce aside, and toast English muffins on the round side under a hot broiler. Then turn muffins over and on flat side spread some Italian sauce, pieces of mozzarella cheese, pieces of Canadian bacon, and slices of mushrooms. Complete by sprinkling a little Parmesan cheese on top. Place under a hot broiler and heat until the mixture is melted together. A dash of oregano gives the true Italian touch.

These Piccadilly Pizzas are good for outdoor dining, they make excellent cocktail canapés, and in no time they will be a solid family favorite in your home.

Of all the herbs used in American foods, mint is the most easily identified. There are half a dozen varieties of mints grown for their aromatic leaves, but only peppermint and spearmint reach our spice shelves as dried flakes or leaves. Obviously these two mints have the most intriguing aroma.

Spearmint was once called spiremint, because of its steeple-shaped habit of growth. This must have been the mint to which Pliny referred when he stated, "The smell of mint doth stir up the minde and taste to a greedy desire of meat."

The Romans carried mint as far north as Britain and, centuries later, John Gerard praised it: "The savour or smell of water Minte rejoyceth the heart of man, for which cause they use to strew it in

Pineapple

2 teaspoons mint flakes, crumbled
3 tablespoons boiling water
½ cup butter or margarine
¾ cup sugar
1 cup (12-oz. jar) pineapple preserves
2 eggs, separated
2 cups sifted all-purpose flour
1 teaspoon baking soda
⅛ teaspoon salt
½ cup coarsely chopped nuts

chambers and places of recreation, pleasure, and repose, and when feastes and banquets are made." In France spearmint was called "Menthe de Notre Dame," and in Italy, "Erbe Santa Maria."

Peppermint is a comparative latecomer, for it seems to have appeared in England in the 17th century. Like spearmint, it has an aroma that is strong and sweet with a cool aftertaste.

Either spearmint or peppermint can be used when making mint-flavored dishes. Most popular uses of mint in this country are in fruit cups, in mint jelly and sauce for lamb, in chocolate desserts, in iced tea and fruit beverages. Commercially, mint is used in all kinds of candies and in the liqueur crème de menthe.

Mint Cake

Combine mint flakes with boiling water; cover and let steep 7 minutes. Strain and cool minted water. Reserve 1 teaspoon of the softened mint flakes. Cream butter and sugar in large mixing bowl until light and fluffy. Combine minted water, reserved mint flakes, pineapple preserves and egg yolks in a small bowl. Blend well. Sift together flour, baking soda, and salt. Add to butter mixture alternately with preserve mixture. Stir in nuts. Beat egg whites until stiff but not dry. Fold into batter. Turn into a lightly greased and floured 9x5x3-inch loaf pan. Bake in a preheated moderate oven (350 degrees) for one hour and 20 minutes or until a cake tester inserted in the center comes out clean. Allow to cool in the pan 10 minutes, then turn onto a wire rack. Serve warm or cool, with whipped cream if desired. Recipe makes one 9-inch loaf.

A psychologist wrote not long ago that many women feel guilty about using mixes and convenience foods; that these descendants of hard-working pioneers sense that they should be contributing something energetic to the creation of a cake, cookies, or a batch of muffins. That's why some mix manufacturers call for one or two ingredients to be added, to give women the feeling that they have earned any compliments they collect.

For all of their rabbit-out-of-a-hat convenience, many baking mixes and brown-and-serve breads lack individuality as processed and sold. Here certain flavoring ingredients—like the baking seeds—can satisfy the creative instinct of the cook and, at the same time, add delightful fragrance and toasty crunchiness to the product.

The "baking seeds" are poppy and caraway. Poppy seeds are just what you'd think—the seed of the beautiful flower. We import all of our poppy seeds from the Netherlands, Turkey, and Poland. Poppies bloom in all kinds of places, and poppy seeds have been a

Poppy Seed

FILLING:

½ cup poppy seed
3 tablespoons honey
½ teaspoon grated lemon peel

Combine poppy seeds with ¼ cup water and honey in small saucepan. Bring to boil and cook 5 minutes. Add lemon peel. Cool.

BISCUIT DOUGH:

2 cups sifted all-purpose flour
2 tablespoons sugar
3 teaspoons baking powder
½ teaspoon salt
¼ cup shortening
¾ cup milk
¼ cup butter or margarine, melted
2 tablespoons honey

famous ingredient since Greek and Roman times, but nobody has ever topped Central Europe as users of these tiny blue seeds. From these people we've learned to use poppy seeds as topping for rolls and breads; as a filling for cakes, coffee cakes, and pastries, and in noodles and salads.

Caraway seed is another aromatic product of the Netherlands, although it can be grown in the Western Hemisphere. This pleasing, slightly sharp-sweet seed that has been known and used so long was discovered by archaeologists in the debris left by Swiss lake-dwellers some 4,000 years ago. In addition to rye bread, have you tasted caraway seeds in cheeses, sauerkraut, new cabbage, soups, stews, and with fish and meats such as pork? You'll love it. A very popular cordial, kümmel, has caraway seeds as its principal ingredient.

The following recipe blueprints a delightful way to incorporate poppy seeds into our everyday biscuit-making.

Biscuits

Sift together flour, sugar, baking powder, and salt. Cut in shortening with pastry blender or 2 knives to crumb consistency. Stir in milk. Knead 20 seconds on lightly floured board. Roll into 12x2x¼-inch rectangle. Brush surface with 2 tablespoons of the melted butter. Spread with Poppy Seed Filling. Roll, starting at 12-inch side, in jelly roll fashion. Cut into slices 1 inch thick. Combine remaining 2 tablespoons butter and honey; place 1 teaspoon in each of twelve 2-inch muffin tins. Place a biscuit in each section. Bake in preheated hot oven (400 degrees) 20 minutes or until browned. Serve hot. Recipe makes 12 biscuits.

Imitation is the sincerest form of flattery, and I was doubly flattered last month when I opened my television show mail to find two recipes which two different gourmet fans had sent me with the recommendation "you may want to try this on the show sometime." Both recipes were my own and had been given several years ago on "The Gourmet Show." One correspondent said her sister gave her the recipe with high praise; the other related she had the dish at a church dinner and asked for the recipe. Just proves a good recipe gets around, providing pleasurable dining for many along the way. Word of mouth—or word of taste—is the best advertising after all.

Good cooks are always sending me, or telling me recipes. I seem to attract food ideas wherever I go, at home and abroad. Everyone loves good food. It is often impossible, however, to get an exact recipe from a cook. It is true that many good cooks cook from their heads, so they don't write down exact measurements, temperatures, or procedures. Without these specific facts, you get maybe-so-maybe-not results. Mistakes are costly.

You probably have had the experience yourself of trying to get a recipe down in black and white, and getting instructions like "Put enough flour in until it is stiff." How stiff? Stiff enough for what? Then they say, "Cook until done." How done? When it's brown, thick, bubbling, or, alas, when it has burned? Or, "Add about a handful of sugar." Whose hand? A man's hand, a woman's hand? A giant? A midget? But my favorite is "Mix until it looks right!"

The Power of

HUNYADY TORTE:

- 12 egg yolks
- 1½ cups sugar
- 6 squares of bittersweet chocolate, melted
- 16 ounces chestnut purée (or 24 chestnuts puréed)
- 12 egg whites
- 1 pint whipping cream
- ¼ teaspoon vanilla
- 3 tablespoons sugar

Foodstuffs are variable enough without these guessing-game measurements. How can these great recipes be preserved for posterity without someone carefully translating them into the language of fine food preparation?

My policy continues to be this, however: if Bonnie and Clyde had a good recipe—you should listen!

So I have often questioned recipe-givers at length when I thought I was on the verge of possessing a great recipe. They say, "Add a few dashes of cayenne pepper." Well, a little cayenne pepper goes a long, long way. So you ask, "Would you say 2 or 3 dashes?" Answer: "More than that." "Well, half a teaspoonful?" Answer: "Not that much."

Whereupon the formerly cooperative recipe-recommender begins to get nervous, what with all these questions, and tries to sneak away with a "When my mother gave me this recipe, she never really said how much cayenne pepper. Actually, I made it one time and forgot the cayenne and it turned out just fine." Well, you can't win them all.

I'm convinced this is how mixes began. Someone couldn't stand it any longer and vowed he'd give directions in 25 words or less of perfectly exact instructions.

But here's one I had the patience to see through until I got the whole, complete, and delicious recipe. This ethereal confection amply illustrates the rewards of patience and dedication, and the power of positive cooking.

Positive Cooking

Beat egg yolks with sugar, add chestnut purée and bittersweet chocolate which has been melted. Beat these ingredients well together. Beat egg whites in a separate bowl. Fold egg whites into the chocolate mixture.

Bake in three or four layer-cake pans in a preheated 325-degree oven. Beat whipping cream with sugar and vanilla and put between layers, lathering each thoroughly. Save a generous portion of the whipped cream to cover the top of the cake.

"Mystique" is one of those fifty-cent words we are hearing more and more often. The dictionary defines it as "a framework of doctrines, ideas, beliefs or the like constructed around a person or object, endowing him or it with enhanced value or profound meaning."

Chili con carne has a dandy mystique. Chili lovers have endowed it with enhanced value and profound meaning from coast to coast. Many books and articles have been written about it and there is a Chili Appreciation Society whose national membership has fun arguing about the relative merits of chopped or cubed meat, tomatoes, beans, or spices as authentic chili ingredients.

There must be as many chili con carne recipes as there are chili cooks. As with the pease porridge of old, "Some like it hot; some like it cold." Not cold, of course, but less hot. Most Texas and Southwestern chili aficionados demand a good hot "bowl of red," with the liveliest kind of spicing. This is the all-American dish they long for when traveling in Hong Kong, Istanbul, or Rome. Chili con carne recipes have all kinds of imaginative names: Jail House Chili, Fire House Chili, Two Alarm Chili, Hatless Chili, and Pedernales Chili, made famous by former President and Mrs. Johnson.

While there are those who prefer a chili con carne which is frankly pungent, most Americans want it richly, rather than hotly, spiced. Youngsters of all ages love it this way, as do their elders.

Most all chili con carne is seasoned with convenient chili powder. This is a blend of ground chili peppers, oregano, cumin, garlic, and

Ranch Hash with

2 tablespoons instant minced onion
2 tablespoons water
1 tablespoon oil
1 15½-oz. can corned beef hash
1½ teaspoons chili powder
⅛ teaspoon instant garlic powder
4 poached eggs
Chili powder

salt. Depending on the brand, chili powder may also contain a bit of clove, allspice, or onion. It is one of the best sellers on the spice shelf for it is delicious in hamburgers, gravies, stews, and sandwich fillings; in omelets and egg dishes; with all kinds of cheeses; with shellfish and oyster cocktail sauces.

Chili powder seems to have been invented about a century ago, probably in San Antonio. It's one of those things which just had to be invented. Chili con carne and Mexican-type dishes were very popular with cowhands. A ready-to-use mixture of the right spices and herbs would make the by-gosh-and-by-golly cooking at the chuck wagon ever so much simpler. Obviously its fame spread so that today it is used in many kinds of dishes and it can be purchased in even the smallest grocery store.

While chili powder is an excellent blend as purchased, some hobby cooks, given to lily-gilding, may want to step up one or two of the spices. There's no law against adding additional oregano or garlic or sneaking in a little extra cayenne if you like it that way.

One bit of advice applies to the use of chili powder as it does to most ground spices and herbs. Make sure your supply is reasonably fresh. Tired spices make a dull dish, boring to the tastebuds, no matter how much time you spend cooking it.

For a supper dish which is both easy and excellent, season canned corned beef hash with a little chili powder, onion, and garlic.

Poached Eggs

Mix instant minced onion with water and let stand 10 minutes to soften. Heat oil in medium-size skillet. Stir in softened onion, corned beef hash, chili powder and garlic powder and mix well.

Cook over moderate heat, occasionally pressing down gently with a large spoon, until the bottom is browned. Serve hot, topped with poached eggs. Sprinkle eggs lightly with chili powder. Recipe serves 4.

We don't know exactly when the word dessert was first used, but we do know the first time it appeared "on the record." It was in 1717, when Lady Baillie, a Scottish woman who lived in Edinburgh, gave a dinner party for 12 guests and called the last course a "deseart." This was a new word which had recently been adopted from the French word "disserve," which meant to clear away. It all goes to show you that even then people associated desserts with something they deserved!

Lady Baillie's "desearts" were on the sweet side, too, just as ours are. One of the dishes she served was called a syllabub, and sometimes it was called sillibubbles! It was a foamy, light custard of eggs, milk, and spices, and a favorite concoction of British queens, so maybe it wasn't as bad as it sounds.

Raspberry Apple

1 6-oz. package raspberry gelatin
2 cups boiling water
1½ cups cold water
¼ cup sugar
1 can (1 lb., 4 oz.) pie-sliced apples, drained
1 10-oz. loaf pound cake
1 cup heavy cream

Dissolve gelatin in boiling water. Stir in cold water.

Set aside ¾ cup gelatin in skillet. Chill remaining gelatin until thickened. Add sugar to gelatin in skillet. Add pie-sliced apples and simmer about 5 minutes or until apples are glazed. Drain off any remaining syrup. Dice apples, reserving 12 slices for garnish. Cool.

Cut pound cake lengthwise into 7 slices. Cut each slice in half.

Although apples and other fruits are among the oldest-known foods, it was not until the time of Queen Elizabeth I of England, in the 16th century, that fruits were first used all by themselves to make a pie.

When speaking of spectacular desserts, one has to mention a dessert that was made for Henry VII of England which must still hold the record for sheer spectacle. It was called a "custard pie," and it was carried into the banquet hall by four strong men who placed it on the King's table. When His Majesty cut the first slice, out flew fifteen pigeons followed by one small man!

Here is a cloud-light apple dessert that is especially desirable for any festive occasion.

Crown

Whip ¾ cup heavy cream until stiff. Fold cream and diced apples into thickened gelatin. Place pound cake squares on bottom and around sides of a 9-inch spring form pan to form crown. Pour in gelatin mixture. Chill until firm.

To serve, remove sides of pan and place on serving dish. Whip remaining cream and spread on sides of crown. Garnish with reserved glazed apple slices.

The canals of Venice are famous. The gondolas which grace the canals are famous, too, and uniquely Venice, since this is the only city in the world where the streets are all rivers. This presents not so much a problem as a situation to be handled. How do you get the work done, and how do you go from place to place? It is all very well for romantics to go gliding around in gondolas, but who makes the deliveries, how do you get to the hospital, or to the cafes, or repair places? You get a boat. So, in Venice, on Sundays you see church-goers catching a water bus to church; other days motor boats back up to the dock to discharge a crew of carpenters and painters; a boat ambulance will pick you up and float you to a hospital should you need one; and the shopping for the restaurants is done by boat.

The first stop on the morning shopping agenda will be the Pescheria, the famous fish market. What you will see here will delight any lover of seafood. The Pescheria is a covered, open arcade, or what is really many arcades around a central columned area. The choice before you, displayed on paper, or leaves, or mats, will be everything from eels and octopus, to scampi, crabs, shrimps, bass, sole (not exactly like Dover sole, a bit more diminutive, but very good), trout, and a fish well thought of in Italy, turbot. Placing the order for the day, the boat loads up on fish, and then is under way to the market near the Rialto Bridge where vegetables, flowers, souvenirs, fruits, and almost everything, is sold. One man will have a stall of spices;

Rialto Stuffed Clams

⅓ cup soft butter, unsalted
2 tablespoons chopped shallots
2 tablespoons chopped parsley
1 tablespoon chopped chives
1 tablespoon chopped chervil
  Several dashes Tabasco
  Salt and pepper to taste
24 clams in shells
  Rock salt, enough to cover
  bottom of broiling pan

another, flowers; another, quail and chicken; and many are the dealers in vegetables. The mushrooms here are large, fresh, and especially appetizing; the zucchini is young and tender and sets a gourmet's mind to sorting out recipes for it. Here, you will often see a gondolier buying flowers for his boats—perhaps the occasion is a wedding, or he may have been hired to paddle honeymooners around the town —and he decorates fittingly.

The market is a busy, bustling, happy place, as only the Italians can be busy, bustling and happy in their daily shopping and buying. One fancies that Browning and his Elizabeth may have strolled along here during their residence in Venice, shopping and composing sonnets; or Casanova, buying flowers for his lady love; Bertini, assaying the vegetable stalls as a subject worthy to be included in his painting; or Lord Byron, or Goethe—any number of the world's great who lived in Venice or visited her lengthily—enjoying the gaiety of this place and finding inspiration. Certainly the gourmet finds delight here. How many chefs, restaurateurs, and gourmets have found the stimulus here to create a new food as worthy of genius as poetry and painting?

Of course, I can't say how many, but I can tell you about one recipe which combines the produce of the market with the catch from the Pescheria. I think it has an exciting touch of gourmet genius.

Venetian Style

Cream together butter, shallots, parsley, chives, chervil, Tabasco, salt, and pepper. With a small amount of water in a saucepan (just enough water to cover bottom of pan well), place the clams in the pan. Heat, shaking the pan periodically until the clam shells open. Throw away the empty shell halves, but place the clams in their half-shell on a layer of rock salt which has been heated until very hot in a shallow broiling pan. Cover each clam with the butter mixture and broil for about 5 or 6 minutes with the clams about 5 inches from the heat. Serve clams hot.

Recipe serves 4.

There is a story about an unemployed school teacher who needed a job very much, and right now. He was having an interview with the local school board, and he was fielding each question carefully in order to impress the board members. Finally, he was asked a question which gave him pause. "Sir, will you teach our students that the world is round or flat?" "Well," considered the unemployed teacher deliberately and thoughtfully, "I can teach it either way."

This is about what the world can do with rice: cook it—not just either way—but all ways. Teaching rice-lovers only one way to cook rice is an impossibility. It is not even possible to point to one recipe and say, "This, my friends, is the best rice recipe in the world."

Consider for a moment: Rice is the staple diet of more than three-fourths of the world's peoples. For five thousand years most of earth's population has depended upon rice for life and health. During these centuries nations have invented and produced an infinite variety of great rice recipes, each a self-expression of the people of the nation or region. If one were to gather all the rice concoctions in the world he would truly have a United Nations of Food Cookbook.

So, the Spanish have their famous paella, the Italians their risotto; the Chinese like it fried, Louisianians like it Creole style, the Eng-

Rice

3 tablespoons butter or margarine
1 onion, chopped
1 small clove garlic, crushed
3 or 4 leaves green lettuce, shredded
2 fresh pork sausages, sliced
3 mushrooms, sliced
3 tomatoes, peeled, seeded and diced
1 cup raw rice
2 cups boiling water or chicken broth

1 teaspoon salt
Dash pepper
½ cup cooked peas
1 diced pimiento
2 tablespoons raisins
Butter or margarine

Melt butter or margarine over low heat and add onion. When onion is brown, add garlic, lettuce, sausages, mushrooms, tomatoes, and raw rice. Mix well. Add boiling water or chicken broth, salt,

lishman boils it, the Japanese not only eat it but make a wine—sake —with it. Indians curry it; Mexicans spice it up, too, and call it Spanish Rice; Indonesians stake their claim on the best rice recipe with their Nasi Goreng, and . . . well, you can see what a quandary this puts a gourmet in. . . . How **could** one say that any of these were the only, or the best way, to prepare rice? And the above-mentioned are only a sampling.

What I will say is that Rice à la Grecque is a classic Greek recipe which is fashioned in the Mediterranean style. When you read the recipe you will quickly note that this is more than a "side dish": it can be a whole meal, but it can also be a sophisticated stuffing for poultry or veal, and it complements lamb, veal, or poultry as an entremets.

Epicurus, the Greek philosopher of good living, must have enjoyed this recipe or one much like it; that is recommendation enough for those of us who enjoy good food, and gets me out of hot water (if you'll pardon a pun) by not having to say Rice à la Grecque is the best rice recipe in the world. Epicurus cannot be reached for comment.

à la Grecque

and pepper. Cover tightly and continue cooking for 20 minutes. Mix well with fork. Add peas, pimiento, raisins (which have been sautéed in butter or margarine). Serve in any of the above recommended ways. Makes approximately 4 cups.

According to folklore, the herb rosemary is a great reanimator and general pepper-upper. There is the legend of the aged queen who lamented that her dancing days were over. She consulted her favorite alchemist, who considered the problem. A rosemary concoction would do the trick, he told her. (As you may know, the "chem" of "alchemist"—later, "chemist"—comes from a Greek word meaning juice. Chemistry was originally the art of extracting juices from medicinal plants.) Three times a day the queen bathed in the rosemary water. Soon she became so young and lovely that she began looking for a handsome young husband. We may assume that she soon found him and that they lived happily ever after.

In an old Italian formula the flowers of rosemary, sage, fennel, marjoram, and other herbs were recommended for the preservation of youth. From another old herbal comes this advice: "Make thee a box of the wood of rosemary and smell to it and it shall preserve thy youth."

Rosemary has been famous in many, many ways. In Ophelia's mad

Rosemary

2 lbs. ground beef (preferably round steak)
½ lb. ground pork
½ lb. ground veal
1 tablespoon flavor salt
3 eggs
½ teaspoon rosemary
1 small jar chopped pimiento
1 cup soft bread crumbs
2 teaspoons onion flakes

scene in Hamlet, she says, "Here's rosemary for you, that's for remembrance." That's surely the best known quotation on rosemary.

Because rosemary was a symbol of remembrance it was always used in wedding bouquets—to make sure the bride would not forget her childhood home. A sprig of rosemary was tucked in the bouquet, another flavored the bride-cup which she carried before her.

There was rosemary for the bridegroom, too. Several centuries ago it was customary, in England, for the bridesmaids to present the bridegroom with a bunch of rosemary bound with ribbons. We haven't discovered what he did with this bouquet, but the tradition is no more. Probably because more and more bridegrooms began hearing the little saying that "where the rosemary flourishes, the lady rules"!

Using the following rosemary recipe any lady can rule, not only the kitchen, but her household as well.

Meat Loaf

2 teaspoons parsley flakes
1 can condensed cream of
    tomato soup, diluted with
    ½ can water

Combine ingredients, and mix well. Shape into a loaf, and bake one hour, uncovered, at 350 degrees. Recipe serves 6.

I receive numerous telephone calls and many letters from the "executive wife" with a variety of food questions. These ladies come in for a great deal of scrutiny these days. More and more corporations want to know ever so much about a man's wife before they employ him, or later, promote him. Not only is she responsible for the management of home and children, but she serves as her husband's public relations counsel, helping him to march ahead, best foot forward. One of her most important tasks is that of entertaining, of serving patrician food in gracious, well-mannered surroundings.

I always suggest to the smart executive wife, or any other smart wife for that matter, that she start with a well-stocked spice shelf and learn how to use it. Expanding your knowledge of spices not only is fun, but essential to your becoming an outstanding hostess. For example, are you familiar with the herb marjoram?

A very versatile herb, marjoram is "the herb of a thousand uses." Add ¼ to ½ teaspoon of marjoram to stews, soups, or casseroles to serve four. Fish and egg dishes are enhanced with the aroma of marjoram, and it brings out the intrinsic flavor of such vegetables as peas, snap beans, lima beans, spinach, and Swiss chard.

Marjoram comes in whole or ground form. Add the marjoram during the last 5 minutes when simmering a stew, soup, or such slow cooking foods. In a stuffing, naturally, we must add the herb along with other ingredients. When preparing roast beef, sprinkle on a

Scalloped

1 7¾-oz. can red or pink
   salmon
1 tablespoon lemon juice
1¼ cups cracker crumbs
⅓ cup butter, melted
1 teaspoon salt
1 teaspooon powdered mustard
¼ teaspoon ground black
   pepper
¼ teaspoon marjoram leaves,
   crumbled

flurry of marjoram before putting it in the oven; then freshen up the intriguing flavor by adding a hint more to the gravy which is made at the last minute.

People have always loved marjoram as a flavoring for foods, but throughout the ages it has had many other uses. Marjoram was strewn here and there at public functions and banquets to sweeten the air. Sweet marjoram was also an ingredient in the perfumes the ancients used after the bath. Marjoram attended weddings and funerals. It had countless uses as a medication, and was considered to be especially effective when treating ailments of the head and stomach.

Marjoram, like many other herbs, is native to Western Asia and the Mediterranean. The Roman Army no doubt hastened marjoram's migration to other parts of Europe. Marjoram came to America with the first settlers and was a treasured plant in the herb garden.

Marjoram is closely related to oregano, the pizza herb. Both plants are members of the big mint family. Oregano is the Spanish word for marjoram and was once called "wild marjoram." Marjoram's aroma is sweeter and more delicate than that of oregano, and it is often called "sweet marjoram" or "garden marjoram."

We import most of our marjoram from France, Portugal, Greece, and Rumania. I have found that the following recipe very effectively demonstrates the unique qualities of marjoram.

Salmon

¼ teaspoon instant onion, powdered
1 cup milk, scalded
Lemon slices for garnish
Parsley flakes for garnish

Drain and flake the salmon, and mix with lemon juice. Combine cracker crumbs, butter, salt, mustard, black pepper, marjoram, and onion powder. Place half of the seasoned crumbs in a 9-inch pie plate. Over it spread the salmon mixture. Pour milk over all. Top with remaining crumbs. Bake in a preheated hot oven (400 degrees) from 20 to 25 minutes. Garnish with lemon slices and parsley flakes. Recipe serves 4.

An old Creole custom is to give "lagniappe," a little something extra with a purchase. Well, there is "lagniappe" in Shrimp Diable. The something extra is "the devil"—diable, in French.

The something extra of Creole cooking was the arrival of the French in what is now Louisiana. Before the coming of Bienville in 1722 with his small colony of Frenchmen, the cooking of the region was Spanish (Spanish explorers having just recently departed), Negro, and Indian. Frenchmen brought with them over five centuries of skill and appreciation in the culinary arts. From the distillation of hundreds of years of experience in the kitchen arts—a fame which was to go around the whole world—they gave Creole cooking its "lagniappe." The main secret of their talents was the knowledge of the use of spices, and the mastering of the sauce mystique which is still with us today.

Shrimp Diable

Although my Shrimp Diable is not Creole, it is an apt illustration of "lagniappe" in a recipe. Furthermore, much in it can be found in common with Creole cooking. Sauce Diable will be recognized as one of the famous French sauces, and this sauce more than any other highlights the artful spice-blending which has also made Creole cooking famous. The recipe's star is shrimp, so plentiful throughout Louisiana.

Escoffier did not think much of shrimp, apparently, for he says in his writing, "As regards shrimps, their use in Europe is generally limited to garnishes, hors d'oeuvres and the preparation of soups, shrimp butters and creams." I do think much of shrimp, and have found it an absolutely perfect companion for Sauce Diable.

1½ lbs. peeled and deveined shrimp
4 tablespoons olive oil
1 shallot or green onion, chopped
1 clove garlic, chopped
1 teaspoon cracked black pepper
1 teaspoon of chervil or parsley, chopped
⅓ cup brandy
2 cups rich, brown beef sauce
1 tablespoon Worcestershire powder
Juice of ½ lemon
2 teaspoons dry English mustard
2 tablespoons catsup

Allow peeled and deveined shrimp to thaw completely.

Place the olive oil into a skillet and sauté the shrimp until they are pinkish-red. Next add shallots, garlic, cracked black pepper, and chervil. Briskly sauté this mixture for 3 or 4 minutes. Add brandy, brown sauce, Worcestershire powder, lemon juice, dry mustard, and catsup. Cover the skillet and simmer the shrimp for 15 additional minutes. Serve over a bed of rice. Recipe serves 8.

Almost every country in the Middle East has its own favorite version of shish kebab. It's a favorite food in Greece, Turkey, Lebanon, Rumania, Iran, even the Orient. And in the Caucasian region, shish kebab is called shashlik. Greeks also apply the name souflaki to this traditional food. In each case it's the same delicious concoction, just called by a different name. In many areas it is sold in street stands, much like our own hot dog and hamburger stands.

Alexander Dumas wrote this in his classic "Dictionary of Cuisine," published in 1873: "From remotest antiquity to the present time, lamb has been the favorite dish of the eastern peoples. The Greeks gave few feasts at which lamb was not the important dish. One of the prophets rebuked the Samaritans for eating too much of it. At one time its use was forbidden to the Athenians." I, for one, am certainly glad that we do not have laws like that these days.

Shish kebab is always made with boneless lamb, of course, cut into cubes of varying sizes, depending on your own preference. "Tiny lamb kebabs for" hors d'oeuvres are made with half-inch cubes; for main course kebabs, the size is usually 1½ to 2-inch cubes.

Most of today's shish kebab recipes list boneless leg of lamb as the cut to use for the meat. You can use boneless shoulder of American lamb for shish kebabs, too.

Sometimes the fruits and vegetables in shish kebabs cook more quickly than the meat, so you might like to prepare them on separate skewers, or else partially cook the lamb, remove it from the skewers with tongs, and then rethread the vegetables or fruits on the same skewers with the lamb and return the skewers to the grill.

When broiling kebabs over charcoal, broil all sides until they are deep brown in color, lifting the skewers to roll them in barbecue sauce, or brush with the marinade or oil frequently.

When you are preparing shish kebabs in the open broiler, place the skewered lamb on a rack about 3 inches from the flame. Turn and baste the shish kebabs frequently until they are done. This will take about 20 minutes or so in the broiler, depending on the size of the lamb cubes. Remember that since American lamb is such a tender meat, it tastes best when cooked medium or rare.

To serve your shish kebabs, slowly push the skewer contents onto plates with a fork. You might prefer to push off the bottom half of the shish kebab first; then the rest, in order not to mash the fruits or vegetables.

The recipe for Souflaki which I am presenting here I obtained from Mr. Chris Semos, owner of the famous Greek restaurant The Torch, in Dallas, Texas. Mr. Semos mentioned that beef cubes can be substituted for the lamb.

Souflaki à la Torch

2½ lbs. lamb, filet of veal, filet
    of beef or lean pork
1   tablespoon oregano
1   tablespoon salt
    Pepper to taste
1   tablespoon cooking wine
½   cup olive oil
    Onions, cut in quarters
    Green peppers, cut in quarters
    Tomatoes, cut in quarters
    Lemon juice

Cut desired meat into cubes (12 to the pound) and place in bowl. Pour combined oregano, salt, pepper, cooking wine, and olive oil over meat. Let stand in refrigerator 6 to 8 hours, stirring occasionally. Remove meat from marinade. Place 6 pieces of meat on each of 5 skewers. If desired, place quarter sections of onion, green pepper, and tomatoes between meat cubes on skewers.

Broil 3 inches from full flame 15 minutes. Sprinkle with fresh lemon juice and serve hot. Makes 5 servings.

Restaurante Antiqua Casa Sobrino de Botin, Calle de Cuchilleros 17, Madrid, Spain, is world-famous not only for roasted suckling pig and roasted baby lamb prepared in the old style, but for the now famous people who like to dine there. Casa Botin is featured in two of Ernest Hemingway's books, Death in the Afternoon and The Sun Also Rises, and naturally so, because this was one of Hemingway's favorite Spanish restaurants. Bullfighters are often seen here during the season (March to October) and Spanish movie stars, writers, artists, students, and tourists—many tourists.

Once the Casa Botin was a small inn where muleteers and traders rested at the end of their journeys. Calle de Cuchilleros means, literally, "street of the cutlers," the name being derived from the fact that many workshops where knives and swords were made were situated here. In 1725 the building was restored, as attested to by the date inscribed above the entrance door. The suckling pig or the baby lamb you order will be cooked in the original oven built as part of the house. Wood of evergreen oak is used for the heat, and this gives

Spanish

4 artichokes
   Water to cover artichokes
1 tablespoon salt
   Juice and rind of 2 lemons
2 teaspoons butter or
   margarine
1 green onion, finely chopped
1 lb. crab meat, flaked
   Salt and pepper to taste
3 or 4 drops liquid red pepper
   seasoning
4 crackers, crumbled
1 tablespoon cream sauce

the roasted meats a very special flavor when added to the ingredients used according to very old tradition. No wonder Castilian roasted meat is a food highly esteemed all over the world.

Today, the old Botin de Cuchilleros is more famous than ever since its customers have spread the word by book or word of mouth that the Casa Botin is a must for dining in Madrid. When you enter the old restaurant, you will want to dine in the lower floor section which was once an old wine cellar. You go down a winding, narrow, bricked-in stairway to a narrow, tunnel-like room, also bricked in uneven patterns. Old lamps with crushed-in shades give off enough light to read the menu. The tablecloths are old and well worn, benches provide seating against the wall, and extra chairs fill the rest of the spaces, except a small path which the waiters must navigate.

Prices are not expensive, and the food is very good, with large servings of meat, and a few vegetables. Spanish Artichokes Antiqua is representative of the latter, and a recipe I think you will enjoy.

Artichokes Antiqua

Cut off stem and, with scissors, cut off top of each leaf from the artichokes. Tie with soft cord to keep the leaves from spreading out. In a large saucepan, over medium heat, bring to boil enough water to cover artichokes. To this water add one tablespoon of salt and the juice and rind of 2 lemons. Add artichokes and cook until bottoms are tender. Remove from heat. Drain and core, leaving leaves and bottom intact.

Melt in saucepan over low heat the butter or margarine. Add the green onions and cook until tender. Add crab meat, salt, pepper, liquid red pepper seasoning, crackers, and cream sauce, cooking until thoroughly hot.

Now fill the cored artichokes with the blended crab mixture. This recipe serves 4.

Have you recently eaten in one of those very dimly lighted restaurants? A restful, romantic atmosphere, but it's doubtful that you have much memory of whatever you ate. The look of food plays a very important role in the total pleasure of eating, especially for Americans. This is even truer now than in 1900, as witness the quantity of colorful paprika sold today. More than 12 million pounds of this brilliant "cosmetic spice" were used in the United States last year.

Though we do not taste color or the substances that are responsible for it, color catches the eye first, and we tend to associate color with flavor, texture, nutritive value, and wholesomeness. Color makes a food "look good enough to eat," and what we eat with enjoyment surely digests much more easily.

Paprika, one of the most popular "cosmetic spices," isn't all just for show, however. It has a mild, pleasant odor and an agreeable, slightly sweet taste. Some varieties may also have a little nip to them. In addition to pleasing flavor it is chuckful of vitamins. More than 25 years ago Prof. Albert Szent-Gyorgyi, a Hungarian scientist, won a Nobel prize for his work on paprika and the discovery of a new group of

Spanish

2 tablespoons olive (or salad oil)
1 tablespoon instant minced onion
¾ cup boiled dried beans or diced cooked potatoes
½ teaspoon salt
⅛ teaspoon ground black pepper
5 large eggs
Paprika for garnish

substances which we now call bioflavonoids. These nutrients, which are also present in citrus and certain other vitamin C-rich fruits, have the valuable ability of increasing the effectiveness of this vitamin.

Then chemists asked, "What makes paprika red? Does this redness add to its food value?" Research showed that the redder the paprika, the more pro-vitamin A it contained. ("Pro-vitamin" means that it becomes true vitamin A only after we've eaten and digested it.)

Paprika is made from sweet, mild-mannered capsicums, or pod peppers. They have nothing to do with either black or white peppers, which are berries. There are hundreds of capsicum cousins, some big, some little; some hot, some sweet; some red, white, orange or green in color. It's very easy to develop new varieties because these plants have sweet, nectar-bearing flowers which are very attractive to bees. Many of the hundreds or thousands of capsicum varieties probably were lucky accidents. But most of the reddest, prettiest paprika peppers were developed under the eagle eye of plant breeders.

Omelet

Heat oil in a 10-inch skillet. Add onion and beans or potatoes. Add salt and ground black pepper to eggs and beat **only** until mixed and barely frothy. Pour in skillet over beans or potatoes. **Cook over very low heat.**

As the mixture sets at the edges, gently pull edges toward the center with a fork and tip the pan so that uncooked mixture flows under the cooked portion. Do not let the omelet brown. Turn off heat the last few seconds. Fold over and slip onto a platter. Garnish with a sprinkling of paprika. Serves 4.

Does it seem that you have trouble shaking pepper freely from some of your handsome old-fashioned pepper shakers? Well, it's not your imagination. Pepper is being ground more coarsely than it used to be, say about thirty years ago. Even "normal grind" isn't as fine as it was before World War II. Larger than normal grind is "coarse grind" black pepper and coarsest of all is cracked black pepper or "butcher's grind."

The reason for this is very simple: We love black pepper. We love to taste pungent flecks of black pepper on our green salads, steaks or chops. America uses almost one-third of all the black pepper grown in the world, even though we have only one-sixteenth of the population.

America has always been a great pepper-importing country. As early as 1672, Boston-born Elihu Yale went to Madras, India, to begin making his fortune in pepper and other spices. (He used some of his pepper fortune to give Yale University its start.) Toward the end of the 18th century, more than a century after Yale went to India, a young and daring Yankee sea captain, Jonathan Carnes, made a trip to the Far East which started our spice trade in earnest. His voyage by sailing vessel took between two and three years and was very

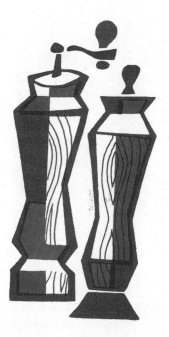

Steak

4 teaspoons coarsely ground
  black pepper
3½ lbs. sirloin steak, cut 1½-in.
  thick
1 teaspoon salt
3 tablespoons butter
2 tablespoons salad or olive oil
½ cup boiling water, wine, or
  brandy

dangerous, but the owners realized a 700% profit from the pepper he brought back. For the next ninety years, from the Revolutionary War to just after the Civil War, American sailing ships made 1,000 trips, each covering some 24,000 miles. In 1822, when there were barely ten million people in the United States, our ships brought in 18,650,000 pounds of pepper. Of course, some of this was reshipped to other countries, but even so, the import duties collected in the pepper port of Salem, Massachusetts, were enough to pay 5% of the expenses of the new American government.

We enjoy black pepper about eleven times more than we do white pepper, judging from relative sales. Black pepper is more pungent, white pepper is more subtle. Black pepper seems to go best with our favorite American dishes. Both black and white pepper come from the same vine, of course. Piper nigrum is the botanical name. It grows in some of the hottest, steamiest, most exotic places in the world: India, Indonesia, Ceylon, and Brazil.

With the festival season approaching, more and more men will be donning chef caps and aprons and performing on the patio. The following recipe is a particular favorite among men.

au Poivre

Rub coarsely ground black pepper into both sides of steak. Sprinkle lightly with salt. Heat butter and oil in a heavy skillet over high heat. Add steak and sear on both sides. Cook 6 to 7 minutes on each side. Remove to serving platter. Add to the pan ½ cup boiling water, wine, or brandy and heat for one minute. Pour over steak. Recipe serves 6.

Some years ago one of the world's most distinguished scientists and his wife were guests at a dinner in their honor. On each lady's plate, as the guests sat down, lay a beautiful corsage. The scientist's wife was extremely nearsighted. Picking up her fork, she cut away polite portions of the flower petals and ate the corsage. The other ladies, to avoid embarrassing her, bravely ate their flowers, too.

Actually, there is nothing especially "brave" about eating flowers. Two or three centuries ago, before so many New World vegetables became common in Europe, the people of England ate all kinds of flowers. Marigold buds were boiled and served with butter and vinegar. Primrose leaves were stirred into scrambled eggs. Violets and wild onions were served as a salad. Jam was made of red rose petals. Cowslips appeared in apple tarts.

In modern times we've developed an appetite for such flower buds as broccoli, cauliflower, and artichokes. The broccoli, which looks so beautifully green on our dinner plates, is a cluster of thickened, undeveloped flower buds. Left to their own devices, out in field or garden, the green buds would burst into bright yellow, four-petaled flowers.

Broccoli, like its cauliflower sister, is a cranky grower, even though it belongs to the cabbage species. That's why it was hardly known in the United States until just after World War I. That's when the first ice-packed broccoli was sent East from California, where it grows most happily. Before this time, consumption of broccoli was almost entirely limited to people of Italian background. It was grown in

Steamed Fresh Broccoli

2 lbs. fresh broccoli
1 teaspoon salt
2 packages Hollandaise sauce mix
2 teaspoons fresh lemon juice
½ cup heavy cream, whipped

limited amounts, more as a curiosity, in the elegant gardens of southern plantations. Several broccoli recipes appear in a book of late 18th and early 19th century recipes. In Italy and around the Mediterranean, broccoli has been prized for twenty centuries or more. Several ways of preparing it are given in a Roman cookbook written about 1500 years ago.

Broccoli of good quality is crisp, clean and of a darkish or purplish green. Since the whole stalk is eaten, tenderness is essential. Be critical of toughness of stalk or leaves with a yellowish cast. Even though we have just pointed out how often flowers have been eaten, broccoli is overmature when the full yellow or purple color of the blossom is distinct.

Broccoli can be cooked by several methods. Some cooks like to use a steamer, but others prefer the quicker open kettle methods. By the upright method, tie the broccoli in a bunch and stand it in the bottom part of a double boiler containing one inch of boiling salted water. Cook 5 minutes uncovered. Then cover with inverted top of double boiler and cook 10 to 15 minutes or until crisp-tender.

By the saucepan method, run one inch of boiling salted water in a saucepan. Cook uncovered first 5 minutes. Then cover and cook another 10 to 15 minutes, until crisp-tender.

I am a champion of serving broccoli in its natural form, not camouflaging its intrinsic flavor with too much embellishment. The following recipe, I believe, is a sensible balance.

with Mousseline Sauce

Wash and trim broccoli. Cut large stalks in halves or quarters. Make lengthwise gashes in stalks to cook uniformly. Place on collapsible steamer rack and lower into large saucepan containing hot water to level of upper part of feet of the rack. Cover securely and cook over low heat 15 to 20 minutes until stalks are crisp-tender.

To make Mousseline Sauce: Prepare Hollandaise sauce mix according to package directions. Then stir in lemon juice and cook until thickened. Fold in whipped cream. Serve broccoli hot with Mousseline Sauce. Recipe yields 6 servings broccoli, 2 cups sauce.

Even if you have eaten Sukiyaki in America, you will find it different in Japan. The centuries-old tradition back of Japanese food customs gives them a reverence for food and a ritual of serving which impresses the Occidental. In Japan, culinary and serving skill approaches a true art and ranks with any of the fine arts.

Each piece of food is prepared, handled, and cooked with utmost care and delicacy. The scarcity of food (for Japan is a tiny island with many people) has always been a challenge to the Japanese to use every morsel with ingenuity. That they do. Although their food is simplicity itself, in simplicity goodness and quality are never sacrificed.

Westerners find the Japanese were first with instant bite-size pieces. Vegetables are cut into small pieces, the beef cubed or sliced very thin, then all of the Sukiyaki ingredients are rearranged on a plate or tray in a pattern like a colorful mosaic. In an authentic Japanese

Sukiyaki

1½ *lbs. sirloin steak (cut into thin slices or cubes)*
2 *tablespoons butter*
⅓ *cup cooking sherry*
1 *cup green onions (sliced into thin one-inch strips)*
1 *cup mushrooms*
2 *cups bamboo shoots*
1 *cup celery (sliced into thin one-half inch slices)*
½ *cup green bell pepper (sliced into thin one-half inch strips)*

Sukiyaki restaurant the cooking will be done at the table to your own taste, on a table grill or a hibachi; then you will eat with chopsticks (the reason for the bite-size pieces).

Sukiyaki beef is usually especially grown for this national dish. Certain areas of Japan, in the western part of Honshu, are beef towns. Omi, Kobe, Matsuzaka are known for their quality beef. The meat is even labeled by the town, for instance, Omigyu. Gyu means beef in Japanese and Omi signifies from whence it came.

Sukiyaki is always served with rice. Not only is it good with Sukiyaki, but hardly a meal in Japan is served without rice. The rice can be served in a large bowl from which guests may serve themselves, if you so desire. If you wish to serve from a chafing dish it substitutes nicely for a hibachi and it can be used for cooking, too.

¼ *cup beef stock (canned beef consommé may be substituted)*
¼ *cup soy sauce*
2 *tablespoons sugar*
1 *cup blanched almonds*
2 *cups cooked rice*

Melt butter in skillet and sauté cubes of sirloin steak. When steak cubes are browned, add onions, sherry, mushrooms, bamboo shoots, celery, green pepper, beef stock, soy sauce, sugar, almonds, and salt and pepper to taste. Cover skillet and simmer for about six minutes.

The items in this recipe should not be overcooked, but rather should remain crisp. Serve on a platter over a bed of cooked rice. Recipe serves six.

Acapulco, sometimes called the Riviera of the Americas, is a tropical paradise with superb beaches and fine hotels, a happy nightlife, and a quaint marketplace for shoppers, a sea view which is surely one of the prettiest in the world and good food. To enable tourists fully to enjoy all of these delights Acapulco offers a casual, slowed-down pace which is completely relaxing.

The Mexicans say that this resort has a special, very special, quality which they call "ambiente." "Atmosphere," we would say. That Acapulco certainly has, and so does Tamale Pie Acapulco.

There are probably hundreds of tamale pie recipes. After having searched for a number of years for a hallmark recipe for this dish, I savored this one when vacationing in Acapulco, and I pronounce it the very best of many.

Tamale Pie

¼ lb. bulk pork sausage
1½ tablespoons cold water
1 lb. ground lean beef
1 cup onion, diced fine
½ cup chopped celery
½ cup green bell pepper, diced fine
2½ cups sieved tomatoes
1¼ cups whole kernel corn (12-oz. can, drained)

2 teaspoons chili powder
1 teaspoon salt
½ teaspoon MSG powder
¼ teaspoon black pepper
1 cup cold water
½ cup yellow corn meal
1 cup sliced ripe olives
1 cup grated sharp Cheddar cheese (3 ozs.)

Acapulco

Place sausage into a large cold skillet and break meat into small pieces with a fork. Add one and a half tablespoons cold water to the skillet. Cover and cook slowly, approximately 8 minutes. Remove skillet cover and pour off fat. Mix in the ground lean beef. Brown the meat over medium heat, stirring occasionally and pouring off fat as it collects. When meat begins to brown, add onion, celery, and green bell pepper and continue to cook slowly until vegetables are soft. Mix in tomatoes, corn, chili powder, salt, MSG powder, and pepper. Cover skillet and simmer slowly for 15 minutes.

Mix together one cup cold water and ½ cup yellow corn meal and blend gradually into the recipe. Continue to cook slowly while stirring until recipe thickens. Mix in sliced olives and turn into a 2-quart greased baking dish. Place in preheated 350-degree oven and bake for one hour. Remove from oven and sprinkle grated cheese on top. Return to the oven for 5 minutes or until cheese is melted. Garnish with whole ripe olives and parsley. Serves 8.

Tamale Pie Acapulco should, of course, be served hot. You can make a complete meal of this Mexican-American favorite.

When an American thinks of steak, he probably has visions of a big T-bone or Porterhouse steak, or rib-eye, charcoal broiled and appropriately seasoned. When an Englishman thinks of steak, it's probably a sirloin of beef, just broiled, with perhaps a dash of Worcestershire sauce. (Actually, the Porterhouse steak is English too, having been served by Mr. Porter in England at his hotel or "house"—thus Porterhouse—but has been popularly adopted in America, with an especially large number of fans in the Midwest.)

But when a Frenchman's choice comes up it will be filet mignon. Filet means boneless, mignon means delicate and pleasing, and this steak is often referred to as "a woman's steak," perhaps because of its nature and its petite size. Endless varieties of filet mignon appear on French menus. Of these the epitome is the tournedos.

Tournedos is the cut of about one inch thickness, maybe a little more, from the lower, narrow portion of the filet de boeuf, between the chateaubriand cut and the filet mignon. Naturally lean, the cut desires sautéeing. Use a heavy skillet and sauté it in butter with a drop or two of olive oil to keep the butter from browning too rapidly.

Tournedos of Beef

2 tablespoons chopped scallions (green onions)
1 tablespoon chopped onion
½ clove minced garlic
6 tablespoons butter or margarine
1 tablespoon curry powder
1 teaspoon ground ginger
2 tablespoons chili sauce
1 tablespoon soy sauce
1 canned tomato, finely chopped
1 tablespoon lemon juice
2 tablespoons flour
1 cup beef broth
2 teaspoons Kitchen Bouquet
12 beef tenderloin tournedos (3½ to 4 ounces each)

Cook over high heat, searing juices in, for only two or three minutes; then reduce heat and cook to the rare point (which is preferred). If, however, you should broil the tournedos, do it with a strip of bacon across the top, or a couple pats of butter.

Now, all of these different preferences of the different nationalities are **cuts**. All are different one from the other, but can come from the very same beef animal. In the case of the tournedos, the French, as is their custom, change the tournedos according to the sauce in or with which they serve it. Thus, with Madeira Sauce garnished with a truffle, it is *Tournedos Rossini;* served with *Sauce Champignons* (Mushroom Sauce) it becomes *Tournedos aux Champignons.* So it is no wonder that the French-trained and French-dominated society of the Vietnamese tried for a tournedos recipe all their own with *Tournedos of Beef, Saigon.*

This is a delicious rendition of tournedos which I have simplified for American kitchens with a few shortcuts not practiced in Saigon— or in France, for that matter.

Saigon

Sauté scallions, chopped onion, and garlic in butter or margarine for one minute. Blend in curry powder, ginger, chili sauce, soy sauce, chopped tomato, and lemon juice. In a separate container combine flour, beef broth, and Kitchen Bouquet, mixing well, and add to sautéed mixture. Bring to boil, stirring constantly. Cook over very low heat for 2 minutes.

Broil the 12 slices of beef tenderloin tournedos two minutes on each side.

Arrange filets on wild rice or toasted bread trimmed to the shape of the tournedos. (Tournedos, being a small piece of meat, are always raised above the garnishes by serving on toast, croutons, or rice to give them their proper center of attention.) In this Saigon recipe, naturally, wild rice is appropriate. Garnish with sliced water chestnuts, bean sprouts, and sautéed black or wild mushrooms. Serves 6.

When the dust is settling on the Christmas presents, will you, just like last year, be looking for a new method to use the rest of the giant turkey you roasted for Christmas dinner? Search no more. Here is a haute cuisine recipe for the remains of that bird of tradition, the best "leftover" you ever tasted—Turkey Émincé New Orleans.

You don't need to use leftover turkey, of course. This dish is elegant anytime, but the beautiful part of it is you **can** use leftovers for it. Once you accomplish Turkey Émincé New Orleans you will cook turkey all through the year just to emince (meaning: to mince the meat) them for this New Orleans style turkey recipe.

So don't hesitate to serve the bird again. No one will recognize it as a leftover. With this recipe you can keep the after-the-Big-Event meals on an upbeat taste theme. Baptized in spices, herbs, sauce, and united with rice, the turkey becomes a gastronomical symphony with a flavor beguiling and satisfaction in tastemaking guaranteed.

Turkey Émincé

Fat from ½ pound of cooked bacon
2 medium onions, diced fine
1 green bell pepper, diced fine
1 large can of mushrooms
1 small can tomato paste
1 small can tomato sauce
1 16-oz. can peeled tomatoes
1 tablespoon garlic salt
 Dash of pepper
 Dash of Tabasco
 Dash of Worcestershire powder
2 oz. white wine
4 cups of cooked rice
1 roast turkey

New Orleans

Place the bacon fat into a skillet. (Do not use the bacon.) In this bacon fat sauté onions, green bell pepper, and mushrooms until soft. Then add tomato paste, tomato sauce, peeled tomatoes, garlic salt, pepper, Tabasco, Worcestershire powder, and white wine. Cover and simmer for 12 minutes.

Place a bed of rice on a serving tray. Cover rice with slices of roast turkey, both dark and white meat. Over turkey and rice pour the sauce sautéed in the skillet. (This recipe uses 4 pounds of turkey and the above mixture will serve 6.)

Garnish Turkey Émincé New Orleans with green bell pepper rings, ripe olives, strips of pimiento, or parsley.

They say that if we don't learn from our mistakes, then there is no use making any. Well, if you have ever made a mistake in cooking a turkey, then you may be ready to learn something new. Or, perhaps you are less than satisfied with the way it usually turns out for you— maybe a little too brown, or underdone, or tough, or something that doesn't measure up to the perfection you'd like to achieve.

If you will try my Turkey-in-a-Sack method I can guarantee you will eliminate all mistakes in your turkey-cooking future. This is the easiest, cleanest, most fool-proof technique I know.

Turkey-in-a-Sack

1 *teaspoon pepper*
2 *teaspoons salt*
3 *teaspoons paprika*
4 *teaspoons hot water*
1 *cup peanut oil*
1 *turkey, 14 to 16 pounds*

Combine pepper, salt, paprika, and hot water. Let stand at least 10 minutes. Add peanut oil and mix thoroughly. Select turkey carefully. It should not exceed 16 pounds. Wash and dry. Rub some peanut oil mixture into inside and outside of turkey. Truss as desired. Pour remaining oil and additional oil into large paper sack (type used in your grocery store—large,

heavy-duty type with no holes). Rub oil into inside of sack until every pore in every inch of the sack is sealed with oil mixture. Place turkey in sack, breast up. Fold end of the sack over and tie securely. Bake in a moderate oven (325 degrees) approximately 10 minutes per pound. Since the sack is airtight, the turkey is cooked by live steam; therefore, when sack is opened, be careful!

You will not have to baste this turkey since the oil-sealed sack is self-basting. You will not have to watch it carefully. The turkey comes out tender to the bone and golden brown. Your turkey is done, ready to serve, and you can

wrap up the sack, after the bird has been removed, and throw it away. There is not even a roaster to scrub and wash. It is a good idea, however, to rest the sack on a cookie sheet as some of the oil may seep through to the outside of the sack.

Words of caution: Do not substitute any other oil for peanut oil. Only peanut oil will work, and it also imparts a wonderful flavor to the fowl. Also, do not attempt to substitute aluminum foil in place of the sack. It will not work. Again, be careful when you open that sack—open end farthest from you first.

If you desire to gild this turkey with a glaze, here is one I recommend:

4 *tablespoons butter*
4 *tablespoons flour*
½ *teaspoon salt*
2 *cups milk*
2 *tablespoons unflavored gelatin*
6 *tablespoons water*
1 *cup mayonnaise*

Melt butter over slow heat, add flour and salt, mix until blended. Then add milk and stir until thickened. Mix gelatin with water and add to the mixture. After this mixture has cooled, add mayonnaise. When turkey has cooled, coat with mixture.

Venice-watching should really be done in the off-season, which is November to mid-March. Since almost three-quarters of a million tourists pay their respects to the Venetian past every year, and since most of them arrive during the "season," you'll have a difficult time seeing anything but fellow tourists if you go then. The joys of sight, sound, and atmosphere will be severely diminished. But during the winter season which the citizens of Venice call "Venice for the Venetians," the hotels have better accommodations, you can roam freely around the islands and participate in the passeggiata (the promenade the Venetians so dearly love), and since there are no automobiles there, strolling and window shopping have otherworldly quality. No one hurries; gaggles of Venetians stop to exchange the gossip and visit, drop into the coffee bars for an espresso, and happily go their way in peace. (I must mention one winter inconvenience— since it gets cold in Northern Italy there will often be fog which hampers island hopping.)

Even though the Venetians know that without the tourists Venice would be a forgotten city (Venice is among the first five tourist attractions in the world and some put it number one), still the return to "normal" where they **live** with Venice's past when she was the city of Europe, is welcomed like a long-awaited holiday.

Venice began A.D. 452, founded deliberately to enable its citizens to defend themselves against enemies on the sound premise that an

Venetian

½ cup olive oil
1 tablespoon chopped garlic
1 tablespoon chopped parsley
1 tablespoon chopped celery
1 tablespoon chopped green
  pepper
2 cups solid pack tomatoes
1 cup tomato purée
  Salt and pepper
  Paprika
  Few leaves sweet basil
1 cup red wine
2 dozen clams

army could not attack an island city. Consequently, Venice soon became a world sea power being dependent upon and rich in ships. Surrounded by a beautiful lagoon and the Adriatic Sea, Venice was destined to become the merchant city of the world with wealth untold shipped in from the opulent East.

During the offseason the food service is more than superb. Regiments of precision-trained waiters and their helpers surround you to do your bidding. Here, dining is not for snacking, but rather full course dinners are the rule. The vaporetto, the Venetian water-bus, or a boat-taxi will whisk you up the Canal Grande to a famous cafe. Having placed your order with the headwaiter, sit back, wait, and watch while the water boy, coffee boy, and the silver boy busy themselves adjusting every detail in preparation for your meal. It will not be long until the sommelier will appear (keeper of the keys to the wine cabinet) to suggest wines from the wine list.

A covey of waiters soon will spring forth from the kitchen in march tempo. The order here seems to be the head man, the assistant, and the assistant-to-the-assistant, with the wine man in a class by himself, and the underlings being apprentices to the men who perform with real skill. This is food drama at its best, a full-scale demonstration of the European reverence for fine food with a flourish of perfectly executed gourmetmanship.

Chiopino

3 lbs. fish fillets (bass, haddock, or cod), cut into small pieces

1 lb. raw shrimp, cleaned, shelled and deveined

1 small lobster or crab, shelled and cut or broken into pieces

Heat olive oil in a Dutch oven or large kettle over a medium heat. Add garlic, parsley, celery, and green pepper. Cook until lightly browned. Add tomatoes, tomato purée, salt and pepper, paprika, sweet basil, and red wine. Reduce heat to low and cook for one hour. Wash and steam clams in small amount of water, just until the shells open. Strain the liquid from the clams and add the liquid to sauce. Add now the fish-fillet pieces, shrimp, and lobster, and cook until tender. Add the clams at the very end of the cooking time. Serve in bowls accompanied by red wine and plenty of toasted French bread. This recipe will serve 6.

First among the fine arts of the kitchen, and possibly the most ancient of them, is la patisserie, dating back as it does to the centuries before Christ, when angry pagan gods could be propitiated by sacrifices of sweet cakes. From rude beginnings, pastry cooks have evolved confections that represent the apex of refinement and imagination. The ephemeral Torten of Vienna, the fabulous gateaux of Paris, the flaky, juicy fruit pies of New England—all are fit for any man and his gods.

Good pastry cooks never lack ingenuity, know no poverty of invention. A good pastry cook must first possess a fertile imagination, then learn to command a handful of basic doughs, batters, and pastes. From these basics, a creative cook can work endless variations.

I learned years ago that often after spending laborious hours in the kitchen preparing a special meal for honored guests, it is the simplest concoction that is received as the pièce de résistance. On one occasion when I hosted a special dinner party for Jock Mahoney (at that time

Viennese

4 tablespoons (½ stick) butter
   or margarine
¾ cup firmly packed light brown
   sugar
⅛ teaspoon salt
1 can (1 lb., 4 oz.) unsweetened
   pitted red tart cherries
1 package devil's food cake mix

Melt butter or margarine in 9x9x2-inch baking pan. Stir in brown sugar and salt. Heat slowly, stirring constantly, just until bubbly; remove from heat. Drain cherries, saving liquid for cake. Spoon cherries over sugar mixture in pan.

the Tarzan of the movies) along with other selected guests, I imported selected filets of cobra from India for hors d'oeuvres and Kobe beef from Japan at $6.25 per pound to be served as the entree. There were numerous other creations that I spent hours in the kitchen negotiating for this special party. As I was staging this meal, I suddenly realized that my preparation time was almost over and I had not as yet accomplished a dessert. Using the limited remaining time, I went to my pantry and withdrew a can of tart red sour cherries and a box of devil's food cake mix. Adding several other items to these prepackaged convenience foods, I turned out a Viennese Upside-Down Cake. To my great surprise, all of the guests insisted that this dessert was a work of the gods.

I suggest that you add this recipe to your files of pastry-making and I am sure you will find, as I have, that simple recipes sometimes are more popular with your family and guests than the more elaborate ones.

Upside-Down Cake

Prepare devil's food cake mix, following label directions but using liquid from cherries as part of liquid called for on package. Pour over cherries in pan.

Bake in moderate oven (350 degrees) 1 hour, or until top springs back when lightly pressed with fingertip.

Cool on wire rack 5 minutes; cover pan with serving plate; quickly turn upside down, then carefully lift off baking pan.

Cut into squares; serve warm, plain or with milk, cream, or ice cream. Makes 9 servings.

Those of you who consider yourselves strictly meat and potatoes people and who don't think a meal is a meal without both may be surprised to know that potatoes were once thought to cause fevers and strange maladies, including leprosy. This was in Europe in the 1700s, and only the King of France, Louis XIV, could convince his subjects that potatoes were an edible food by ordering them served at the palace. His Majesty even went so far in his palace-to-subjects public relations program as to wear a potato flower in the buttonhole of his suit. No doubt his subjects watched the palace staff with some apprehension to observe if they dropped dead; or was this some scheme to rid the country of the weaker citizens during a food shortage?

As it turned out, all that happened was that people began to like potatoes more and more, until today the yearly world crop of potatoes is over 8 million bushels.

White Wine

4 *large potatoes or 8 new*
  potatoes
½ *cup white wine (Riesling,*
  Hock Sauterne, or Chablis)
¼ *cup salad oil*
3 *tablespoons vinegar*
1 *tablespoon sugar*
3 *tablespoons minced onion*
  Salt and pepper to taste

There is an old expression, "strictly cold potatoes," which generally refers to a person without warmth, or unfriendly, or to a situation or deal that is now a dead issue. This would seem to make cold potatoes equivalent to nothing good; in fact, with such an introduction, a recipe using cold potatoes sounds downright impossible. But you take a few cold potatoes and you begin adding a little salad oil, a little onion, salt, and pepper and you are on your way to potato salad.

Of course, you may say that there is nothing unusual or new about potato salad. It's served at every picnic, and many, many times between picnics. But here again, you take some otherwise plain potato salad and add some white Riesling or Chablis wine and voilà! Kitchen magic transforms it into a food with a flair. Such is the evolution of a creative recipe.

Potato Salad

Cook the potatoes in ½ inch boiling water in a covered saucepan until tender. Then drain, cool, peel, and slice into a bowl. Add white wine, mixing lightly until the potatoes are well moistened. Now add salad oil, vinegar, sugar, minced onion, salt and pepper to taste, and mix together thoroughly, but lightly. Store in the refrigerator for at least one hour before serving. This recipe makes 6 servings.

Make White Wine Potato Salad the center of a buffet and surround it with selections of cold cuts, sliced hard-boiled eggs, sliced tomatoes, sliced cucumbers, olives or pickles. What an elegant luncheon this makes for the gourmet.

Sweet potatoes are one of the most all-round-nutritious foods of the world. They are so nutritious that people have gotten along for considerable periods on a diet made up almost solely of this vegetable. They not only have a high initial content of carotene—which is converted to vitamin A in the body—but the carotene increases during the usual period of storage before they reach the retail market.

The sweet potato was growing over much of what we call Latin America when Columbus first landed. In Peru they probably grew thousands of years before the first Spanish explorers set eyes on them. When Columbus returned in triumph to the Spanish Court he brought with him all kinds of American plants and animals. The sweet potato was a great success in Europe and was given its American name, "batatas." (It's easy to see how this got to be "potato.") Sweet potatoes were imported from Spain by the English and Henry VIII was one of the great sweet potato-eaters of his day—he particularly liked them in pies, well-sweetened and spiced. When Shakespeare wrote that the sky was "raining potatoes," he meant sweet potatoes, of course.

Herbalist Parkinson called them "Spanish potatoes" in the early 17th century and gave these cooking hints: "The Spanish potatoes are roasted under the embers, and being pared, or peeled or sliced, are put in sacke [meaning wine] with a little sugar, or without, and is delicate to be eaten. They are used to be baked with marron, sugar and other things in pies, which are dainty and costly dish for the table. The comfit makers [meaning candy-makers] prefer them and

Yam Peanut

4 cups mashed yams
3 tablespoons butter or margarine
2 tablespoons brown sugar
½ teaspoon ground nutmeg
½ teaspoon ground cinnamon
½ teaspoon salt
1/16 teaspoon ground black pepper
1 egg, lightly beaten

candy them as diverse other things, and so made are very delicate, fit to accompany such other beautiful dishes."

The very sweet orange-fleshed, copper-skinned sweet potato, called a "yam" in North Carolina, where it grows so happily in modern times, was probably brought there from Europe at least three centuries ago. These would have been planted in family gardens, for home use only. Then in the 1930s North Carolina farmers and gardeners realized that they had a very good thing growing for them. They began to plant yam acreage which enabled them to ship sweet potatoes throughout the country. Research has made it possible to grow as many as 800 bushels of yams per acre. New curing techniques have made it possible to store and market North Carolina yams for ten months in the year.

The yam growers of the Tarheel State want us to enjoy their sweeter sweets with the moist, orange flesh. Here are some of their yam-cooking rules: Yams are rapid cookers, in the oven or out. Bake them in a moderate oven always. They are so full of sweetness that they may "leak" if baked too long, or at too hot a temperature. Press them, rather than piercing with a fork, to test for doneness. Wash yam skins before baking, to please the peeling-eaters at the table. Boil yams in a deep, heavy pot with just enough water to keep them from scorching. Remove from heat and drain as soon as done.

The following recipe is one that I am certain you will enjoy.

Puffs

2 *apples, peeled, cored and cut into 12 wedges*
1 *cup peanuts, coarsely chopped*
2 *tablespoons butter or margarine, melted*

Combine yams, butter, sugar, nutmeg, cinnamon, salt, black pepper, and egg. Mix well. Surround each apple wedge with a portion of the mixture and shape into balls. Roll each yam ball in peanuts. Place on greased baking dish. Pour melted butter over each ball. Bake in preheated moderate oven (350 degrees) 25 to 30 minutes.

Recipe makes approximately twelve 1½-inch balls.

TABLE OF MEASUREMENTS
AND SUBSTITUTION

WEIGHTS AND MEASURES

60 drops ...... 1 teaspoon
3 teaspoons .... 1 tablespoon
2 tablespoons .. 1 liquid ounce
4 tablespoons .. ¼ cup
16 tablespoons . 1 cup
2 cups .... 1 pint
2 pints .... 1 quart
4 quarts .... 1 gallon
8 quarts .... 1 peck
4 pecks .... 1 bushel
16 ounces ..... 1 pound
1 peck potatoes . 15 pounds
1 bushel plums . 50 pounds
1 bushel pears .. 48 pounds
1 bushel
  peaches ...... 48 pounds
1 bushel apples . 44 pounds

COCOA AND CHOCOLATE

For 1 ounce (square) cooking
  chocolate use 4 tablespoons
  cocoa and ½ tablespoon fat.
For ¼ cup or 4 tablespoons cocoa use 1 ounce (square)
  chocolate and omit ½ tablespoon fat.

GENERAL EQUIVALENTS

2 cups butter or margarine = 1
  pound
1 bouillon cube = 1 teaspoon
  beef extract
1 tablespoon unflavored gelatin
  = ¼ ounce or 2⅔ leaves of
  leaf or French gelatin
Horseradish, 1 tablespoon fresh
  grated = 2 tablespoons bottled
1½ cups molasses = 1 cup sugar
1 tablet rennet = 1 tablespoon
  liquid rennet

MILK

For 1 cup fresh sweet milk in
batters use:
  ½ cup evaporated milk and ½
    cup water.
  1 cup sour milk with ½ tea-
    spoon soda as leavening.
    Omit 2 teaspoons tartrate or
    1 teaspoon double-action
    baking powder.
  1 cup buttermilk with ½ tea-
    spoon soda as leavening.
    Omit 2 teaspoons tartrate or
    1 teaspoon double-action
    baking powder.
  1 cup skim milk and 2 table-
    spoons fat.

FLOUR

For 1 cup sifted enriched flour use any one of the following (sifted if possible):

- 1 cup cake flour + 2 tablespoons flour
- ⅓ cup corn meal + ⅔ cup enriched flour
- ½ cup corn meal + ½ cup enriched flour
- ¾ cup bran + ¼ cup enriched flour
- ½ cup bran + ½ cup enriched flour
- ½ cup rye flour + ½ cup enriched flour
- 1 cup rye flour
- ½ cup whole-wheat flour + ½ cup enriched flour
- ¾ cup whole-wheat flour + ¼ cup enriched flour

SUGAR

For 1 cup granulated sugar use:

- 1 cup brown sugar, well packed
- ¾ cup honey and reduce liquid by 3 tablespoons
- 1½ cups molasses and reduce liquid by 6 tablespoons
- 1½ cups sorghum and reduce liquid by 6 tablespoons
- 2 cups corn syrup and reduce liquid by ½ cup
- 1½ cups maple syrup and reduce liquid by ½ cup

INDEX

T

V